Narratives of Dislocation in the Arab World

This monograph explores and investigates narratives of physical, psychological, and emotional dislocation that take place within the Arab world, approaching them as manifestations of the Arabic word *ghurba*, or estrangement, as a feeling and state of being.

Distancing itself from the centrality of the "West" in postcolonial and Arabic literary studies, the book explores experiences of migration, displacement and cosmopolitanism that do not directly ensue from the encounter with Europe or the European other. Covering texts from the Levant, Egypt, the Arabian Peninsula and beyond from the 19th, 20th and 21st centuries, the book grounds narratives of dislocation in the political, social and cultural structures that affect the everyday lived experiences of individuals and communities. An analysis of Arabic, Turkish and English texts – encompassing fiction, memoirs and translations – highlights less visible narratives of *ghurba*, specifically amongst ethnic minorities and religious communities. Ultimately, the chapters contribute to a picture of the Arab world as a place of *ghurba* where mobile and immobile subjects, foreigners and local inhabitants alike, encounter alienation.

Bringing together a diverse range of academic perspectives, the book will be of interest to students and scholars in postcolonial and comparative literary studies, history, and Arabic and Middle East studies.

Nadeen Dakkak is Lecturer in World and Postcolonial Literatures at the University of Exeter. She was IASH-Alwaleed Postdoctoral Fellow at the University of Edinburgh in 2021–2022 and completed her PhD in English and Comparative Literary Studies at the University Warwick. Her research examines literary and cultural productions on migration in the Gulf.

Routledge Advances in Middle East and Islamic Studies

23 Dissident Writings of Arab Women
Voices Against Violence
Brinda Mehta

24 Higher Education Revolutions in the Gulf
Globalization and Institutional Viability
Fatima Badry and John Willoughby

25 Knowledge Production in the Arab World
The Impossible Promise
Sari Hanafi and Rigas Arvanitis

26 Palestinian Culture and the Nakba
Bearing Witness
Hania A.M. Nashef

27 Orientalism, Zionism and Academic Practice
Middle East and Islam Studies in Israeli Universities
Eyal Clyne

28 The Migrant in Arab Literature
Displacement, Self-Discovery and Nostalgia
Edited by Martina Censi and Maria Elena Paniconi

29 Bildungsroman and the Arab Novel
Egyptian Intersections
Maria Elena Paniconi

30 Narratives of Dislocation in the Arab World
Rewriting *Ghurba*
Edited by Nadeen Dakkak

For more information about this series, please visit: www.routledge.com/middleeaststudies/series/SE0728

Narratives of Dislocation in the Arab World

Rewriting *Ghurba*

Edited by Nadeen Dakkak

LONDON AND NEW YORK

First published 2023
by Routledge
4 Park Square, Milton Park, Abingdon, Oxon OX14 4RN

and by Routledge
605 Third Avenue, New York, NY 10158

Routledge is an imprint of the Taylor & Francis Group, an informa business

© 2023 selection and editorial matter, Nadeen Dakkak; individual chapters, the contributors

The right of Nadeen Dakkak to be identified as the author of the editorial material, and of the authors for their individual chapters, has been asserted in accordance with sections 77 and 78 of the Copyright, Designs and Patents Act 1988.

All rights reserved. No part of this book may be reprinted or reproduced or utilised in any form or by any electronic, mechanical, or other means, now known or hereafter invented, including photocopying and recording, or in any information storage or retrieval system, without permission in writing from the publishers.

Trademark notice: Product or corporate names may be trademarks or registered trademarks, and are used only for identification and explanation without intent to infringe.

British Library Cataloguing-in-Publication Data
A catalogue record for this book is available from the British Library

Library of Congress Cataloging-in-Publication Data
Names: Dakkak, Nadeen, editor.
Title: Narratives of dislocation in the Arab world : rewriting ghurba / edited by Nadeen Dakkak.
Description: Abingdon, Oxon ; New York, NY : Routledge, 2023. |
Series: Routledge advances in Middle East and Islamic studies |
Includes bibliographical references and index.
Identifiers: LCCN 2022042759 (print) | LCCN 2022042760 (ebook) |
ISBN 9781032294780 (hardback) | ISBN 9781032294797 (paperback) |
ISBN 9781003301776 (ebook)
Subjects: LCSH: Alienation (Social psychology)–Middle East. |
Place attachment–Middle East. | Environmental psychology–Middle East.
Classification: LCC HM1131 .N387 2023 (print) |
LCC HM1131 (ebook) | DDC 302.5/440956–dc23/eng/20221222
LC record available at https://lccn.loc.gov/2022042759
LC ebook record available at https://lccn.loc.gov/2022042760

ISBN: 978-1-032-29478-0 (hbk)
ISBN: 978-1-032-29479-7 (pbk)
ISBN: 978-1-003-30177-6 (ebk)

DOI: 10.4324/9781003301776

Typeset in Times New Roman
by Newgen Publishing UK

Contents

List of Contributors	vii
Introduction NADEEN DAKKAK	1

PART I
***Ghurba* in Narratives of Slavery and Racism**   23

1   Dissolving into the Nile: Ottoman Reformism and
Maternal Slavery in *Sergüzeşt*   25
BURCU GÜRSEL

2   Re-writing the Other: Uncovering the Legacies of Slavery
in Suad Amiry's *My Damascus*   47
ARTHTHI SATHANANTHAR

PART II
***Ghurba* in Narratives of Displacement**   65

3   *The Woman from Tantoura*: Structural Marginalisation
and the Re-Making of Home among Palestinian Refugees
in Lebanon   67
ROBA AL-SALIBI

4   Memory and Resistance in Susan Abulhawa's *Against the
Loveless World*   84
BENAY BLEND

vi *Contents*

5 The Refugee as a "Russian Doll": Haitham Hussein's
   Readings of *Ghurba* and Exile at the Time of the Global
   "Migration Crisis"   101
   ANNAMARIA BIANCO

PART III
Religious Spaces of *Ghurba* and Belonging   121

6 *Ghurba* and the Emergence of a Gendered Pious
   Consciousness in Popular Religious Novels
   by Arab Women   123
   HAWRAA AL-HASSAN

7 Can the Qazani Speak? Nineteenth Century
   Naqshbandi Migrants and Translators in Mecca
   during the Age of Print   138
   MARIAM ELASHMAWY

PART IV
Negotiating National Imaginaries of Belonging and Exclusion   161

8 Spectral Migrant Workers and the Paradox of
   Modern Nation-Building in Deepak Unnikrishnan's
   Temporary People   163
   LAVA ASAAD

9 The Arab-African Cultural Identity in Idris Ali's *Dongola*   179
   RANIA SALEM

   Index   197

Contributors

Hawraa Al-Hassan is Research Associate at the University of Cambridge, where she completed her doctorate in the Faculty of Asian and Middle Eastern Studies. She is the author of *Women, Writing and the Iraqi Ba'thist State: Contending Discourses of Resistance and Collaboration (1968–2003)* (Edinburgh University Press, 2020). Her areas of interests include the novel and the state, and the modern cultural history of the Arab world.

Roba Al-Salibi is a PhD candidate at the Institute of Arab and Islamic studies at the University of Exeter. Her research examines themes of border, home, belonging and futurity in Palestinian, Syrian and Iraqi exile literature. Al-Salibi's main areas of interest are gender studies, refugee studies and postcolonial literature.

Lava Asaad is English Lecturer at Auburn University. She received her doctoral degree from Middle Tennessee State University (2019). She is the author of *Literature with a White Helmet: The Textual-Corporeality of Being, Becoming and Representing Refugees* (Routledge, 2020) and the co-editor of *In the Crossfire of History: Women's War Resistance Discourse in the Global South* (Rutgers University Press, 2022).

Annamaria Bianco holds a PhD from Aix-Marseille University (IREMAM) and University of Naples "L'Orientale" (DAAM). She is the author of thesis « *Adab al-malga' » : représenter le refuge dans le roman arabe du XXIe siècle* (2022). She is currently an associate researcher at IREMAM and a teaching assistant in Arabic language and literature at Jean Jaurès University of Toulouse. Her research interests include cultural productions of Arab migrants, refugees and exiles and the representation of human rights in fiction. She is an editor of the junior scholars journal *Maydan – rivista sui mondi arabi, semitici e islamici.*

Benay Blend is retired professor of American and Native American history. Her work includes "'I Learnt All the Words and Broke Them Up/To Make a Single Word: Homeland': An Eco-Postcolonial Perspective of Resistance in Palestinian Women's Literature," *Ecofeminist Dialogues* (2017). She also publishes articles in the *Palestine Chronicle*.

viii *List of Contributors*

Nadeen Dakkak is Lecturer in World and Postcolonial Literatures at the University of Exeter. She was IASH-Alwaleed Postdoctoral Fellow at the University of Edinburgh in 2021–2022 and completed her PhD in English and Comparative Literary Studies at the University Warwick. Her research examines literary and cultural productions on migration in the Gulf.

Mariam Elashmawy is a doctoral student in Arabic studies at Freie Universität Berlin. She has a MA in Arabic Studies, with a concentration in Middle East history from the American University in Cairo. She is currently the Managing Editor at *Alif: Journal of Comparative Poetics*. Her research interests focus on print and manuscript culture, intellectual Middle East history and Islamic mysticism.

Burcu Gürsel is Assistant Professor at Western Languages and Literatures at Kirklareli University, Turkey, where she teaches both in English and in Turkish. She received her PhD in Comparative Literature from the University of Pennsylvania, and was a postdoctoral fellow at the Forum Transregionale Studien. She works on transimperialism, colonialism, slavery and the role of intellectuals, especially in the Ottoman Empire and Europe.

Rania Salem is Lecturer at the British University in Egypt. She defended her PhD thesis entitled "Cultural Identity in Selected Arab-African Novels" at the Faculty of Arts, Ain Shams University, with first-class honors, in March 2022. She received her MA in English and Comparative Literature in 2014 from the American University in Cairo.

Arththi Sathananthar is Lecturer at the Department of Minorities & Multilingualism at the University of Groningen. She completed her PhD in English at the University of Leeds. Her research lies at the intersection of life writing and de/postcolonial studies with a focus on diaspora, transculturalism and home.

Introduction

Nadeen Dakkak

Despite being often translated as estrangement or exile, the Arabic word *ghurba* carries multiple layers of meaning that make it versatile and encompassing of various kinds of experiences. It is at once the fact of being physically distant as a foreigner far away from home, a psychological and emotional state of alienation and estrangement, and a reference to the foreign place itself, the land where one becomes a stranger and suffers the challenges that accompany this position, be they mundane, everyday struggles of adaptation, or the deeper strains of homesickness. What perhaps echoes the versatility of the word is its common everyday usage, as well as its recurrence in literature and popular culture that have long been a space for Arab poets, writers, and intellectuals to express alienation and the pain of separation from homeland and loved ones. Arab literature and culture are replete with narratives of dislocation in which the *ghurba*, here both a place and the fact of being away from home, swallows immigrants literally and figuratively, either detaching them from the homeland and preventing possibilities of return, or transforming them to the extent that they become strangers in their own home countries after their return. At other times, *ghurba* is more a destiny and a state of existence imposed upon generations of displaced individuals for whom feeling at home in one place is impossible. In such narratives of dislocation, *ghurba* describes the feelings of alienation that infiltrate or completely shape an individual's experience in the *manfa* (exile), or a community's experience in the *shatat* (diaspora). In other words, *ghurba* as a concept can be arguably understood and used in a similar way to how concepts like exile and diaspora have been used to theorize the affective state of immigrants, refugees and other displaced individuals away from their physical or imagined homelands. At the same time, the word accommodates a vast array of meanings and cannot be restricted to this usage. *Ghurba* as a concept and a state of being can allow us to understand narratives of dislocation in a more expansive way, first by situating these narratives within the Arab world, and even within the boundaries of the homeland itself, and second by disentangling them from experiences of migration, exile and diaspora. Because it describes feelings of alienation that emerge in different states of estrangement, including but not exclusively those caused by

DOI: 10.4324/9781003301776-1

2 *Nadeen Dakkak*

migration and exile, it has the capacity to function as a tool for nuancing our understanding of the region as not only the home away from which estrangement takes shape but as a site of dislocation as well, a place where estrangement can be experienced by local inhabitants and foreigners alike.

The word *ghurba* is no doubt mostly associated with displacement and migration to foreign places, particularly Europe and North America, because it is primarily in such experiences that an individual feels detached from place and people due to differences in language, culture and religion, amongst other factors. Indeed, narratives of migration and exile in Europe and North America have been at the center of numerous works of literature by Arab writers, including those who were preoccupied by the encounter with colonial modernity in metropolitan centers throughout the twentieth century. Recent political conflict in the region has intensified the movement of refugees and migrants out of the Arab world, producing an even larger body of work in Arabic and other languages. What is overshadowed by these narratives is the fact that the region constituting what we understand today as the "Arab world" has always been experienced as a place of *ghurba* by migrants, refugees, travelers, slaves and other mobile subjects. Mobilities and diasporic communities in the Arab world itself tend to be marginalized, despite the significant political, social, and cultural implications of their presence. This volume thus seeks to depart from the focus on the encounter with the "West" by investigating narratives of dislocation set within the "Arab world"—neither of which are seen as bounded or homogenous entities—whether dislocation is the result of inter-Arab migration and displacement, or foreign encounters. After all, the conditions that have triggered migration from the Arab world to the West and elsewhere are often interlinked with factors that have led many Arab states to become a place of *ghurba* for migrants and displaced people, the most evident of which are authoritarianism and exclusionary notions of national identity and citizenship.

While the region has historically been a hub of movement and is associated with mobility in contemporary times due to the outflow of people seeking refuge from war and economic crises, the circumstances that give rise to *ghurba* as a feeling and a state of being have not always been the outcome of spatial distance from the homeland. In fact, the focus on mobility risks marginalizing articulations of *ghurba* that demonstrate how the act of staying at home itself heightens feelings of alienation, and how these feelings are entwined in many ways with experiences of migration and displacement. Central to the study of migration is "the relationship between mobility and immobility and the extent to which 'migration' and/or 'staying put' are entangled rather than mutually exclusive in the contemporary 'mobile world'" (Fortier 2014, 66). The Arab world has been a place of *ghurba* for sedentary peoples during periods of turmoil and transformation, as well as for ethnic, religious, and linguistic minorities at various historical junctures. In some cases, *ghurba* can be the impetus for leaving the homeland, an act that then either generates other forms of *ghurba*, or offers possibilities of belonging in a new place. In

Introduction 3

other cases, *ghurba* is a position that individuals actively embrace or adopt to assert their difference in places or societies that reject their presence, or to seek refuge from systematic marginalization. Herein lies its value as a word that simultaneously captures different forms of estrangement and that allows this volume to bring together various narratives which paint a more nuanced picture of the Arab world as a site of mobility and alienation. *Narratives of Dislocation in the Arab World* does not have an expansive scope that is able to cover all experiences of estrangement in all parts of the region. Similarly, this introductory chapter does not aim to offer a conclusive understanding of *ghurba* as a concept or a tool against already existing theorizations of migration, exile, displacement, and diaspora in narratives set within and away from the region. Rather, it seeks to question why some narratives are more dominant than others by arguing for the need to explore other experiences of estrangement as well. What we hope will emerge from this collection of essays is an affirmation of the fact that there is no uniform narrative of dislocation in the Arab world, and that any attempt to construct a holistic yet heterogeneous narrative will have to decentralize the unidirectional story of South–North mobility and to recognize psychological and emotional out of placeness as forms of dislocation.

Theorizing *Ghurba*

Spatial distance, absence, and unfamiliarity are all at the heart of the etymology of *ghurba*.[1] The verb *gharab* means to travel or migrate, and to go away. It is the verb used to describe the sun as it goes away and disappears in its hiding place during sunset. *Gharab* is also used for when something is far or absent from one's thinking. The extent to which going away or being absent from one's homeland have negative connotations, because of the detachment and estrangement they cause, possibly derives from the fact that excessiveness is another meaning for words sharing the root gh-r-b. *Ighrab* is excess or the act of going too far when doing something. For example, the verbs *aghrab* and *istaghrab* have been used to describe someone who has exaggerated or gone too far in their laughter. The noun *al-gharb*, which we now use to refer to the West as well as the direction itself, was used to refer to extremeness and going too far in something, which connects with the meaning of *al-gharb* as the act of going away from the homeland. Excess is also there in the verb *aghrab* which, when used to mean travel in the land or from one land to another, suggests exaggeration in the sense that someone has gone too far or spent too long in the act of traveling. We see spatial distance as well in the nouns *al-gharab* and *al-gharba*, which both refer to remote, faraway places, with the latter closely resembling the way in which *al-ghurba* refers to foreign places in contemporary everyday usage. All four nouns, *taghreeb*, *tagharrub*, *ightirab*, and *ghurba*, mean being distanced from the homeland and are commonly used today but with variations. *Al-taghreeb* refers to the displacement or forced migration of an individual or a people, while the meaning of the other

4   Nadeen Dakkak

three can be inclusive of voluntary and involuntary migration. *Ghurba* recurs in everyday usage and captures the emotional strains of physical dislocation and psychological alienation, while *tagharrub* and *ightirab* carry more official references to migration and detachment from the home country in Modern Standard Arabic. *Mutagharrib* and *mughtarib*, which mean the emigrant or the person who lives outside their home country, also vary in usage, with the latter being visible in the state discourses and emigration policies of some Arab countries.

Like *mutagharrib* and *mughtarib*, the noun *al-ghareeb* refers to the person who is at a distance from the homeland, but it also means the stranger. *Ghareeb* as an adjective refers to anything that is strange, in the sense of being ambiguous and unfamiliar. Here we see how words with the same root gh-r-b can have meanings related to both strangeness and being away from a place, typically the homeland. *Al-mughrib* is both the person who travels too far and the person whose talk is ambiguous or who speaks of strange things. Similarly, the superlative adjective *al-aghrab*, which in contemporary usage means the strangest, refers to both the furthest away and the most ambiguous. The correlation between being away from home and being a stranger implies the inevitability of detachment and estrangement as a result of migration or displacement. Estrangement is expectedly central to the experience of being forcibly displaced from one's home country, but the seeming simultaneity of the act of moving away with the fact of becoming a stranger also reflects common understandings as well as condemnations of migration in Arab culture. After all, migration involves the distress of being perceived and treated as an outsider and of having to survive away from the comforting familiarity of home and to adapt to the unfamiliar, but it also involves the prospect of an endless estrangement that takes the form of being stuck away from one's home country or of continuing to feel and be perceived as a stranger after returning to it. At the same time, the above sketch of the meanings associated with the word *ghurba* reveals that the connection between estrangement and being away from the homeland does not in the first place derive from the encounter with the foreign. While the association with excess could suggest the long distance between home and away, distance is always relative to perceptions of space in the same way in which foreignness is relative to changing perceptions of what is unfamiliar and different. The perceived foreignness of a place is not necessarily an indication of its remoteness and vice versa. More importantly, the above definitions of *ghurba* and its derivatives put emphasis on the act of moving away itself, or the fact of being away and absent, rather than on the place to which one has moved. Estrangement, in other words, can be said to be the result of detachment from the homeland rather than of feeling estranged or of being perceived as a stranger in any particular foreign place. This understanding of *ghurba* suggests its capaciousness and demonstrates its ability to articulate the estrangement that ensues from different experiences of detachment from the homeland, regardless of where one moves or is forced to move.

Introduction 5

We can theorize *ghurba* then as a concept that contains within it an acknowledgment of how an individual's detachment from their home makes them vulnerable to feelings of alienation and to occupying the status of a stranger no matter how near or far displacement and migration take them. In this way, *ghurba* enables us to push against and go beyond the emphasis on the encounter with the "West" in narratives of dislocation, which is primary to this volume's aim of centralizing experiences of displacement and migration that take place within the Arab world. If we understand distance in the above definitions of *ghurba* and its derivatives figuratively and not only literally as the geographic space separating one from the homeland, it becomes possible to further disentangle dislocation from experiences of displacement and migration and to recognize how it takes the form of psychological and emotional detachment as well, which is the second primary aim of this volume. Here being a stranger is not necessarily correlated with being away from home, and estrangement can be experienced within the homeland, which is exactly what the word *ghareeb* allows with its multifaceted meanings. The two plurals of *ghareeb*, *ghurub* and *ghuraba'*, are similarly inclusive of the different meanings that can be associated with being a stranger and more commonly refer in contemporary usage to those who are perceived as unfamiliar and different, regardless of whether they are at home or away. Even *ightirab* and *mughtarib* can be used more broadly to refer to alienation and the person who is alienated, respectively, as in Halim Barakat's book *al-Ightirab fil Thaqafa al-Arabiyya* where he understands *ightirab* as a state of inner and social alienation in the Arab reality in which dominant regimes marginalize Arab peoples and cause their paralysis (2006, 27–28). For Barakat, *ghurba* combines both *ightirab* (alienation) and migration, which makes it inclusive of feelings of alienation at home, but also exclusive of migratory experiences in which assimilation occurs with neither nostalgia nor continued attachment to the homeland (2006, 145).

The usefulness of *ghurba*, therefore, derives from its versatility and its ability to encompass experiences that are excluded from words that describe particular forms of mobility, such as *hijra* (migration), *nuzuh* (displacement), *nafy* or *manfa* (exile), and *shatat* (diaspora). The English word estrangement conveys the psychological and emotional detachment of a foreigner or someone who is made to feel like a stranger, and it is often used as the translation of *ghurba*. However, it does not capture the word's versatility and leaves out the loose yet significant connections that *ghurba* contains between movement, distance, absence, and strangeness, as outlined above. Using the Arabic word instead of the translation in this chapter and throughout the volume should not be understood as an indication of its untranslatability, but rather of the attempt to capture the diversity of narratives of dislocation in the Arab world and the desire to bring them together without privileging the lens of social, psychological, and emotional detachment, or that of spatial mobility. What this volume hopes to also achieve by using the original Arabic is to transport the affect that the word *ghurba* often evokes from the locations

6 *Nadeen Dakkak*

with which it is easily associated, namely the "West" with its perceived foreignness, to less obvious locations that may be more hesitantly described as foreign or as sites of *ghurba*, namely the Arab world itself, notwithstanding heightened experiences of alienation that take place within it. *Ghurba* entails distance, absence, and the encounter with the unfamiliar but also the vulnerability to social exclusion and hostile reception by the host state and its policies. All this explains its perceived threat on individuals and the communities they leave behind as well as the negative affect it evokes, which makes it all the more important to bring *ghurba* closer and even place it inside the boundaries of the familiar in order to unsettle assumptions of what constitutes it and who its subjects are.

Dissociating *ghurba* from its typical location within the unfamiliar and the faraway is essential for highlighting not only estrangement at home but also disjunctures and contradictions between assumptions of what home, belonging, or the familiar should be like, and the reality of hostile borders, exclusionary migration regimes, and systematic social marginalization within the Arab world. For example, cultural, linguistic, and religious affinities may suggest that displacement in or migration to a neighboring Arab country cannot be identified as a form of *ghurba*, but everyday lived experiences, such as the ones depicted in narratives discussed in this volume, question these affinities and underscore the role of political, economic and social structures in shaping and even producing dislocation (Chapters 3, 4, and 5). Criticism of these structures frequently invokes discourses of regional, Arab, Islamic, Third World, or even global South solidarity in order to point out the hypocrisy of governments and the dissonance between their empty slogans and laws towards migrants and refugees. Other narratives make it clear that being a citizen of an Arab country does not make one at home within it, which importantly foregrounds factors that make *ghurba* a condition for immobile subjects as well (Chapters 5, 6 and 9). There are also the experiences and narratives of those who arrive from outside the region and encounter racism, discrimination as well as hostile borders and migration laws that in many ways echo the ones encountered by migrants and refugees fleeing Arab countries into Western Europe and North America (Chapters 2 and 8). Many Arab countries are thus both at the receiving end and perpetrators of the violence and subjugation caused by regimes of migration and border governance. Nodes in the inherently unequal modern global system of (im)mobility, they are places of *ghurba*, unfamiliar and alienating to many migrants, refugees, and others who may or may not find in them possibilities of refuge or belonging away from home. Taking the word *ghurba* from its Arab linguistic and cultural settings and using it to approach the experiences of non-Arabic speakers can challenge ethnic, linguistic, cultural, and geographical borders in Arab countries and societies, or in what we understand as the "Arab world," thus blurring the boundaries of the familiar and the unfamiliar.

Notwithstanding all of the above, expressions of *ghurba* within the Arab world have not been the subject of much attention, and this is where

Introduction 7

the contribution of this volume comes. More emphasis has been put on experiences of estrangement in the West and on migration and other kinds of mobilities from the Arab world to mainly Western destinations. This is not unique to research on the region and is arguably a reflection of migration research trends in the Social Sciences. There has been much criticism against the dominance of migration studies by movement from the global South to the global North despite the fact that South–South migration is greater in terms of numbers (Fiddian-Qasmiyeh 2020, 2–6). The alignment of migration research with the interests of state agendas and its reliance on state funding have, among many other reasons, contributed to its Eurocentrism, its silence on the role of colonialism and colonial legacies in shaping (im) mobility and borders, and its preoccupation with South–North migration, primarily its impact on Northern immigration states (Mayblin and Turner 2021, 10–12, 34–36). A growing body of scholarship has been seeking to centralize the global South in migration research in order to question classical concepts and frameworks, and to propose alternative theorizations that contest Eurocentric assumptions of universality (e.g., Nawyn 2016; Adamson and Tsourapas 2019; Crush and Chikanda 2019; Fiddian-Qasmiyeh 2019). Within the Arab world, inter-Arab labor migration and regional displacement have been the subject of research focusing on inter-state relations as well as the political, economic and social repercussions of migration on sending and receiving states (e.g., Tsourapas 2019; Thiollet 2011; IOM 2004). The Gulf States in particular are at the center of much of this research because of the large numbers of migrants they have received from neighboring Arab countries and from other regions, especially South Asia, in the decades following the growth of the oil industry and rapid modernization (e.g., Abdulhadi, AlShehabi and Hanieh 2015; Babar 2017). There has also been increasing interest in the case of other Arab states, like Lebanon and Jordan, that host large populations of migrant workers from Asian and African countries and that adopt similar discriminatory migration and labor policies (e.g., Eyadat 2013; Pande 2014). Scholarship on Arab migration regimes is needed to recognize and critique the role of modern European imperialism and colonialism, whether past or present, in the construction of borders and racial hierarchies that control mobility in the region but also to exceed the postcolonial analytical lens in order to create possibilities for theorizing and understanding local dynamics of migration from within the region itself (Mayblin and Turner 2021, 154–157).

Beyond migration studies in the Social Sciences, research on the historical and contemporary diasporas of the Arab world underscores its cosmopolitanism and contributes to understanding the political, social, and cultural implications of migration to and within the region (e.g., Gorman and Kasbarian 2015; MEI 2010; Gorman and Irving 2021). As with migration structures, cosmopolitanism in the Arab world cannot be understood without recognizing the role of modern colonialism and imperial domination in shaping mobilities and everyday relations between migrant communities

8 *Nadeen Dakkak*

and local populations. Examining past and present realities of diasporas in the global South counters the tendency to prioritize movement from "peripheral" colonies to "central" metropoles and foregrounds displacement and migration between colonies (Mayblin and Turner 2021, 14, 36). At the same time, cosmopolitanism in the Arab world cannot be understood only in relation to European imperial and colonial control, for it is the result of multiple histories, including those of non-European empires, as well as contemporary factors (Chapters 1 and 7). The diverse societies and cultures of the Arab world were both entangled with and existed independently from the encounter with European modernity. *Narratives of Dislocation in the Arab World* follows in the footsteps of this research that reconstructs histories of migration, diaspora, and cosmopolitanism in the region but by looking in particular at narratives of estrangement set within it, and by departing from the emphasis that is typically placed on the encounter with the "West" when approaching Arab literatures of migration.

Beyond the Encounter with the "West"

Contrary to the silencing of colonialism and its legacies in a large part of core migration research in the Social Sciences (Mayblin and Turner 2021, 1–4), critical approaches to migration, exile, and diaspora in literary and cultural studies have been strongly informed by postcolonial theory. Notwithstanding its inadequacy for exploring all kinds of movements around the globe and the fact that it "has mostly been elaborated from an Anglocentric perspective," the centrality of postcolonial approaches for understanding modern and contemporary narratives of migration and diaspora stems in the first place from the extent to which these narratives in many parts of the global South have revolved around the encounter with Europe (Bromley 2000, 8). In the case of the Arab world, before the formation of diasporas and the emergence of the figure of the exilic Arab writer, nineteenth- and early twentieth-century Arab thinkers have been concerned with questions of modernity and tradition in the encounter with the European, "Western" or "occidental" other (El-Enany 2006), an encounter that led many to even espouse the Orientalist and colonial ideology that equated progress with the adoption of European values (Hassan 2019, 49). In subsequent years and until today, physical encounters with European metropoles and other Western centers found a large space in Arab fiction, but literary expressions of migration and exile, at home and in the diaspora, have been as manifold as the historical and cultural moments in which they occurred.

In the late nineteenth and early twentieth century, the emigration of writers and intellectuals from the Levant to North and South America caused the flourishing of diasporic literary circles and produced a large amount of work that came to be identified as *adab al-mahjar* (literature by immigrants), which was very influential on the development of modern Arabic literature (Civantos 2015, 295–301). It is telling that the first novel

Introduction 9

to be written by an Arab in English, *The Book of Khalid* by the Lebanese American writer Amin Al-Rihani, published in 1911, is a reflection on the cultural encounter between the "East" and the "West" through a narrative depicting the migration and return of two boys from Lebanon to New York. In later years, many writers narrated stories of travel to Western Europe that either reinforced the East–West dichotomy, or that used the discourse on European modernity to criticize and indict Arab societies and the state of political disintegration in the aftermath of defeat in the 1967 Arab-Israeli War (known as the *Naksa* or setback), which caused an intellectual crisis for Arab writers and thinkers (Sellman 2018, 756–759). But even before that, particularly as a result of the 1948 dispossession of Palestinians after the creation of Israel (known as the *Nakba* or catastrophe), the West had become the place where many Palestinian writers formed their exilic subjectivities and reflected on displacement, exile, and their role as committed intellectuals. In the last two decades of the twentieth century and in more recent years, the growth of Arab diasporas in Western Europe and North America have additionally given rise to a large body of diasporic writing in Arabic and other languages (Salhi and Netton 2006; Al-Maleh 2009; Hassan 2011; Gana 2013; Bayeh 2015).

The above is by no means a comprehensive sketch of the myriad ways in which Arab writers from different parts of the region have responded to experiences of migration, exile, and displacement. It is beyond the scope of this introduction to illustrate the extent to which the encounter with European colonialism and modernity has been crucial to both these experiences and to the body of writing they made possible. Suffice it to say that postcolonial approaches—with their investment in tracing and contesting the hegemonic and oppressive structures of imperialism and colonialism in their past and contemporary forms as well as their potential for resisting nationalist post-colonial political regimes (Ball and Mattar 2019, 5; Moore 2017, 11–12)—are essential for appreciating the significance of this writing and have indeed been usefully employed in Arab literary scholarship (e.g., Hassan 2011; Gana 2013; Sellman 2018), despite being slow in adequately engaging with the Arab world and its literary and cultural productions (Moore 2017, 4–6). At the same time, the centrality of postcolonial approaches for understanding modern and con-temporary narratives of migration and diaspora from around the world is entwined with their limitations. Postcolonial theory initially gained promin-ence in English Literary Studies and in later years played a significant role in transforming the discipline of Comparative Literature in the US academy in particular (Hassan 2019, 44, 48). This has led it to gradually become influential in other fields of literary study, including modern Arabic literature in which it enabled a methodological shift and a more evident interrogation of the role of imperial and colonial domination (Hassan 2019, 47–48). Notwithstanding the importance of this interaction, the Anglocentrism of postcolonial theory raises questions not only about its adequacy for approaching all narratives of migration, as previously mentioned, but also about the extent to which its

10 Nadeen Dakkak

influence may have contributed to the centrality of Europe or the "West" in Arabic and comparative literary studies.

Because "postcolonial criticism is as inherently comparative as Orientalism" in the way in which it stopped short of dismantling the East–West or South–North axis, it has allowed the continued centrality of Europe in "a kind of reverse Eurocentrism," even with the aim to contest its hegemony, and this is evident in the unequal public and critical reception of literary texts (Hassan 2019, 50). I quote Waïl Hassan at length here because his investigation of the implications of bringing together postcolonial theory with Arabic literary studies, primarily within the domain of Comparative Literature, is useful for my aim in this Part to highlight the limitations of approaching narratives of migration and displacement in relation to the West. Giving the example of Sudanese novels that have received much less visibility than the work of Tayeb Salih, known for his *Season of Migration to the North*, which was published in 1966, Hassan argues:

> The agenda of comparison remains Eurocentric. Texts that dialogue with European works, themes and motifs enjoy greater visibility than those less, or not at all, oriented toward Europe. This is as true with Arab readers as with the paradigms of Comparative Literature as an academic discipline. … [P]ostcolonial studies has enabled the entry of modern Arabic literature into the realm of comparison, of dialogue with other literary critical fields through the metalanguage of theory, and with that has come increased sophistication and attention to questions of method. At the same time, however, this has confined Arabic literary studies to the North-South, or centre-periphery, paradigm that defines the postcolonial (in its literary-historical sense), foreclosing questions relevant to more recent periods, strictly local conditions or cultural, historical and political ties among regions of the Global South.
>
> (2019, 51)

Hassan identifies the South–South paradigm that has been enabled by comparative literary studies as a small, recently emerging domain, but with much potential for challenging the boundaries and the "verticality" with which postcolonial studies as well as Arabic literary studies tend to operate (2019, 52). The South–South paradigm would make it possible to recognize "'horizontal' links that are often overlooked in studies that re-inscribe European primacy in 'vertical' relations that radiate unidirectionally between the metropolitan centre and each of its colonies" (2019, 52). This "horizontal" comparativism does not imply decontextualization from European colonialism but a "reconceptualization" of these fields of study through a "triangulated model of comparison" which, as Anna Ball and Karim Matter put it, "responds to discourses and practices of colonialism, imperialism and global capitalism in the Middle East without sacrificing the specificity of the local" (Hassan 2019, 53; 2019, 8). Despite the breadth of Hassan's

Introduction 11

concerns with the "epistemological, disciplinary and institutional limits of Arabic literary studies today," his critique of the persistence of East–West dualism and of the "principle of absolute Otherness" that it relies on raises similar points to the ones I make here on the need to go beyond the "West" when approaching narratives of dislocation in the Arab world (2019, 54). The East–West dualism and the easy association of *ghurba* with what is typically perceived as the "foreign" and alienating "West" are manifest in the centrality of narratives of migration, exile and displacement in the "West" and the marginality of narratives in which *ghurba* is articulated in closer, less "foreign" places, or even at home.

Although the notion of *manfa* or exile, which is a prominent aspect of modern Arab writing on displacement, conveys feelings of loss and estrangement *away* from the homeland rather than *in* any particular locale, it has arguably taken shape in the encounter with the "West" or in relation to Western or European modernity. In the writings of exiled Palestinian intellectuals, and in Edward Said's theorization if it, the contemporary experience of exile is not simply associated with artistic creativity and modernist experimentation, as it was celebrated in European literature, but also grounded in the reality of dispossession and displacement that has become a marker of Palestinian literature and culture until today (Mattar 2019, 34–35). As Mattar argues, exile cannot be reduced to the "empty discourses of a free-flowing, hybridising transnationalism" of some postcolonial approaches that distanced Said's work from its Palestinian origins (2019, 35–36), which is not to say that it was not understood as an empowering position. Exile for many Palestinian writers like Said, Mahmoud Darwish, and Jabra Ibrahim Jabra, is an "enabler of creativity and criticism … a state of displacement that is at once tragic and a catalyst for change" (Halabi 2017, 97). It is at the heart of Said's "secular criticism," which allows the intellectual to develop a political commitment and a critical perspective that transcend nationalist, ideological and other primordial attachments (Halabi 2017, 101; Mattar 2019). Here, it is important to understand exile both literally and metaphorically, for it is not just an enforced physical displacement from the homeland but a deliberate distancing of the self from centers of political power, one in which intellectuals critically position themselves against colonialism as well as "endogenous structures of oppression," both of which cause their alienation (Halabi 2017, 11–12). These are the circumstances that have given rise to the figure of the exilic Arab intellectual whose "physical and intellectual displacement and liminality" allow them to push for change through art and writing that embody their modern subjectivity (Halabi 2017, 103). Therefore, in this notion of exile, estrangement is not only experienced away from, but also vis-à-vis the homeland from which the exilic writer has been uprooted. Even in writings that do not explicitly engage with the experience of exile, this double estrangement has been central to the Arab literary tradition in the aftermath of the 1967 *Naksa*, which caused the disillusionment of writers with Arab nationalism and signaled a state of political impasse. In such writings, alienation can be

12 Nadeen Dakkak

understood as a response to the social and political changes that led the "old conflict between the 'self' and the 'other' [to be] replaced by conflicts within the self" (Hafez 1994, 95–96).

However, even when the notion of exile encompasses material, psychological and intellectual estrangement, the "West" remains paramount to it. It is the center from and against which the exilic intellectual derives and builds the humanist sensibility and worldview that mark their exilic modern subjectivity and give them "cultural capital" (Halabi 2017, 102). As Zeina Halabi makes clear, the nineteenth-century Arab Enlightenment era with its investment in reconciling Western modernity with local Arab and Islamic culture paved the way for the emergence of the modern subjectivity that would subsequently allow twentieth-century Arab intellectuals to build their emancipatory projects against colonialism and local oppression (2017, 8–9, 16–17). Even though Jabra, for example, was exiled in Iraq, central to his experience and to the archetypal exilic figure he creates in his fiction is the "Western humanist tradition" through which he and other Arab intellectuals at the time sought to find answers for the political and cultural predicaments of the Arab world, including Palestinian displacement (Halabi 2017, 104). Therefore, the notion of exile as it has been articulated in modern Arabic literature is, to borrow Hassan's words again, "oriented toward Europe" and thus often produced texts that "dialogue with European works, themes and motifs," even when they are not set outside the Arab world (2019, 51).

Aside from this orientation, the "West" is also the place with which exile is mostly tied in imagined trajectories of Arab displacement and migration because its unfamiliarity and distance allow it to best harbor the solitude and alienation of the exilic experience. Barakat expands the notion of exile beyond forced displacement to include voluntary exile as well, both of which are characterized by a deep sense of alienation as a result of "holding on to Arab identity and Arab cultural belonging," contrary to migration that causes "integration within the new society" (2006, 145). He differentiates between "external" and "internal" exile, the former located in Europe and the United States to which increased migration throughout the second half of the twentieth century have given more prominence to the relation between *ghurba* and literary creativity (2006, 145), and the latter occurring within *al-watan* or the homeland (2006, 149). This he understands as both the home country, where exile takes the form of estrangement rather than physical dislocation, and as *al-watan al-arabi*, or the Arab homeland (2006, 149). For Barakat, internal exile is "worse and more miserable" than external exile, but what is clear from the differentiation he makes between the two is that the perils of internal exile derive from feeling alienated and suffocated by the political and cultural climate that Arab regimes impose on Arab peoples, rather than the fact of being physically distanced from home and feeling as an outsider in a strange place (2006, 148–149). Exile in this sense is mostly located within the unfamiliar and does not encompass the alienation, nostalgia and intercultural encounters that arise from experiences of physical dislocation, whether

Introduction 13

enforced or voluntary, within the Arab world. Furthermore, even though Said grounded exile in the material circumstances of displacement, its association with modernist writing, solitude, creativity, and the critical positioning of the self has traditionally led exiled intellectuals to be differentiated from refugees, a term evoking mass displacement and victimhood (Sellman 2018, 758–759). This hierarchy has made the notion of exile inadequate for approaching all narratives of displacement in Arabic literary studies.

In more recent literary criticism, exilic literature as a genre has come to be understood as the literature of the Arab diaspora or *al-shatat* where diasporic fiction, whether written in Arabic or other languages, "bears the marks of both the writers' country of origin and their host country" and "acts as a bridge" between them (Salhi 2006, 3–4). However, most of the scholarship that addresses Arab diasporic writing is centered on migration to the West, particularly Europe and North America (Aberrezak 2016; Fadda-Conrey 2014; Hassan 2011; Al-Maleh 2009; Salhi and Netton 2006; Bayeh 2015). This does not mean that recent and contemporary migration from Arab countries to Western destinations has continued to take the same patterns which marked earlier migration in the second half of the twentieth century. Political conflict and economic crises have given rise to a large number of migrants, refugees and asylum seekers who do not encounter the "West" or write about exile like their predecessors. Johanna Sellman notes,

> Cities such as Berlin, Stockholm and Amsterdam have become important centres for Arab cultural production in Europe, displacing the primacy of London and Paris. Newer diasporas are reshaping the field of Arab and Arabic cultural production in Europe. Literary narratives themselves are shifting away from the themes and contexts of colonial and post-colonial Arabic exile literature, and exploring new aesthetics and modes of representing migration in a global context. In Arabic literature, the "cultural encounter" frameworks, "political commitment" and modernist understandings of exile of the 20th century have been giving way to new approaches to writing migration […].
>
> (2018, 754)

Focusing in particular on Arabic literature of "forced" or "precarious migration" to Europe, Sellman argues that this literature should still be read in relation to earlier postcolonial fiction and by making use of postcolonial approaches because it "evokes north–south axes of power such as unevenly distributed access to mobility and the economic realities shaping migration" (2018, 755). However, even if such contemporary migration narratives echo global experiences of mobility and border-crossing and do not exactly reiterate earlier tropes of migration to colonial or former colonial metropoles, their settings remain characteristically "Western." After all, cities like Amsterdam and Berlin share many similarities with Paris and London, and contemporary Arab migrants and refugees may associate them with the same

14   *Nadeen Dakkak*

values of modernity that have marked colonizing nations and their metropoles, or have similar ambivalent attitudes towards their societies and cultures. In other words, the contemporary migration narratives that Sellman highlights may be global in their focus and in the way they negotiate postcolonial exile literature, but they follow the same trajectory that pushes migrants from the margin to "Western" centers in the world of global capitalism.

The above overview does not aim to give a comprehensive picture of how Arab narratives of dislocation have been approached in postcolonial, comparative, and Arabic literary studies. This would potentially be the subject of a much larger discussion that takes into account commonalities and differences between Arab fiction on dislocation in Arabic, English, French, and other languages from within and outside the region, and that investigates more thoroughly the possibilities and limitations offered by postcolonial, comparative and world literary frameworks, as well as by exile and diaspora as analytical tools. Rather, the purpose of this overview has been to namely highlight the centrality of the "West" in narratives of dislocation and how they have been approached in order to propose a more capacious understanding of dislocation in the Arab world, one that is attentive to different forms of *ghurba* that take place within it. The contention here is not that migratory encounters with the "West" should be less central, but that they should not determine how we conceptualize dislocation in a way that eclipses other narratives.

Rewriting *Ghurba*

The nine chapters included in this volume examine mostly fictional, but also autobiographical narratives of physical, psychological and emotional dislocation in what is understood as the "Arab world" or, in some cases, in the wider "Middle East" region. Borders are porous and the location of these narratives is oftentimes ambiguous, in between places and cultures. On the one hand, this in-betweenness dispels assumptions on the existence of an "Arab world" that is underpinned by uncomplicated geographical, ethnic, cultural and linguistic boundaries, and it additionally reveals the impossibility of not understanding the region or parts of it as an extension of, and a focal point to others that lie outside these perceived boundaries. Indeed, one aim behind the inclusion of contributions which tackle non-"Arab" narratives of migration and displacement in a volume focused on articulations of *ghurba* is to challenge these boundaries and to suggest different avenues for approaching literary and cultural production from/about the region. On the other hand, the cosmopolitanism of the Arab world and the transnational connections that shape its contemporary reality are not sufficient to dismantle or claim the irrelevance of these boundaries. All the chapters in this volume ground narratives of dislocation in political, social and cultural structures and practices that show how boundaries manifest in everyday lived experiences and have real effects on the individuals and communities whose stories they tell. With the exception of a few, the chapters do not all explicitly engage with the notion of *ghurba* and a number of them look at non-Arabic texts by Arab and non-Arab authors. However, what brings them together despite their multifarious themes and concerns, and despite their different theoretical and methodological approaches, is the fact that they all contribute to painting a picture of the Arab world as a place of *ghurba* where mobile and immobile subjects, foreigners and local inhabitants alike, encounter alienation. In that sense, the chapters make it possible to see the region from a different light by focusing on less visible narratives, ones that do not fit typical understandings of *ghurba* as primarily located in the realm of the unfamiliar and the faraway.

The chapters are not ordered chronologically, but this volume starts with an early form of mobility that has been central to the shaping of economic relations and cosmopolitan societies in the region, but that has not received adequate attention despite its contemporary legacies of racism and racial hierarchies. The forced mobility of enslaved women from Caucasian and African descent across the Ottoman Empire in the nineteenth and twentieth century raises questions about the extent to which slavery narratives have found a space in literary production from/about the region. The two chapters in Part I, *Ghurba* in Narratives of Slavery and Racism, highlight how the issue of slavery was tackled in the biographical fiction and memoirs of authors whose lives were entangled with those of the enslaved characters they write about. In Chapter 1, Burcu Gürsel examines how maternal slavery and displacement appear in anti-slavery literature by late nineteenth-century Ottoman reformist writers, particularly Sami Paşazade Sezai's novel *Sergüzeşt*, published in 1888, where his depiction of the enslaved female protagonist can be understood as partially mourning the displacement of his formerly enslaved mother from the Caucasus. The repetitive forced displacement of the enslaved female protagonist in *Sergüzeşt* from her homeland to Istanbul to Egypt reveals the economic and social networks that were enabled by the slave trade across the Ottoman Empire and its provinces. At the same time, Gürsel shows how this physical displacement is entwined with Sezai's own deliberate displacement of slavery itself from the Imperial metropole to the Egyptian province as part of his attempt to balance between his anti-slavery stance and the need to face up to European imperialism and its pressures on the Ottoman Empire to abolish slavery. By investigating the liminal position of exiled Egyptian Turks between the province and the metropole, their Westernization and, accordingly, what is perceived as their different or less "humane" treatment of enslaved people than in Istanbul, the chapter reveals power dynamics at the intersection of European colonialism, Ottoman Imperialism and nineteenth-century slave trade.

In Chapter 2, the experiences of enslaved women are shaped by a different dynamic, that of Arab racism against people of African origins, and blackness in particular, but they are similarly characterized by immobility and vulnerability to sexual exploitation. Arthti Sathananthar highlights the marginalization and othering of black "maids" in the affluent Damascene household that Suad Amiry depicts in *My Damascus* (2016), which narrates the stories

16 *Nadeen Dakkak*

of multiple generations of women in her family throughout the twentieth century. The chapter notes the importance of Amiry's inclusion of their voices in her family narrative, a decision that reflects their intimate connection with the family as well as Amiry's own literary attempt to bring to the foreground the region's history of slavery, and to address contemporary issues of Arab racism and anti-blackness, especially in the Levant. At the same time, Sathananthar traces Amiry's racialized representation of black and mixed-race characters to demonstrate the narrative's uncritical reproduction of racist tropes, thus revealing a process of textual othering that calls into question the ways in which Arab literary and cultural production have struggled to adequately engage with histories of slavery from the African continent, or with continued anti-black racism (Kareem 2019).

We move to more contemporary forms of othering and marginalization in Part II, *Ghurba* in Narratives of Displacement, but even here the experiences of refugees and asylum seekers cannot be disconnected from their political and socioeconomic histories and are a continuation of an already existing state of *ghurba*. In Chapter 3 and Chapter 4, the trauma of Palestinian dispossession is passed on from one generation to the next, and *ghurba* is renewed in every new location in which the Palestinian characters are displaced, thus making it a permanent state of existence rather than a temporary experience bound to a certain place. In Chapter 5, *ghurba* is a pre-existing condition in the "homeland" for Syrian Kurds even before they experience marginalization and alienation as a result of forced migration or asylum within the region and in Europe. By focusing on narratives of displacement in Arab countries, including Lebanon, Kuwait, Jordan, and Egypt, this Part foregrounds the systematic exclusion, both social and institutional, which migrants and refugees from the region are subjected to in neighboring Arab countries. Roba Al-Salibi's analysis of Radwa Ashour's *al-Tanturiya* (2010; translated as *The Woman from Tantoura*) in Chapter 3 looks at the structural marginalization of Palestinian refugees in Lebanon, particularly during the period of the Lebanese civil war, but by privileging the subjective lens of the female protagonist. Alsalibi grounds the novel in the political and socioeconomic reality of Lebanon as well as the 1948 Nakba which marked the moment of rupture and displacement for Palestinians, but she shows how the Palestinian characters still manage to build homes and maintain intimate communal ties through the use of memory as a tool that enables them to push against this reality and preserve their identity. By focusing on the centrality of the subjective and the affective in Ashour's novel, the chapter thus demonstrates the necessity of going beyond both dominant colonial and humanitarian narratives that homogenize Palestinians and affirm their victimized status without recognizing their agency in the face of settler-colonialism and exclusionary migration structures.

Memory is similarly represented as a tool of resistance in Susan Abulhawa's *Against the Loveless World* (2020), as Benay Blend shows in Chapter 4, especially when it is used by Palestinian women to subvert the more familiar

Introduction 17

nationalist male perspectives that have tended to dominate historical narrations of Palestinian dispossession and displacement. Both here and in Chapter 3, gender determines Palestinian experiences, with women taking on the responsibility of supporting the family, materially and emotionally, and building networks that sustain the collective identity of Palestinians. However, in the context of Kuwait where Abulhawa's novel is partially set, Blend shows how this collective identity, alongside the country's exclusion of non-citizens and its hostility against Palestinians after the 1990 Iraqi invasion, plays an important role in preventing the assimilation of Palestinians and in preparing the protagonist for her physical and emotional return to Palestine, despite earlier feelings of attachment to Kuwait and her distance from her Palestinian identity. The chapter thus not only sheds important light on the Palestinian presence in Kuwait, but it also demonstrates how experiences of *ghurba* in a place that does not reciprocate the attachments which diasporic communities have for it can become the impetus for rebuilding stronger connections to the physical or imagined homeland, or even for sparking political commitment to its cause, as in the case of Abulhawa's protagonist.

Contrary to Palestinian displacement, which has been central to Palestinian literary and cultural production since 1948, the more recent experiences of Syrian refugees have triggered new reflections on *ghurba* that rethink earlier Arab literary conceptions and representations of migration and exile (Sellman 2018). In Chapter 5, Annamaria Bianco investigates thematic and aesthetic shifts in contemporary literature of forced displacement (*adab al-tahjir*) and asylum (*adab al-luju'*) by looking at the journey of Syrian-Kurdish writer Haitham Hussein to Europe across several locations, and by examining his memoir *Qad la yabqa ahad, aghatha kristy ... ta'aly aqul laki kayfa a'iysh* (2018; translated as *No One May Remain. Agatha Christie, Come, I'll Tell You How I Live*). Hussein's personal and literary reflections on his experience of repression in Syria, and of exclusion in the United Arab Emirates, Egypt, and Turkey before finally deciding to apply for asylum in the United Kingdom allow him to criticize discourses of Arab, Islamic and humanitarian hospitality and to reveal the double marginalization of Kurdish people. Bianco shows how Hussein's writing returns to the roots of feeling out of place within the homeland, which ultimately contributes to shaping his perspective on the virtues of *ghurba* as a way to "come out of one's self" in order to reflect on meanings of identity, home and belonging.

If physical *ghurba* away from one's homeland is identified as a site of identity construction in Chapter 5, social and psychological *ghurba* within the homeland can also be a refuge from marginalization, a position that one willingly adopts to maintain distance and assert their non-belonging. In Part III, Religious Spaces of *Ghurba* and Belonging, we see how Islamic belief encourages the adoption of this position, but also how religious communities in general offer a refuge for migrants from the perils of alienation away from home. Islam has notably endowed *ghurba* with positive connotations by promising happiness in the afterlife for believers who are estranged from the

18   Nadeen Dakkak

rest of society because of their beliefs. Prophet Mohammad's hadith, "Islam began as something strange (*ghareeb*) and will go back to being strange, so glad tidings to the strangers (*al-ghuraba'*),"[2] emphasizes spiritual *ghurba* and is commonly evoked in religious discourses to maintain the morale of Muslim believers amidst what is perceived as a time of corruption, even if the meaning of *ghuraba'* can be interpreted differently. Being a *ghareeb* has its own significance in Shia Islam, as we see in Chapter 6 where Hawraa Al-Hassan examines political expressions of spiritual *ghurba* in popular religious novels by two Shia women writers from Iraq and Kuwait, Amina al-Sadr's *al-Fadila tantasir* (Virtue Prevails, 1969) and Khawla al-Qazwini's *'Indama yufakkir al-rajul* (When a Man Thinks, 1993). Published in response to increasing state-led secularization in the region and primarily aimed at young female readers, the chapter shows how this genre of religious fiction emphasizes the virtues of *ghurba* when it arises from the marginalization of pious Shia communities in a secular country or from political oppression against Muslim communities. At the same time, Al-Hassan argues that these writers turn *ghurba* into an empowering state by making it essential for the religious awakening of characters and an impetus for asserting Islamic values in society and claiming the public spaces from which they are excluded. In this way, Islamic belief does not only offer a refuge from *ghurba* by embracing it and turning it into a private space of belonging, but it spurs the consciousness that pushes individuals to counter their *ghurba*, to change their political and social reality so that they cease to be strangers.

In Chapter 7, religion similarly offers a space of belonging and a refuge from alienation in a strange land, as Mariam Elashmawy shows in her reading of the intellectual and migration story of the Naqshbandi scholar Muhammad Murad al-Qazani (d. 1352/1935) from the historical Volga-Ural region to the Hijaz, where he stayed for 36 years in Mecca during the late nineteenth and early twentieth century. Focusing in particular on the circumstances which led al-Qazani to translate the historical Naqshbandi text *Rashahat 'ayn al-hayat* by Fakhr al-Din 'Ali (d. 940/1533) from Persian into Arabic, Elashmawy foregrounds the role of diasporic Sufi networks in Mecca as well as the neglected intellectual and translation circles that operated between the Arabian Peninsula and peripheral Islamic regions. The chapter examines the choices that al-Qazani made in his translation and other writings from this period of his life first to show the extent of his homesickness and feelings of marginality and insecurity about his intellectual prowess as a non-native Arabic speaker, and second to demonstrate how he found solace and a form of spiritual belonging in Sufi religious spaces as well as the texts that he engaged with and translated. This intellectual history reveals the cosmopolitanism of Mecca and the intellectual role of Muslim migrant communities, but it also raises questions about the reception of non-Arab Muslim scholarly productions, the treatment which these migrant communities received, and continuities between past and contemporary marginalization.

Introduction 19

Nowhere are histories of cosmopolitanism as important to emphasize as they are in the Gulf States where modern national identities and narratives derive legitimacy from the exclusion of cosmopolitan pasts and contemporary migrant communities. The last Part of the volume, Negotiating National Imaginaries of Belonging and Exclusion, begins with stories that disrupt such narratives by shedding light on the lives of South Asian migrants in the United Arab Emirates. Deepak Unnikrishnan's *Temporary People*, the subject of Lava Asaad's analysis in Chapter 8, depicts multi-layered Indian experiences of marginalization and belonging that all disrupt the illusion of homogeneity in a country that both relies on and excludes migrant workers. While their *ghurba* is a direct result of their alienation in Abu Dhabi, Assad shows that the migrant worker experience is one of double exclusion and detachment from both home and host country, and that the middle-class migrant experience is similarly characterized by an "anxious belonging" that is as fragile as the romanticized and imagined ideas of India as home. The chapter foregrounds the aesthetics of narrating the stories of such disjointed beings and critiques the marginalization of their experiences in contrast to their counterparts in Western immigrant destinations.

Although the status of minorities and their inclusion/exclusion in nation-building is different from that of migrants in the Gulf who remain legally excluded from pathways of citizenship and official belonging, their marginalization within the homeland and their alienation from homogenizing national narratives arguably result in experiences of "anxious belonging" as well. Such is the case of Nubians in Egypt, as we see in Rania Salem's analysis of Idris Ali's *Dongola* (1993) in the last chapter. Unlike other experiences of psychological *ghurba* within the homeland, however, here the physical displacement of Nubians from their indigenous lands characterizes their dislocation and has been at the center of literary works by Nubian writers from the 1970s onwards, including Ali. Despite being accused of espousing a separatist ideology that disrupts national unity, Salem notes that Ali sought harmony rather than radical separatism and considered himself part of the Egyptian literary realm, a position that she argues is at the heart of his critical depiction of the radicalism of *Dongola*'s protagonist. The chapter shows how Ali's own ambivalent identity as a Nubian writing in Arabic and his conception of an Arab-African cultural identity are expressed in the protagonist's struggle to find belonging in either northern and southern Egypt and to reconcile the displacement and marginalization of his community with his belief in political possibilities of national integration. Here we see how *ghurba* takes the form of estrangement not only in the homeland, but within one's own ethnic and cultural community because of conflicts between how they envision their place within the Egyptian nation.

These chapters do not cover literary evocations of *ghurba* in all geographical and thematic areas, and there is indeed much room for further investigation of how *ghurba* manifests as an affect, an experience, a state of being and a concept in a wider body of literature beyond the contexts included

20 *Nadeen Dakkak*

in this volume. For example, the geographical focus of the chapters mostly excludes countries in North Africa where writers have been preoccupied with questions of slavery, race and migration. Similarly, the *ghurba* of religious and ethnic communities excludes non-Muslim minorities, indigenous peoples, and their literatures and languages. Despite the emphasis on gender and sexuality through the prioritization of women's experiences in some of the chapters, the volume also does not address recent writings on sexual minorities which could shed new perspectives on how we conceptualize *ghurba* within places that are both familiar and strange. These are only some examples of what is left out of this volume, but we nonetheless hope that its rewriting of *ghurba* within this modest scope would contribute to and introduce important avenues for future scholarship on dislocation within the Arab world.

Notes

1 In this section, I rely on definitions and examples from different dictionaries and sources collated in *The Doha Historical Dictionary of Arabic*, dohadictionary.org, and Almaany.com.
2 The Hadith is from *Sunan Ibn Majah*, Vol. 5, Book 36, Hadith 3986, available in Arabic and English translation: https://sunnah.com/ibnmajah:3986.

References

Abderrezak, Hakim. 2016. *Ex-Centric Migrations: Europe and the Maghreb in Mediterranean Cinema, Literature, and Music.* Indiana: Indiana University Press.
Adamson, Fiona B., and Gerasimos Tsourapas. 2020. "The Migration State in the Global South: Nationalizing, Developmental and Neoliberal Models of Migration Management," *International Migration Review* 54(3), pp. 853–882, doi.org/10.1177/0197918319879057
Al-Maleh, Layla (ed.). 2009. *Arab Voices in Diaspora: Critical Perspectives on Anglophone Arab Literature.* Amsterdam: Rodopi.
Babar, Zahra (ed.). 2017. *Arab Migrant Communities in the GCC.* Oxford: Oxford University Press.
Ball, Anna, and Karim Matter. 2019. "Dialectics of Post/Colonial Modernity in the Middle East: A Critical, Theoretical and Disciplinary Overview." In *The Edinburgh Companion to the Postcolonial Middle East*, ed. Anna Ball and Karim Mattar. Edinburgh: Edinburgh University Press, pp. 4–22.
Barakat, Halim. 2006. *al-Ightirab fil Thaqafa al-'Arabiyya: Matahat al-Insan baynal Hulm wal-Waqi'* [Alienation in Arab Culture: The Dilemmas of Man between Dream and Reality]. Beirut: Markaz Dirasat al-Wihda al-'Arabiyya.
Bayeh, Jumana. 2014. *The Literature of the Lebanese Diaspora: Representations of Place and Transnational Identity.* London: I. B. Tauris.
Bromley, Roger. 2000. *Narratives for a New Belonging: Diasporic Cultural Fictions.* Edinburgh: Edinburgh University Press.
Civantos, Christina. 2015. "Migration and Diaspora." In *The Modern Companion to Modern Arab Culture*, ed. Dwight F. Reynolds. Cambridge: Cambridge University Press, pp. 293–311.

Crush, Jonathan, and Abdel Chikanda. 2019 "South–South Migrations and Diasporas." In *Routledge Handbook of South-South Relations*, ed. Elena Fiddian-Qasmiyeh and Patricia Daley. New York: Routledge, pp. 380–396.

El-Enany, Rasheed. 2006. *Arab Representations of the Occident: East-West Encounters in Arabic Fiction*. London: Routledge.

Eyadat, Zaid. 2013. "Balancing Security and Human Rights: The Case of Female Migrant Workers in Jordan." In *Migration, Security, and Citizenship in the Middle East: New Perspectives*, ed. Peter Seeberg and Zaid Eyadat. New York: Palgrave Macmillan, pp. 43–63.

Fadda-Conrey, Carol. 2014. *Contemporary Arab-American Literature: Transnational Reconfigurations of Citizenship and Belonging*. New York: New York University Press.

Fiddian-Qasmiyeh, Elena. 2019. "Southern-led Responses to Displacement: Modes of South-South Cooperation?" In *Routledge Handbook of South–South Relations*, ed. Elena Fiddian-Qasmiyeh and Patricia Daley. New York: Routledge, pp. 239–255.

Fiddian-Qasmiyeh, Elena. 2020. "Introduction: Recentering the South in Studies of Migration." *Migration and Society* 3(1), pp. 1–18, doi.org/10.3167/arms.2020.030102.

Fortier, Anne-Marie. 2014. "Migration Studies." In *The Routledge Handbook of Mobilities*, ed. Peter Adey, et al. London: Routledge, pp. 64–73.

Gana, Nouri (ed). 2013. *The Edinburgh Companion to the Arab Novel in English: The Politics of Anglo Arab and Arab American Literature and Culture*. Edinburgh: Edinburgh University Press.

Gorman, Anthony and Sarah Irving (eds.). 2021. *Cultural Entanglement in the Pre-Independence Arab World: Arts, Thought and Literature*. London: I. B. Tauris.

Gorman, Anthony and Sossie Kasbarian (eds.). 2015. *Diasporas of the Modern Middle East: Contextualizing Community*. Edinburgh: Edinburgh University Press.

Hafez, Sabry. 1994. "The Transformation of Reality and the Arabic Novel's Aesthetic Response," Bulletin of the School of Oriental and African Studies 57(1), pp. 93–112. www.jstor.org/stable/619498.

Halabi, Zeina G. 2017. *The Unmaking of the Arab Intellectual: Prophecy, Exile and the Nation*. Edinburgh: Edinburgh University Press.

Hassan, Waïl S. 2011. *Immigrant Narratives: Orientalism and Cultural Translation in Arab American and Arab British Literature*. Oxford: Oxford University Press.

Hassan, Waïl S. 2019. "Postcolonialism and Modern Arabic Literature: Twenty-First-Century Horizons." In *The Edinburgh Companion to the Postcolonial Middle East*, ed. Anna Ball and Karim Mattar. Edinburgh: Edinburgh University Press, pp. 43–56.

Helene Thiollet. 2011. "Migration as Diplomacy: Labor Migrants, Refugees and Arab Regional Politics in the Oil-Rich Countries," *International Labor and Working-Class History* 79, pp. 103–121, doi.org/10.1017/S0147547910000293.

International Organization for Migration. 2004. *Arab Migration in a Globalized World*. https://publications.iom.int/system/files/pdf/arab_migration_globalized_world.pdf

Kareem, Mona. 2019. "Arabic Literature and the African Other." Africa is a Country, https://africasacountry.com/2019/05/how-do-arabs-talk-and-write-about-black-people [accessed 23 March 2022]

Khalaf, Abdulhadi, Omar AlShehabi and Adam Hanieh (eds.). 2015. *Transit States: Labour, Migration and Citizenship in the Gulf*. London: Pluto Press.

22 *Nadeen Dakkak*

Mattar, Karim. 2019. "Edward Said and the Institution of Postcolonial Studies." In *The Edinburgh Companion to the Postcolonial Middle East*, ed. Anna Ball and Karim Mattar. Edinburgh: Edinburgh University Press, pp. 23–42.

Mayblin, Lucy, and Joe Turner. 2021. *Migration Studies and Colonialism*. Cambridge: Polity Press.

Middle East Institute. 2010. *Viewpoints: Migration and the Mashreq.*

Moore, Lindsey. 2017. *Narrating Postcolonial Arab Nations: Egypt, Algeria, Lebanon, Palestine*. London: Routledge.

Nawyn, Stephanie J. 2016. "Migration in the Global South: Exploring New Theoretical Territory," *International Journal of Sociology* 46 (2), pp. 81–84, doi.org/10.1080/00207659.2016.1163991

Pande, Amrita. 2014. "Forging Intimate and Work Ties: Migrant Domestic Workers Resist in Lebanon." In *Migrant Domestic Workers in the Middle East: The Home and the World* Fernandez, ed. Bina Fernandez and Marina de Regt. New York: Palgrave Macmillan, pp. 27–49.

Salhi Zahia, Smail, and Ian Richard Netton (eds.). 2006. *The Arab Diaspora: Voices of an Anguished Scream*. New York: Routledge.

Salhi, Zahia Smail. 2006. "Defining the Arab Diaspora." In *The Arab Diaspora: Voices of an Anguished Scream*, eds. Zahia Smail Salhi and Ian Richard Netton. Routledge, pp. 1–10.

Sellman, Johanna. 2018. "A Global Postcolonial: Contemporary Arabic Literature of Migration to Europe," *Journal of Postcolonial Writing* 54(6), pp. 751–765, doi.org/10.1080/17449855.2018.1555207 [accessed August 9, 2020]

Tsourapas, Gerasimos. 2019. *The Politics of Migration in Modern Egypt: Strategies for Regime Survival in Autocracies*. Cambridge: Cambridge University Press.

Part I

Ghurba in Narratives of Slavery and Racism

1 Dissolving into the Nile

Ottoman Reformism and Maternal Slavery in *Sergüzeşt*

Burcu Gürsel

Despite the fast growing number of studies on Ottoman slavery and dependency—an inevitably haphazard collective effort, given Ottoman slavery's myriad forms over six centuries on three continents—literary scholarship on anti-slavery literature in the late Ottoman period is scant.[1] The Tanzimat (reform) period, officially starting with Sultan Abdülmecid's Edict of Gülhane in 1839 and lasting until the first constitution in 1876, ultimately stretched to the Young Turk revolution in 1908 that ended Abdülhamid II's long reign, and even up until the Republican era. This period came to encompass extensive reforms throughout the empire after an initial promise of equal protection to non-Muslim subjects. It also saw a translation movement and the appearance of the genres of the novel and drama in the Ottoman world. The untapped corpus of anti-slavery writing by those late-nineteenth century Ottoman reformists whose own mothers had been purchased as young concubines from the Caucasus is haunted by the auto/biographical elements of inherited trauma, namely maternal slavery and displacement. The writers persistently narrate slaves' passage from a mythologized motherland to their demise or salvation in the fatherland. In so doing, they employ ambivalent filial, sexual, or paternal overtones in their attitudes toward the literary character of the slave girl, who might represent the mother when young, a love object, or an adopted former slave.

For the novelist whose mother was a slave girl, this literary character can only be a barred object of desire, since the writer wishes to have been a father to his own mother when she was enslaved. These sons repeatedly deliver the symbolic mother from slavery to new, rightful families of her own—else, the mother will die, and the sons remain unborn.[2] Alternately, she is driven headlong to her death, as in the melancholic subject's wish for "matricide," of killing the unmourned but internalized mother. Whether in the form of sentimental-realist fiction, historical fabulation, or pan-Ottomanist allegory, these writings reveal writers who are anti-slavery as sons, but sovereign as potential masters. Attempting to mourn their own traumatized and emotionally absent mothers, they find themselves taking on the mother's mourning for her own lost mother, mother tongue, and mother land. And yet, as patriarchs,

DOI: 10.4324/9781003301776-3

26 *Burcu Gürsel*

authors, and statesmen, they rally just as strongly in defense of the state, especially when it is pitted against Western imperialism: slavery is deplorable; the lasting institution of Ottoman slavery less so. Among the towering figures whose mothers were formerly enslaved are first Ahmet Midhat (1844–1913), the prolific novelist who established the genre in the Ottoman Empire, and who demonstrated a lifelong obsession with the topic of slavery in various literary genres. In fact, scholars only assume his mother had been a slave, perhaps since her exodus from the war-torn Caucasus was similarly traumatic—an assumption that points to the slippage between slavery and wartime immigration or other forms of dependency.[3] Second, Abdülhak Hamid Tarhan (1852–1937), known as "the great poet" (*şair-i azam*) well into the Republican period, wrote both autobiographically and symbolically about slavery, making it integral to his plays and memoirs in addition to a long narrative poem, "My Mother."[4] Finally, Sami Paşazade Sezai (1859–1936), who was most celebrated for his anti-slavery novel *Sergüzeşt* (1888)—the poster child of all Ottoman anti-slavery literature, published the year after his mother's death—also pioneered the genre of the modern short story (including a few on slavery) in Turkish.[5]

This chapter first delineates the theoretical potential and originality of the subgenre of intimate biofiction by the sons of formerly enslaved mothers, in counter-distinction from first-person "slave narratives"—a pillar on which theories of trauma, affect, and the sentimental novel stand. This subgenre likewise remains unassimilable to general anti-slavery literature on account of the writers' intimate connection to the subject matter and their compound trauma, melancholy, and even guilt. Elite sons of formerly enslaved mothers not only represent her in writing as the mother when young/love object/ adopted daughter, but also project her through a splintered narratorial standpoint of victim by inheritance, witness, potential master and perpetrator, and downright state representative. This section of the chapter will therefore argue that scholarly emphasis on authority and paternity in late-Ottoman literature, no doubt warranted by the elite status of the writers, comes at the expense of the formerly enslaved mother. As this section also suggests, the relatively few but insistent retranslations from European Enlightenment in this period are of works that merely broach the issue of slavery, while nineteenth-century abolitionist literature remained untranslated.

As I then argue, intimate biofiction by the sons of formerly enslaved mothers occupies a double time, the time of trauma and the present, or the maternal history of *ghurba* in slavery and history in the making. In the lifetime of Sezai's mother, slave trade in the Caucasus dramatically rose due to unceasing war, genocide, and forced displacement even as the empire was pressured to stop it in its tracks. The global abolition of maritime African slave trade increased cross-desert and intra-imperial trafficking, while new plantation-type agricultural practices in Egypt likewise inflected numbers. The geographic reach of slaves' displacement remained immense, encompassing the empire and also the Caucasus. *Sergüzeşt* (*An Adventure*) maps this reach through the slave trade

Dissolving into the Nile 27

that brings Dilber from the Caucasus to Egypt, and Cevher from the Sudan, and it does so at the height of the European pressure on the Ottoman Empire to abolish slavery. Sezai is at pains to first locate and then displace the entire problem of slavery itself, from the paternalizing slaver ethos of the metropole to the extravagantly Westernized Egyptian Turks now exiled there. Egyptian Turks like Sezai's family, the *pieds-noirs* of Istanbul, are held responsible for a moral depravity that dishonors slave, woman, and literature in one fell swoop. But the displacement does not stop there and is driven home, back to the liberally Orientalized Egyptian province whence those Turks came. The Egypt that once merged with Greco-Roman antiquity and held the promise of the highest East–West synthesis after Islamicization and even British conquest, indeed achieves a perverse synthesis in the depravity of the slave trade. The slaves' *ghurba* can only turn into an absolute and suicidal melancholy in this coalition of civilizations.

The Slave Mother and the Masterpiece: Theoretical Implications

In the Ottoman Empire, girls incorporated into the slave trade could eventually become ladies and mistresses of their homes or, as in the case of Sami Paşazade Sezai's mother, one of multiple wives. The horizon of immense social mobility sustains many a suspense plot in literature. Intimate biofiction by writers whose mothers were former slaves heralds the Ottoman Empire's troubled transition to modernity and channels the return of the foreign slave mother who, according to Fethi Benslama (2009), was meticulously eradicated in the foundational works of classical Islamicate literature. In *Psychoanalysis and the Challenge of Islam*, Benslama argues that although Abraham is the ancestor, the Father of the Genesis to whom Muhammad traces his own pedigree as prophet, Hajar, the slave mother of Ishmael, Abraham's first son, is never mentioned by name in the Kuran. She is the carnal mother whose legitimacy will always be in question but whose presence was necessary to legitimize the spiritual motherhood of Sarah, to whom a son had originally been promised. Locked in an elaborate gift economy, the slave woman herself becomes generative of progeny, and then generative of Sarah's legitimacy (73–108).

When the foreign slave mother of Islamicate literature resurfaces to haunt Ottoman reformism, she relays her unique form of *ghurba*—her displacement and unfulfilled mourning for her own mother, motherland, and mother tongue—to her own son. Furthermore, the repetition of her displacement is imminent. In both the erasure of the foreign slave mother and the obsession with her, we can find a struggle to come to terms with her agency and to assimilate the mother's mourning in the son's work of literature. The character of the slave girl—a triple cathexis as mother, love object, and adopted daughter—must profess voluntary, free love for the master. The author finds himself attempting the double work of mourning on the mother's behalf and his own inability to access the traumatized mother. Two plot resolutions

28 *Burcu Gürsel*

appear. She can be delivered through the salutary achievement of manumission and marriage. Alternatively, the author drives her headlong to her demise in a symbolic "matricide" which, in Julia Kristeva's terms, expresses the (self-) aggression of the melancholic who remains incapable of dissociating himself from the internalized mother (1989, 9–13). The late Ottoman literary context further lays bare the fact that this melancholy is inherited and traceable to the formerly enslaved mother's own internalization of her lost mother.

The pursuit of the formerly slave mother in literature by Ottoman reformists has potent implications for a host of fields. Ottoman slavery was marked by common practices of manumission and marriage to former slave girls. This repeated generational turnover from former slave mothers and their free, elite sons diverges from other contexts of ubiquitous, nation-wide abolition whereby an entire generation of enslaved persons can be followed by an entire generation of free progeny. Where literary theories of trauma, affect and the sentimental rely significantly on arguments on abolitionist literature,[6] the case of the sons of formerly slave women in elite Ottoman households blurs conceptual categories since these sons are simultaneously victim by inheritance, witness, perpetrator, and third person narrator.[7] Through works such as Harriet Beecher Stowe's *Uncle Tom's Cabin* (1852), to which Mizancı Murad in fact refers in his contemporaneous review of *Sergüzeşt* (Kerman 2019, vii–viii), colonial authors elicit and readers enthusiastically supply a "sentimental" rapport toward the characters of enslaved persons, thus conspiring to perpetuate their sovereignty over the enslaved. Even where slavery studies and trauma studies prioritize first person slave narratives,[8] there can be powerful interventions from contemporaneous editors, mediators, or networks enabling their publication, including in narratives by Sudanese slaves rescued by Christian missionaries (Powell 2012). This problem is no less important in the imaginative reconstruction of such lives in historical or biographical scholarship (Toledano 2007; Zilfi 2010).

In the Ottoman context, the proximity to power and radical upward social mobility of some courtly slaves have proven captivating. First-person accounts of palace women from slave origins can impart that their loyalties and nostalgia lie with the court, their high social station, and latent economic power after manumission, rather than with the circumstances and trauma of their childhood enslavement.[9] Such former slaves may even have their own slaves. In a similar vein, Walter Andrews and Mehmet Kalpaklı's *The Age of Beloveds: Love and the Beloved in Early-Modern Ottoman and European Culture and Society* (2005), revels in the subversive poetics of the all-encompassing notion of *kul* in the early modern period, where even the sultan himself would be a slave to god in spirit and a "slave" to his own slave in love. Foreign slaves, men and women alike, came to rise in rank and control the empire through their love relationships with the sultan. However, the extreme circumstances of the slave trade in the second half of the nineteenth century are, by definition, outside the purview of this work. Again, in the Ottoman context, anti-slavery literature by writers, including women, with

Dissolving into the Nile 29

no intimate, personal stakes in the matter, consists typically of one-off works, rather than an obsessive, lifelong preoccupation. Identification with the slave protagonist and character development are scant in such works, which sooner relegate slavery to allegories and metaphors about saving the empire from autocracy or liberating women in general.[10]

By contrast, we find striking personal investment and ambivalence in intimate biofiction, namely *roman de filiation*, or novels fictionalizing auto/ biographical remembrances of a family member, in this case the mother who was a former slave.[11] Attention to Tanzimat writers' slave mothers also shifts contemporary critical emphasis on paternity, paternalization, and authority.[12] The question of maternal slavery may now come to supersede, or at least accede to the level of, the question of paternity, since these writers identify not only with the fatherland that they often officially represent but also with a lineage of unmourned mothers. One can speak of an Oedipal triangle mapped on to the imperial geography of the imperial fatherland, the motherland in the Caucasus, and the son's alternating glance at the two, often from an official mission in the provinces or in Europe. Slavery happens to be the sorest point in his task of diplomatic representation, as he must always answer to Europe about an unforthcoming abolition in the empire, all the while profusely defending Ottoman slavery as more humane, as home.

Considered in its full weight, such anti-slavery writing complicates notions of the trans-imperial transfer of ideas and genres in modernity. On the question of slavery, Tanzimat translators opt for texts from a period and corpus that merely broach the subject. Alongside translating nineteenth-century bestsellers, Tanzimat writers read such contemporary works as *Uncle Tom's Cabin*, but seem to have steered clear of translating them. Instead, a small number Enlightenment works were repeatedly translated that keep at arm's length the subject of slavery and dependency, including indentured labor, *odalık*-like mistress relationships, kidnapping and imprisonment, and metaphorical preoccupations of the enslavement of nations and humanity. As Madeleine Dobie shows in *Trading Places: Colonization and Slavery in Eighteenth-Century French Culture*, eighteenth-century French writers, unwilling to confront plantation slavery in the French colonies, sometimes resorted to images or even metaphors of a displaced, Oriental slavery. Ottoman translation choices, in turn, exploit this ambivalence of the previous century—a trend that has been lost in a "Classics" debate, the terms of which go unchallenged in both modernist and contemporary criticism.[13] Given the outsized importance of "the Enlightenment" (*Aydınlanma*) in Ottoman and Turkish discourse, and its connotations in the word "the intellectual" (*aydın*), the limited number and collective significance of translated European Enlightenment works merit greater attention.[14] These works' method of broaching but not tackling slavery and dependency can be key to understanding Tanzimat writers' approach a century later.

Although tempting, the notion that the advent of the European novel instigated abolitionism in the Tanzimat period is likewise questionable.

30 *Burcu Gürsel*

Narrative genres addressing, but not problematizing, slavery already existed,[15] and the reformists marshaled not only the new genre of the novel but poetry and drama as well. Still, the circumstances of the birth and possibilities of the novel are intimately tied with the changing shape of the family and how the individual can belong in it.[16] The flurry of Ottoman reformist anti-slavery writing might owe less to a direct transfer of Enlightenment notions of equality and freedom or to nineteenth-century abolitionist fiction than a translational loophole through which to broach the subject of slavery without addressing it. In this vein, Sami Paşazade Sezai was able to only partly translate Alphonse Daudet's *Jack,* which features an African prince who was effectively reduced to slavery at school in France. This translation, however, was censored midway, leaving the slave trade with Africa and the position of blacks in nineteenth-century France outside of the Ottoman world of publication (Sezai 2019, II: 191–255).

The Double Time of the Enslaved Mother

Anti-slavery Tanzimat writers knew they would be read for ideology as they answered to a double tribunal: Western accusations of not being abolitionist enough, soon enough, and Ottoman resentment at the moral upper hand of an even more brutal Western imperialism. The general Ottoman literary reduction of slavery to the domestic variety indeed screens greater brutalities and enables a relativistic defense (Toledano 1998). Reading for overt ideology alone, however, overlooks these writers' sense that they owed their very existence to their mothers' enslavement and that children, at least symbolically, guaranteed the mother's eventual legal manumission under Islamic law. Sezai side-steps the question of how close to home—and to his mother's death—his novel *Sergüzeşt* is. The author claims in an interview to have been inspired by the slave girls in his milieu (II: 179), although this novel appeared the year after his mother died and evidently mourns as well as commemorates her life. The writer's mother was abducted from the Caucasus (Circassia or Georgia). Motherhood, pregnancy, and the suffering of women especially in slavery are major themes in his writing, also in such short stories as "Mommy [Anneciğim]," "Mihriban," and "The Wedding [Düğün]." According to Güler Güven, his chief biographer, in his childhood Sami Paşazade preached about freedom to the slaves in the household. When he told his mother about his "inability to process" her suffering, she retorted: "Had I not been a slave, I could not have had children like you" (2009, 38).

Sami Paşazade Sezai was born in a family mansion that was often compared to a town in size, with at least 42 rooms where his father's multiple wives and "more than 40 *cariye* (female slave)" resided (Güven 2009, 89). His grandfather had been a notable of Mora but upon his death the family was ousted to Egypt, leaving some of the writer's uncles behind as hostages. His father became prominent in Egypt and was promoted to director of the Bulaq Press by Muhammad Ali, the former Mamluk autocrat (Güven 2009, 21). The

Dissolving into the Nile 31

family was later effectively exiled to its Istanbul residence, which served as a cultural hub for the well-known literary and political figures of the time. Here, the writer had tutors in Persian, Arabic, and French. A nostalgic representation of this life can be found in *Konak*, an unfinished novel written nearly half a century after *Sergüzeşt*, in 1934–1935. The next-generation patriarch was his eldest brother, who had 23 children and a number of collections, including one of rare books; Sezai himself had a brief marriage that ended due to his impotence, by his own account (Güven 2009, 26, 44). Sezai had a career as a diplomat in London and Madrid, and left for exile in Paris upon the publication of *Sergüzeşt*. There he joined the anti-Abulhamid (II) Committee of Union and Progress (*İttihat ve Terakki*). He often led their clandestine publication activities but took on more active political roles as well. In his correspondence with Besim Ömer Paşa, who later translated and published in Istanbul a French translation of *Sergüzeşt* as *Dilber, esclave, et l'Eunuque amoureux* (1933), Sezai explained that the Censorship Commission shortened the original title from *Bir esirin sergüzeşti* by censoring the word slave (Güven 2009, 82).

The novel *Sergüzeşt* straddles a double historical context: 1888, the year of its publication, also corresponds to the height of predominantly British pressure for abolition in the Ottoman Empire, and a series of conventions leading up to the Brussels conference on slavery in 1889–1890 (Erdem 1996, 132). On the other hand, intradiegetic history, as exploited in the novel, might rather correspond to the time of his mother's enslavement well before his birth in 1859, which in turn corresponds to the waves of exodus from the Caucasus or the Circassian Genocide (Richmond 2013). Specific historical references are far and between in the novel, other than the arrival of Circassian slave girls in Tophane and the increasing population of Turks coming back from Egypt. However, the main male character, Celal, once presented an artwork while studying under Jean-Léon Gérôme in Paris, which hints at a time frame around the artist's meeting with the Sultan Abdülaziz and Hıdıv İsmail in Paris in 1867 and his subsequent stay in Istanbul (Kaya 2006, 75–76). This anchor places the plot in proximity of the probable time of the enslavement of the author's mother.

By the publication date, external pressures for abolition were profoundly contradictory: in 1882 England became the "abolitionist colonizer" of Egypt while in the Ottoman Empire, the rising plantation economy in Egypt, the abolition of the trans-Atlantic slave trade, and the exodus from the Caucasus actually led to an increase in slavery toward its peak in 1881 (Erdem 1996, 58). According to Ehud Toledano, up to one million refugees may have entered the Ottoman Empire between 1855 and 1866, of whom more than 150,000 had slave status in their home country (1997, 84). The Ottoman Empire both attempted to control the narrative and protect the domestic institution of slavery. Every concession to Europe, such as abolishing trade alone, was also a strategy to stall abolition. Abdulhamid could not bring himself to abolish slavery at court, and even anti-slavery officials had slaves of their

32 *Burcu Gürsel*

own. Ironic reversals ensue: just as French Enlightenment literature displaced the issue to Oriental slavery, Ottoman reformist literature displaces the issue back to the more brutal, extensive, and systematic Western plantation slavery. Plantation slavery nevertheless prepared the conditions of its own undoing as modern plantations heralded assembly lines, festering notions of individual subjecthood, freedom, equality, solidarity, and emancipation, all amounting to a kind of class consciousness (Scott 2004). As for the Ottomans in the new world system, the abolition of the African slave trade alone was under-written by the notion that enslaved Africans suffered abject conditions and lack of civilization on trade routes, whereas slaves from the Caucasus enjoyed an upgrade in their state of civilization upon arrival (Erdem 1996, 109). In fact, poverty in the Caucasus may have exacerbated a pre-existent "Istanbul dream" of social mobility (Zilfi 2010, 127–128). Slavery from the Caucasus could thus masquerade as a blessing in disguise compared to the Atlantic slave trade or plantation slavery.

Although prominent in Ottoman historiography as a topic in its own right, slavery does not factor into debates on Ottoman (self-) Orientalism and (post) colonialism, except in the more remote discussion of the Sudan.[17] For instance, Özgür Türesay insists that the Orientalist discourse about the provinces and especially Arab lands falls short of actual colonialism, given constitutional monarchy's insistence on equal political representation. Incorporating a dis-cussion on Ottoman slavery, even in the absence of a dominant slave economy, would make that argument more problematic. Moreover, Edhem Eldem suggests that the metropole could assume that the real object of Orientalist representations was the provinces and not the center (2015). However, the "*pied-noir*" status of Sami Paşazade's family—Egyptian Turks taking root in Istanbul—complicates that argument. For even at the very metropole, "the provincial" and "the slave" are not only close to home—they *are* home, mer-ging notions of the old Istanbulite, the Egyptian, the provincial Turk, and the Westernized one.

Displacing Slavery (Back Home) to the Province: Slaves' *Ghurba*

Sami Paşazade Sezai's *Sergüzeşt* charts the slave girl's constant forced dis-placement in an extended metaphor of water: maritime slave trade from the Caucasus, her first chore in Istanbul of carrying water beyond her capacity, and her suicide by drowning in the Nile. In this metaphorical body of water, through her tears, her body—an empty vessel of suffering—will dissolve. Dilber's tears mark every turning point in the plot, offering protection when nothing else can, providing a ritual of commiseration and marking the stages of her enslavement: "You are a slave!" (6); "I am a slave…" (13), "Let me be *your* slave" (14). Sezai details the slave trade, the girls' ordeal and rebellion in the maritime passage, their intermediary stay in traders' houses, and the process of their sale and resale down to the contracts drawn. Such specifics of the novel are comparable to those in scholarship on individual stories of defiance against slave traders at sea in 1866 (Toledano 2007, 193–194) and on back-alley trading after slave markets were abolished (Toledano 1982, 53–54). The protagonist in Sezai's *Sergüzeşt*, renamed Dilber, is repeatedly sold throughout the novel. In her first household, her abusive mistress is herself domestically abused. Dilber's immediate supervisor there is an intimidating Arab slave woman who mistreats her, indicating the novel's colorist view of the slaves. Her second household models the ideology of raising slaves *as if* they were family, a notion Sami Paşazade echoes in an elegy for a young slave (*cariye*) he may have loved: "this noble Caucasian girl was raised with the love and respect worthy of her good name, virtue, and nobility of nature" (I: 131–132). In the world of the novel, however, the same is said of slaves, including Dilber, who are still sold again on any pretext (I: 22).

Whereas in many a Tanzimat novel the preliminary purchase of a woman as a slave is a perfectly desirable way of meeting and getting to know a potential wife, *Sergüzeşt* rejects the marriage prospects of the concubine to the master. Following the paradigmatic turning point where the slave girl must "voluntarily" fall in love with her master, Celal, an aspiring artist, evolves from an infantile narcissist toying with his slave to a melancholic romantic hero at the mercy of his parents' authority.[18] "Playing doll" by way of dressing Dilber up as an artist's model casts the slave's body, as well as mind, as a mere *tabula rasa*. In Egypt, where Dilber is finally sold, Cevher, a Sudanese eunuch, embodies despairing and fatal desire. The eunuch is a double foil for Celal's unconsummated love and Dilber's "Caucasian" desirability. Through him the plot converges the triangulated imperial slave trade and *ghurba*: the exilic master, the thrice-sold Circassian *odalık*, and the castrated Sudanese.

Even in her depersonalized potentiality, the slave girl remains unpossessable, a perpetual child-bride whose status resides not in her age but in her agency, of which she has just enough to "freely" fall in love with her master. Her hopes for social mobility can now only translate into constant movement and displacement. When sold once again by Celal's mother, she is "unable to feel anything," frozen in a fugue state like a sculpture of Venus (47). Retrenched by her first owners, eliminated overnight by Celal's mother, despairingly adored by Cevher the eunuch but persecuted by the Egyptian patriarch, she finally kills herself, altogether exiting the narrative centered around her. Everybody cries in this sentimental novel and melancholy abounds, but "weeping is the greatest right of slavery. We possess the right" (45). The enslaved person's ritual crying is different from Celal's fatal indulgence in his own melancholy in the clasp of his exacting mother. In the traders' houses, in the slavers' French mansion and in the Egyptian palace, slaves cry for their barely remembered mother/land/tongue. Dilber's fleeting presence through the novel of which she is the protagonist is not unrelated to the emotional absence of a traumatized mother, a former slave.

34 *Burcu Gürsel*

The Exilic Slaver: Egyptian Turks as Istanbul's *Pieds-Noirs*

Sons of formerly enslaved mothers who are now anti-slavery writers take on the double work of mourning, one on behalf of the mother who lost her own, and the other of the writer for whom the mother was emotionally unavailable. In Sezai's *Sergüzeşt*, the topic is broached but constantly displaced to the Egyptian-Turkish constituency and then finally banished to Egypt altogether. Egypt becomes the locus of the greatest threat—that of sexual slavery and compromised chastity. It is also where the heroine attempts a full escape, from the palace and finally from the confines of the entire plot. The Egyptian-Turkish constituency occupies the status of *pied-noir*, despite, or perhaps because of, the excessive level of wealth and Westernization that they brought with them. Their exilic state is in stark juxtaposition to their own slaves' displacement. Also because of the displacement inherent in the *pied-noir* status, Sezai is at pains to distance and displace the problem of slavery to an Orientalized Egypt he fails to cast as other.

Sezai negotiates Orientalist representations, questioning their veracity when the imperial center is in question but condoning their utility in gaining access to a European audience. When it comes to Egypt, the narrator avails himself of Orientalist tropes to spontaneously evoke stock images from a European cultural reservoir, in the same way that Celal cleaves his way into the Parisian salon with a properly Orientalist painting of a harem eunuch chaperoning ladies on a boat:

> His superior talent for the high art of painting having reached the desirable exceptional level by virtue of unsurpassed training and cultivation, he presented to the salon his painting of a six-oared rowboat wading through the whimsical, melancholic waters coursing through the Bosphorus. On board were two ladies, their thin veils revealing rosy cheeks and sparkling black eyes, as well as a harem eunuch standing at the back of the boat whose sides were covered with a fringed shawl.
>
> (26)

Although the narrator affirms Celal's quality European education, it is also clear that his success is conditioned on the decorous use of Orientalist tropes. When the committee objects to the "exaggerated" use of light, Celal stands his ground by insisting that "in the Orient" it is impossible to overdo colors. The Salon is thus ostensibly cautious against heavy-handed Orientalism, and the Ottoman artist avid for it. The historic figure of Osman Hamdi Bey (1842–1910) looms large in the fictional character of Celal, since the pioneering Ottoman painter and archaeologist exhibited his Orientalist work to great acclaim and almost exclusively in Europe.[19]

A decade after the publication of the novel, Sezai questions the indiscriminate use of Orientalist tropes in "The Effects of the First Travel [İlk Seyahatin Tesiratı]" (1898):

Especially the kind of travel writing about us concerns things imagined, not seen. The descriptions and representations in those books can apply, for instance, to Egypt, or Algeria. Descriptions of streets lined with date palms in Istanbul are not rare.

(I: 203)

The veracity of the image is questioned when it concerns Istanbul, but when it comes to Egypt, in this article as in the novel, the setting must unequivocally reflect the European Orientalist imagination. In the novel, a nouveau-riche Egyptian who purchased Dilber has a mansion in "Arab" architectural style imitating "El-Hamra" palace: "That night, one salon was filled with saz players and dancers as if to bring into this world the part of the *Thousand Nights* [*Elf-ül Leyl*] that belongs to the fairies ... A fairy tale!" (I: 66). The two dozen women there are like "angels in heaven," dancing in outfits with "open neck lines revealing their translucent, white breasts, all molded from pure light, with which the beauty-gazing lover would not want to part for days on end" (66–67). Through these idealized descriptions, perhaps also evoking classical *diwan* poetry, the narrator explicitly instructs the Ottoman (then French, in translation) reader to reach into their reservoir of stock Orientalist images, just as they do for Celal's painting: "In this abundant Oriental feast, which, like fairy tales published all around Europe, fuels everyone's imagination, what attracted greatest attention was [Dilber]" (67). The figure of the Oriental despot completes the imagery, but not without distinguishing the center from the periphery: at the palace in Egypt where Dilber is finally sold, her master is about to finally exact sexual services, while Celal in Istanbul had refrained from violating her even as he entered her room while she slept.

When it comes to the metropole, not only does the imaginary European tribunal become harder to satisfy, but the narrator is also hard-pressed to explain how the hollow imitation of Europe—a popular theme of the time—degenerates Ottoman and European literature at once. A two-page "digression" attacks Westernized critics who strive to harass veiled Ottoman women and literary genius alike. In this curious juxtaposition, Sezai's narrator contemplates the veil for a European audience but literature for Ottoman readership, finding that nothing less than "national honor" is at stake. Although "women are veiled in the name of public morality and decorum," they are verbally harassed so egregiously that "we must confess that it is a great contradiction in terms when Europeans inquire as to the rationale of the veil and we answer by saying that it is out of respect for female chastity" (35). Literature occupies a place similar to that of the woman, and suffers the same aggression from Westernized ruffians

with their canary-yellow neck-ties, light-colored jackets with wide black striae, and blue trousers. ... Just as these men harass decent people, they attack literature, of which they have no knowledge. What they clap most

36   *Burcu Gürsel*

in literature are gossips and critics ... [who,] like snakes, ... spit out ink
with their pens at the very face of genius, and, to put it precisely, swear
the most.

(35)

The imitators' ignorance is made apparent as they deride Lamartine, of
whom they have only heard the name, and deem Hugo, of whom they have
only seen a picture, worthy of their appreciation (36). Just as Celal's painting
in the Parisian salon features a eunuch safe-guarding beautiful ladies' chastity, or as the Egyptian palace both cloisters and exposes harem beauties, the
narrator's diatribe associates the honor of the arts with that of the woman. In
all instances, acceptability for a European audience is the ultimate standard
against which contradictions must be resolved.

Locating Ottoman Anti-Slavery Literature in the Provinces

In view of Sezai's inconsistent Orientalist aesthetic, it becomes possible to
say that Dilber's struggle to maintain her chastity as a slave girl at some level
reflects the possibility of Ottoman anti-slavery literature. But the path is tor-
tuous, as when Dilber cries for the death of Virginie (30), whose bliss she
had envied, in Bernardin de Saint-Pierre's immensely popular novel, *Paul et
Virginie* (1788). This allusion shows how late Ottomans channel eighteenth-
century French literature to evoke and elude the topic of slavery. Even Dilber,
whose status as slave is reiterated by everyone including herself, misses the
text's slant references to slavery. Nevertheless, the literature that demands
translation is French, and so is the language that requires learning. In her
second home, where she is "raised," she has had to learn Turkish fast (9),
whereas the old French tutor in the house has picked up only a few words in
her 10 years there. "All human beings are obligated to learn the language of
Voltaire, Hugo, and Jean-Jacques Rousseau," she proclaims, further betraying
her linguistic ignorance by calling Turkish the "Byzantine [language]" or the
Arabic that they speak in Egypt (28).

Just as Muhammad Ali's Bulaq press in Cairo—a family pedigree for
Sezai—pioneered the translation of the Western classics before the imperial
center could, Westernization infiltrated Istanbul via a detour in the Egyptian
province. The phenomenon was most visible in the extravagance of Egyptian
Turks in Istanbul, in full display in Sezai's brother's mansion but absent in his
father's, even though the latter was a legendary intellectual hub (Güven 2009,
26, 32). According to Güven, Cevdet Paşa stressed in his *Ma'rûzât* the great
debt incurred by courtly individuals who emulated their lifestyle: "In short,
those ruffians of Egypt inflicted great harm on the state and the nation by
corrupting the morals of the people of Istanbul" (quoted in 23). In the novel,
the tendency is represented by Celal's father, "who had lived for a long time
in Egypt and accumulated wealth through numerous official posts there, [and]
had now splurged on the construction of a European-style building around

cape Moda" (27). Details of the setting include nude sculptures of mermaids, high-end vases and pottery, an antique table "from the period of Louis the XIVth," a painting of Napoleon Bonaparte, and a piano that Celal's sister plays in the evenings.

This is the very household that will raise Dilber and then disown her by scurrying her back into the slave market. The narrator marshals all human failings to explain this outcome but also strives to differentiate the "Egyptian" and the "European" from the authentically "Istanbulite" slaver household. While this is an Istanbul mansion, it is unrelentingly French in style, but "Egyptian" *pied-noir* in origin. In which dimension are its slaver ways housed?

> Even though the mistress of the house treated her well and courteously in accordance with her urban upbringing, her profoundly belittling and contemptuous regard toward slaves—an attitude she inherited from the Egyptian families of her lineage—was no secret to Dilber, who had experienced the violence and humiliation of humanity. The greater part of [the mistress's] forgiveness and tolerance toward the slave women stemming from this patronizing contempt, she might for instance say, "Whatever! Sliver of a slave!" when she forgave a small offense. This disdainful forgiveness would strike Dilber every bit as damaging as a cruel punishment.
>
> (29)

The mother contemplates the relationship budding between her son and her slave, whether to let him destroy his own future and his arranged match "or to destroy this sliver of a slave who wanted to obstruct his bliss and betrothal." In these moments of free indirect discourse, the narrator slips into the mother's voice and representation of Dilber (44). A multi-cultural coalition of evil—decidedly non-Istanbulite—determines the slave girl's fate:

> Finally, with the love of ostentatious nobility bestowed by the West, the addiction to wealth and fortune born of ambition and desire, and the contempt for slavery's hapless [victims] that can be found among Egyptian families, she decided that Dilber must be sent from the house.
>
> (44)

For Sezai, there must be an authentic Istanbulite "slaver morality" untainted by the new, arriviste Egyptian ethos, which had itself been corrupted by way of Westernization.

On the flipside of this *pied-noir* depravity, however, is an idealized historic version of Egypt that has long synthesized the East and the West to the point of excellence. The author remains committed to an eclectic view of Egypt's supreme value for the Empire and for Islam, all the more for its incorporation of the Western heritage throughout history. *Sergüzeşt* continually evokes classical Greco-Roman heritage through various references to Dilber as Venus

38 *Burcu Gürsel*

(I: 47), as well as to Cleopatra and to Alexander.[20] As late as 1903, Sezai declares in the article "Egypt and Egyptians [Mısır ve Mısırlılar]," that after India, Egypt is "a treasure of wealth for all humanity, and the greatest pillar of Islam," whose conquest meant more than mere imperial expansion but rather the "conquest of the very heart of Islam" (III: 59). When juxtaposed, Selim I, the conqueror, and Abdülhamid II, the present sultan, create a "deplorable contradiction," the first finding the world too small for the extent of his conquest, the latter surrendering Egypt to the British with his "corrupt, treacherous, delirious, and murderous administration and prerogative" under the eyes of all world nations "except for the Turks who owned Egypt" (III: 60). Instead, the English "brought a new era of freedom" to Egypt. The Islam of "the book, the pen, knowledge, and intelligence," rather than of war, can stand to benefit. Al-Azhar might have become the Sorbonne of Islam had Western advancement, expertise and civilization been preached from its lecterns (III: 61). In fact, Hıdıv Abbas Hilmi could achieve just that, since he was educated in the Viennese school of Theresianum, in the "cultural enlightenment of Europe," rather than "at the hands of harem eunuchs from among the dark people of the Sudan and Nubia, at the school desks of the torturous teachers of the Middle East, or in the company of tutors from Kastamonu and Konya." He could have turned Egypt into a philosophical center for both the Empire and Islam. But Egyptians, especially the pashas and beys, lacking in "spiritual fortitude," chose to run away to Paris, "the epicenter of Enlightenment," leaving Egypt to fall prey in the "Darwinian" process of natural "selection" (III: 61–62).

Although Sezai contrasts the exceptional and synthetized culture of Egypt with its disastrous state under Abdülhamid and the corrupt local elite, Güven argues that the Cairo branch of the oppositional Committee on Union and Progress was also the most corrupt among the exilic hubs. By 1896, unlike the groups exiled to Paris and Geneva, the Cairo group became known for their opportunistic and parasitic behavior (2009, 51). While Sezai was popular among the Unionists and directed their important publication, *Şûrâ-yı Ümmet*, as it was moved from Cairo to Paris, he was also close to Mustafa Fazıl Paşazade Mehmet Ali Paşa, the grandson of Muhammad Ali, whose patronage his father had enjoyed (54–59). In *Sergüzeşt,* too, the Egyptian promise of the supreme synthesis of Islam and Europe finally goes rogue, or becomes perverted, at the hands of the Turks returning from the province to the center. The juxtaposition of Paris and Cairo brings to relief how each is filtered through the other's transformative power—Westernization, Orientalism—and becomes further enmeshed in the cultural transformation of Istanbul itself. Not only in this 1903 essay, but also in his 1924 preface to the second edition of *Sergüzeşt*, Sezai continues to see civilizational difference and competition as key to the trajectory of a world history polarized between the ruthless and masculine rationality of the West and the feminine emotionality of the East (1924, 3–7). The writer considers himself not above Eastern, feminine emotionality, which had once failed to survive the Andalusian synthesis of civilizations, whereas for him Namık Kemal exemplifies and in fact

Dissolving into the Nile   39

concedes British civilizational ecumenism. Despite incorporating nation-alist sentiment, this preface demonstrates that, barely a year after the British invasion of Istanbul itself and the founding of the Turkish Republic, Sezai unrelentingly negotiates Ottoman literature and his novel on slavery in civilizational terms.

Melancholy, Black and White: The Slave's Unmournable Mother

In the novel, while Celal represents the itinerancy of the *pieds-noirs* and their depraved, Egyptian style of Westernization, Cevher represents "one of those harem eunuchs who are loyal to their masters to the point of sacrificing their lives for him ... perhaps cursing nature for being black, and the Sudan for being a eunuch" (68). Doing double duty as a foil for both Celal and Dilber, Cevher embodies the castration that Celal projects only symbolically, with his uncon-summated and deranged love. Cevher's enslavement simultaneously contrasts with Dilber's when the black eunuch and the white would-be *odalık* cross paths in Cairo. Like a bird torn from parched lands and brought over, "wings clipped," to fecund lands abounding with natural beauties, he "looks at each beauty descending from the world of wonders with a burning gaze ... aflame in the hellish fire of his lack." A stock character of the black eunuch designed to recall Montesquieu's *Persian Letters*, Cevher not only commiserates with Dilber but also compares himself and traders to her in racial terms. "If my face is black, must my soul also be dark?" (69) he protests, making biology racial and symbolic. Alone with Dilber on a boat on a "lac" (sic.) he remembers how happy he was in the maternal arms that protected him from the dangers of the African desert, and bemoans his lot in both geography and race: "This curly hair is perilous and interlocks the heart like ivy. What do I know, I thought even the proverbial angels in heaven were black. And now! And now! Let us cry for each other's lot" (70). The new object of his impossible longing, Dilber is cause for him to racially compartmentalize the slave trade into African trader and white victim, thereby absolving the empire: "Could a Caucasian tribe that has nobility of nature, qualities of courage, and the most apparent grace, pos-sibly deserve destruction at the hands of African traders? ... Cleopatra, here, captive in a room in Egypt!" (73). This moment reverses another, when Dilber was dressed up as Cleopatra by Celal as if to suggest upward social mobility. Cevher can see no further than Celal could, who, in a delirious and paranoid state, had blamed Dilber's sale on the entire continents of Asia, "that old man expanding in its own blood," and Africa, "which turns a lizard into a crocodile and a cat into a tiger" (61).

While becoming a useful testing ground for notions of slavery and race, the stock character of Cevher also mirrors Dilber's frustrated desire, now fast turning into absolute despair. The first succumbs to the suicidal risk he takes while the latter commits suicide. At the end of the novel, about to die after falling off the ladder with which he attempts to save her, Cevher pleads, "run, quick, to your love and your freedom! May all of Egypt marvel tomorrow

40   *Burcu Gürsel*

upon hearing about a helpless slave who tore open the iron bars of a prison with his weak arms to save a kind, oppressed soul" (75). Cevher can only seek vicarious fulfillment of sexual and romantic desire and an afterlife in public memory. The mother is a constant reference point for the slaves' absolute despair, from Cevher's childhood memory to Dilber's punishment in the closet where she longed for her mother, to her sleeping with a picture in her hand that Celal thought was "of her mother, her only source of consolation" (34), to her memory of "looking for her mother in vain" in the horrific nights spent at slavers' houses (73). The specter of the mother reappears and cannot be mourned, remaining the single point of reference for the absence of lasting and free relationships in slavery. From this vantage point, Dilber's suicide, given the impossibility of her return to Istanbul, is also a return to the maternal womb after an endless journey on the (tearful, rainy) waterways of the slave trade, including the Black Sea, the Bosphorus, the "lac," and finally the Nile. Dilber's suicide by drowning brings her to a state beyond desire, or a post-desire state that inverts the pre-desire state in the womb:

> As she resurfaced in the river on her back, Dilber's long hair undulated along with the water currents, the moonlight falling on the poignant traces of the colorless face that had left behind every desire, hope, and purpose. On that face, where there was no color but the frigid incandescence of the most devastating melancholy, it became apparent that all grief and suffering had become still, all love and desire extinguished. Where, one wonders, are these sinister, fatal whirlpools and floods of the Nile taking poor Dilber? To her freedom!
>
> (78)

The novel's final words on the slave's "freedom" in suicide resonate with Sezai's article, "Egypt and Egyptians," which harps on the imperial loss of Egypt and its unfulfilled promise of synthesizing Eastern and Western high culture. Unimpeded even by the British conquest which, to Sezai's consolation, instilled the latest notions of liberty in Egypt, this promise is ultimately perverted by self-serving Egyptian elites and treacherous Egyptian Turkish administrators alike. By the time of the 1924 preface, the missed moment of "freedom" still lies in the future of the new Republic, having been deferred, not only by the autocratic empire of the first edition, but also by the invasion of those European empires so painstakingly emulated by the homeland.

This novel, banner of all Ottoman "abolitionism," reveals that the slave mother, or love interest, is no mere metaphor to her son, an intellectual and writer, who betrays a precariously direct identification with her. The same empathy for human suffering on the massive scale of war or genocide is not forthcoming in Sezai's political writings on the "Hamidian" Armenian massacres. There, suffering is merely a starting point on the path to declarations of national unity.[21] In *Sergüzeşt*, however, the slave's *ghurba* is the beginning, the middle, and the end in an uncompromising whole, where the heroine's

Dissolving into the Nile   41

end in Egypt highlights her coerced itinerancy, irretrievable homelands, and lost (mother) tongues. Her displacements draw a telling map of the psychological predicament of Ottoman reformists who were personally imprinted by a maternal slavery that they could in turn easily perpetuate. That map has a second layer, too, of trans-imperial colonialism from the unspoken-for stretches of the Caucasus to the Egyptian province and the Sudan. Despite first, and last, hitting "home," maternal slavery is blamed on every place but. Held at arm's length, the slave girl—the mother, the love object, the adoptable child— is here brought to her demise, thus resolving and containing in the Nile her tear-traced errancy and episodes of statuesque, catatonic states of subjection.

Conclusion

In pursuing the unique ambivalences in intimate biofiction by prominent Tanzimat writers whose mothers had been purchased as slaves, this chapter has raised, more than answered, questions about how this corpus may contribute to various areas of study. Neither first-person slave narrative nor distant third-person fiction, this body of ostensibly abolitionist intimate biofiction channels the voice of reformists who identify both with the empire they often officially represent and with the formerly enslaved mother whose trauma they inherit. The plots in their intimate biofiction, which sees the return of the eradicated foreign slave mother in classical Islamicate heritage, seek to resolve this tension either by delivering the mother through lawful manumission and matrimony, or else by liberating her and (and the author) in matricide. Sami Paşazade Sezai's novel *Sergüzeşt*, the best-known work in the corpus, demonstrates how the issue of slavery is often transimperially displaced, as exemplified by its evocation of the French Enlightenment. The novel's displacement strategy is to diagnose slavers' depraved ethos to be not authentically Istanbulite but Egyptian-Turkish—the social segment that ironically pioneers massive Westernization in Egypt and Istanbul alike. In fact, now exilic, these *pieds-noirs* hail from an Egypt that once promised the highest synthesis of Islamicate and European culture but then degenerated into a depravity coded in Orientalist tropes. Egyptian Turks' own exilic and melancholic state is but counterpoint to the differentiated *ghurba* of the Caucasian *odalık* and the Sudanese eunuch, whose melancholy revolves around their lost mothers and motherlands. The plot line of the *odalık*'s subjection, repeated sale, "voluntary" love for the young master, and death aestheticizes the maternal legacy of melancholy for the son—ever a potential master.

Notes

1 See Parlatır's fruitful survey of slavery in Ottoman literature (1992); Sagaster's pursuit of the belatedness of Tanzimat anti-slavery ideology (1997); Powell (2012), more on whom later. Also see Özbay's fascinating tracing of the development of the concubinage system to the "evlatlık" ("child-one," as opposed to adopted child) and "besleme" ("fed one") (2012).

42 Burcu Gürsel

2   The birth of a child, born free, guaranteed that the mother could not be sold, and would be manumitted after her master's death. However, paternity could always be denied, especially by his heirs; she could only go free after all the masters' debt was paid, and in any case the mother could be married off far away from her child, too (Zilfi 2010, 112).

3   Ahmet Hamdi Tanpınar and a long line of scholars after him assume that Ahmet Midhat's mother was a slave (Güven 2009; Parlatır 1992; Toledano 1993, 1998). Her wartime displacement overseas, while pregnant and with a small child, and her poverty in the Ottoman Empire closely resemble her compatriots' journey as enslaved persons. She may presumably have been purchased as a slave by the family of her previous husband. Midhat does not explicitly state this, nor do his son and his friend (Yazgıç 2020; Fahreddin 2018).

4   All translations mine unless otherwise indicated.

5   According to Güven, his mother died in the year 1886–1887 (2009, 38). For biographies of Sami Paşazade Sezai, see especially Güven 2009 and Kerman 2016 and 2019.

6   For the incorporation of slave narratives in affect theory, trauma theory, the sentimental novel and translation studies, see Berlant 2004; Brodzki 2007; Cohen 1999; Festa 2006; Powell 2012; and Samuels 1992.

7   For these specific problems, especially in relation to slavery, war, genocide, etc., see Gilmore 2017; Schwab 2010; and Felman and Laub 1992.

8   On the problem of the slave or a woman slave as a first-person narrator, and the problem of reconstructing an archive see, Hartman 2007 and 2019; Whitlock 2000, Sharpe 2010; Stoler 2002.

9   For the financial power accrued by former palace slaves, see Argit 2020; a memoir by a former palace slave in English translation can be found in Brookes 2008. For a memoir on the elite harem, see Saz 2004.

10 Such authors include Namık Kemal (author of *İntibah* and *Karabela*, a novella about a resentful African eunuch), Recaizade Mahmud Ekrem (*Vuslat*), Nabızade Nazım (*Zehra*), Emin Nihat ("Faik Bey ile Nuridil Hanım'ın Sergüzeşti"), Fatma Aliye (*Muhaderat*), Zafer Hanım (*Aşk-ı Vatan*), Abdülhalim Memduh (*Bedriye*).

11 For the limits of biofiction and autobiography, especially in their relationship to colonialism and gender, see, Lackey 2022; Renders, de Haan, and Harmsma 2017; Smith and Watson 1998 and 1992.

12 Jale Parla capitalizes on the search for paternal figures and equivocal relationships to authority in Tanzimat writers who grew up without a father and were persecuted by the sultan—an observation that has proven influential (1990).

13 The "Classics Debate" of Tanzimat writers and translators pits Romanticism against Classicism and Realism, thereby sidestepping the Enlightenment almost entirely, as do the critics by not asking why those specific and few Enlightenment woks were translated (Tanpınar 1988, c. 1942, 291–293; Parla 1990, 27; Paker 2012, 344).

14 For comprehensive lists of late-Ottoman translations from Europe, see Yağcı 2011, and especially of translations from the French, see Bay 2013 and Anamur 2013.

15 Examples include Evliya Çelebi's *Seyahatname* as well as the narratives embedded in Mevlana's *Mesnevi.*

16 Marital bonds superseding blood ties left their quickest mark on the novel while the creation of characters beyond the scope of maternal supervision is fundamental to the birth of the novel (Perry 2004; Tóibín 2012).

Dissolving into the Nile 43

17 See Türesay 2013 for an overview of the debate in favor of assimilation into equal citizenship. Also see Deringil 1998, 2003; Makdisi 2002a, 2002b; Motika and Herzog 2000; Kuehn 2011; Eldem 2015; Dağlıoğlu 2015; and Minawi 2016.
18 For an unquestioning account of "free love" for the master as it appears in many of Ahmet Midhat's works, see Shissler 2010, 2019 and Green 2020. Tanpınar, for one, sees through the fantasy of "free love" in the context of slavery (1998 [c. 1967], 62).
19 See Çolak for a discussion on the parallel between Celal and Osman Hamdi Bey, who was supported by Sezai's father and brother (2019, 35; 44). In its new location, the Istanbul Museum of Painting and Sculpture has a room dedicated to Osman Hamdi's European certificates for his exhibitions and excavations.
20 The scenes include Celal dressing Dilber up in various disguises and Cevher comparing her slavery in Egypt to Cleopatra's incarceration there (31, 33, 36, 73).
21 See, for instance, "The Armenian Conference [Ermeni Kongresi]" (III: 25–29).

References

Anamur, H. 2013. *Başlangıçtan bugüne Fransızcadan Türkçeye yapılmış çeviriler ile Fransız düşünürler, yazarlar, sanatçılar üzerine Türkçe yayınları içeren bir kaynakça denemesi.* Gündoğan.
Andrews, W. G. 1985. *Poetry's voice, society's song: Ottoman lyric poetry.* U of Washington P.
Andrews, W. G. and Kalpaklı, M. 2005. *The age of beloveds: love and the beloved in early modern Ottoman and European culture and society.* Duke UP.
Argit, B. İ. 2020. *Life after the harem: female palace slaves, patronage, and the imperial Ottoman court.* Cambridge UP.
Bay, Ö. F. 2013. *Fransız edebiyatından yapılan ilk edebi çeviriler üzerine analitik bir uygulama (1860–1900).* Doctoral Dissertation. Hacettepe U.
Benslama, F. 2009. *Psychoanalysis and the challenge of Islam.* Bononno, R. (transl.). U of Minnesota P.
Berlant, L. (ed.) 2004. *Compassion: the culture and politics of an emotion.* Routledge.
Brodzki, B. 2007. *Can these bones live? Translation, survival, and cultural memory.* Stanford UP.
Brookes, D. S. (trans. and ed.) 2008. *The concubine, the princess, and the teacher: voices from the harem.* U of Texas P.
Cohen, M. 1999. *The sentimental education of the novel.* Princeton UP.
Conermann, S. and Şen, G. (eds.) 2020. *Slaves and slave agency in the Ottoman Empire.* Bonn UP.
Çolak, İ. A. 2019. *İmge ve imaj: Türkiye'de resim ve edebiyatta ortak dil.* Corpus.
Dağlıoğlu, E. C. 2015. Bir şiddet formu olarak Osmanlı-Türk Oryantalizmi ve Araplar. In: Kurt, Ü. and Çeğin, G. (eds.) *Kıyam ve kıtâl: Osmanlı'dan Cumhuriyet'e devletin inşası ve kolektif şiddet.* Tarih Vakfı. pp. 434–468.
Deringil, S. 2003. "They live in a state of nomadism and savagery": the late Ottoman Empire and the post-colonial debate. *Comparative Studies in Society and History*, 45(2), pp. 311–342.
Deringil, S. 1998. *The well-protected domains: ideology and the legitimation of power in the Ottoman Empire, 1876–1909.* I. B. Tauris.

44 Burcu Gürsel

Dobie, M. 2010. *Trading places: colonization and slavery in eighteenth-century French culture*. Cornell UP.

Eldem, E. 2015. The Ottoman Empire and Orientalism: an awkward relationship. In: Pouillon, F. and Vatin, J.-C. (eds.) *After Orientalism: critical perspectives on agency and eastern re-appropriation*. Brill. pp. 89–102.

Eldem, E. 2013. Hayretü'l-azime fi intihalati'l-garibe: Voltaire ve Şanizade Mehmed Ataullah Efendi. *Toplumsal Tarih*, 237, pp. 18–28.

Erdem, Y. H. 1996. *Slavery in the Ottoman Empire and its demise 1800–1909*. Palgrave.

Fahreddin, R. 2018. *Ahmet Midhat Efendi*. Mehmedoğlu, Ö. K. (transl.) Ferfir.

Faroqhi, S. 2017. *Slavery in the Ottoman world: a literature survey*. EB-Verlag Dr. Brandt.

Felman, S. and Laub, D. (eds.) 1992. *Testimony: crises of witnessing in literature, psychoanalysis and history*. Routledge.

Festa, L. 2006. *Sentimental figures of empire in eighteenth-century Britain and France*. John Hopkins UP.

Frank, A. 2012. The children of the desert and the laws of the sea: Austria, Great Britain, the Ottoman Empire, and the Mediterranean slave trade in the nineteenth century. *The American Historical Review*, 117(2), pp. 410–444.

Gilmore, L. 2017. *Tainted witness: why we doubt what women say about their lives*. Columbia UP.

Green, O. 2020. Cultivating Ottoman citizens: reading Ahmet Midhat Efendi's *Felâtun Bey ile Râkım Efendi* with Âli Pasha's political testament. In: Ringer, M. M. and Charrière, E. E. (eds.) *Ottoman culture and the project of modernity: reform and translation in the Tanzimat novel*. I.B. Tauris. pp. 65–84.

Güven, G. 2009. *Sami Paşazade Sezayi ve eserleri*. Dergah.

Hanna, N. 2005. Sources for the study of slave women and concubines in Ottoman Egypt. In: Sonbol, A. A. (ed.) *Beyond the exotic: women's histories in Islamic societies*. Syracuse UP. pp. 119–130.

Hartman, S. 2019. *Wayward lives, beautiful experiments: intimate histories of social upheaval*. Norton.

Hartman, S. 2007. *Lose your mother: a journey along the Atlantic slave route*. Farrar, Straus & Giroux.

Kaya, G. S. 2006. Dolmabahçe Sarayı için Goupi Galerisi'nden alınan resimler. In: Taşdelen, Ö. and Baytar, İ. (eds.) *Osmanlı sarayında Oryantalistler*. TBMM Milli Saraylar. pp. 71–91.

Kerman, Z. 2019. Önsöz. In: Sami Paşazade Sezai. *Samipaşazade Sezai: Bütün eserleri*, vol. 1. Türk Dil Kurumu. pp. v–xiv.

Kerman, Z. 2016. Sami Paşa-zade Sezai. In: Parlatır, İ. et al. (eds.) *Tanzimat edebiyatı*. Akçağ. pp. 557–584.

Kincaid, J. 1997. *The autobiography of my mother*. Plume.

Kristeva, J. 1989. *Black sun: depression and melancholia*. Columbia UP.

Kuehn, T. 2011. *Empire, Islam, and the politics of difference: Ottoman rule in Yemen, 1849–1919*. Brill.

Lackey, M. 2022. *Biofiction: an introduction*. Routledge.

Makdisi, U. 2002a. Rethinking Ottoman imperialism: modernity, violence and the cultural logic of Ottoman reform. In: Hanssen, J., Philipp, T., and Stefan, W. (eds.) *The empire in the city: Arab provincial capitals in the late Ottoman Empire*. Verlag. pp. 29–48.

Makdisi, U. 2002b. Ottoman Orientalism. *The American Historical Review*, 107(3), pp. 768–796.

Miller, C. L. 2008. *The French Atlantic triangle: literature and culture of the French slave trade*. Duke UP.

Minawi, M. 2016. *The Ottoman scramble for Africa: empire and diplomacy in the Sahara and the Hijaz*. Stanford UP.

Motika, R. and Herzog, C. 2000. Orientalism alla turca: late 19th/Early 20th century Ottoman voyages into the Muslim "outback." *Die Welt des Islams*, 40(2), pp. 139–195.

Özbay, F. 2012. Evlerde ev kızları: cariyeler, evlatlıklar, gelinler. In: Davidoff, L., and Durakbaşa, A. (eds.) *Feminist tarih yazımında sınıf ve cinsiyet*. İletişim. pp. 13–48.

Paker, S. 2012. Ottoman conceptions of translation and its practice: the 1897 "classics debate" as a focus for examining change. In: Hermans, T. (ed.) *Translating others*, vol. 2. Routledge. pp. 325–348.

Parla, J. 1990. *Babalar ve oğullar: Tanzimat romanının epistemolojik temelleri*. İletişim.

Parlatır, İ. 1992. *Tanzimat edebiyatında kölelik*. Türk Tarih Kurumu.

Perry, R. 2004. *Novel relations: the transformation of kinship in English literature and culture, 1748–1818*. Cambridge UP.

Powell, E. M. T. 2012. *Tell this in my memory: stories of enslavement from Egypt, Sudan, and the Ottoman Empire*. Stanford UP.

Powell, E. M. T. 2003. *A different shade of colonialism: Egypt, Great Britain, and the mastery of the Sudan*. U of California P.

Renders, H., de Haan, B., and Harmsma, J. 2017. *The biographical turn: lives in history*. Routledge.

Richmond, W. 2013. *The Circassian Genocide*. Rutgers UP.

Sagaster, B. 1997. *"Herren" und "Sklaven:" der Wandel im Sklavenbild türkischer Literaten in der Spätzeit des Osmanischen Reiches*. Otto Harrassowitz V.

Sami Paşazade Sezai. 2019. *Bütün eserleri*. 3 vols. Kerman, Z. (ed.) Türk Dil Kurumu.

Sami Paşazade Sezai. 1924. Mukaddime. In: *Sergüzeşt*. 2nd edition. Kitabhane-i Sudi. Istanbul. pp. 3–7.

Samuels, S. 1992. *The culture of sentiment: race, gender and sentimentality in 19th century America*. Oxford UP.

Saunders, R. 2007. *Lamentation and modernity in literature, philosophy, and culture*. Palgrave.

Saz, L. 2004. *Haremin iç yüzü*. Borak, S. (ed.) Kırmızı Beyaz.

Schwab, G. 2010. *Haunting legacies: violent histories and transgenerational trauma*. Columbia UP.

Scott, D. 2004. *Conscripts of modernity: the tragedy of colonial Enlightenment*. Duke UP.

Sharpe, C. 2010. *Monstrous intimacies: making post-slavery subjects*. Duke UP.

Shissler, H. A. 2019. Haunting Ottoman middle-class sensibility: Ahmet Midhat Efendi's Gothic. In: Booth, M. (ed.) *Migrating texts: circulating translations around the Ottoman Mediterranean*. Edinburgh UP. pp. 193–209.

Shissler, H. A. 2010. The harem as the heat of middle-class industry and morality: the fiction of Ahmet Midhat Efendi. In: Booth, M. (ed.) *Harem histories: envisioning places and living spaces*. Duke UP. pp. 319–341.

Smith, S. and Watson, J. (eds.) 1998. *Women, autobiography, theory*. U of Wisconsin P.

46 Burcu Gürsel

Smith, S. and Watson, J. (eds.) 1992. *Delcolonizing the subject: the politics of gender in women's autobiography*. U of Minnesota P.

Stoler, A. L. 2002. *Carnal knowledge and imperial power: race and the intimate in colonial rule*. 2nd ed. 2010. U of California P.

Tanpınar, A. H. 1998 (c. 1969). *Edebiyat üzerine makaleler*. İletişim.

Tanpınar, A. H. 1988 (c. 1942). *Ondukuzuncu asır Türk edebiyatı tarihi*. Çağlayan.

Tóibín, C. 2012. *New ways to kill your mother: writers and their families*. McClelland & Stewart.

Toledano, E. R. 2007. *As if silent and absent: bonds of enslavement in the Islamic Middle East*. Yale UP.

Toledano, E. R. 1998. *Slavery and abolition in the Ottoman Middle East*. U of Washington P.

Toledano, E. R. 1993. Late Ottoman concepts of slavery (1830s–1880s). *Poetics Today*, 14(3), pp. 477–506.

Toledano, E. R. 1982. *The Ottoman slave trade and its suppression: 1840–1890*. Princeton UP.

Türesay, Ö. 2013. L'Empire ottoman sous le prisme des études postcoloniales: à propos d'un tournant historiographique récent. *Revue d'Histoire Moderne et Contemporaine*, 60(2), pp. 127–145.

Walz, T. and Cuno, K. M. (eds.) 2010. *Race and slavery in the Middle East: histories of trans-Saharan Africans in nineteenth-century Egypt, Sudan and the Ottoman Mediterranean*. The American U in Cairo P.

Whitlock, G. 2000. *The intimate empire: reading women's autobiography*. Cassell.

Wright, J. 2007. *The trans-Saharan slave trade*. Routledge.

Yağcı, A. S. E. 2011. *Turkey's reading (r)evolution: a study on books, readers and translation (1840–1940)*. Doctoral Dissertation. Boğaziçi U.

Yazgıç, K. 2020. *Oğlunun kaleminden Ahmet Midhat Efendi ve dönemi*. Vakıfbank Y.

Zilfi, M. 2010. *Women and slavery in the late Ottoman Empire: the design of difference*. Cambridge UP.

Zilfi, M. 2005. Thoughts on women and slavery in the Ottoman era and historical sources. In: Sonbol, A. A. (ed.) *Beyond the exotic: women's histories in Islamic societies*. Syracuse UP. pp. 131–138.

2 Re-writing the Other

Uncovering the Legacies of Slavery in Suad Amiry's *My Damascus*

Arththi Sathananthar

As much as Suad Amiry's *My Damascus* (2016a) is a narrative about an affluent Damascene family, it is also about the enslaved people and the servants who maintain the household. The two key figures I will examine in this chapter are Sajeda and Ghalia. Based on a backdrop of systematic patriarchal and colonial structures, these women are subject to restrictions that impede their agency and mobility. The text illustrates different historical periods in the Levant, ranging from the early twentieth century to the early 2000s, thus revealing how the institution of slavery operates as evidenced by how Sajeda and Ghalia enter the Baroudi family but also the racism that continues as one of its legacies. Amiry refers to all three of them as "maids" when it is only Fatima who is not bartered or bought like Sajeda and Ghalia, which raises critical questions about her authorial representation of these women. The pivotal events of the memoir are centred on the Baroudi mansion or Beit Jiddo, her grandfather's house. Amiry illustrates the interconnected lives of all the women who closely inhabit and shape the family home, which makes her text centred on the way in which the idea of home is produced from the intimate bonds of their relationships. At the same time, disjunctures in these relationships reveal the role of class and racial hierarchies in the household.

My Damascus stages two very different periods in Syria's history: the long past of Greater Syria and the present day of twentieth century Syria. Greater Syria or *Bilad al-Sham* (land to the north or left-side of Hejaz) encompassed Syria, Jordan, Lebanon and Palestine, which are all places that Amiry includes in her family history. The term *al-Sham* was created by the Muslim dynasties preceding Ottoman control of the region; it referred to Damascus, as the city was the epicentre of the region: "Damascus [was] the capital of Greater Syria as it was known then" (Amiry, 2016a, 10). Although the text does not detail the creation of Greater Syria, it describes the extensive borderless world of Jiddo and Teta's time before it was broken up to form individual Levantine states. Therefore, Amiry attempts to bridge both the spatial and temporal changes concerning Greater Syria. The trigger for her to focus on Syrian culture was the Syrian refugee crisis of the twenty-first century (Amiry, 2016b). The text offers a nostalgic portrayal of a city's past to counteract the current setting of an almost decade-long civil conflict in a war-torn and ravaged Damascus.

DOI: 10.4324/9781003301776-4

48 *Arththi Sathananthar*

Suad Amiry is a conservational architect. Her internationally acclaimed organization RIWAQ documents and restores heritage sites across the West Bank and Gaza. She identifies architecture as her primary concern, noting that "I became a writer by accident" (2014, 199). She received international acclaim for her first book, *Sharon and My Mother in Law: Ramallah Diaries* (2003), based on her email correspondence while living under two decades of Israeli occupation. Since then, she has authored several non-fiction books on Palestine and Palestinians: *The Palestinian Village Home* (1989 – co-authored with Vera Tamari), *Nothing to Lose But Your Life: An 18 Hour Journey with Murad* (2010), *Menopausal Palestine: Women at the Edge* (2010), *Golda Slept Here: The Presence of the Absent* (2014).[1] All these works explore the politically fraught subject matter of home and homeland. This oeuvre encompasses tropes that are also developed in *My Damascus*: the depiction of crossing borders and checkpoints to reflect contemporary Israeli/Palestinian reality (*Nothing to Lose But Your Life*); the intimate lives of women in relation to a changing socio-political history (*Menopausal Palestine*); and the story of dispossession through a focus on houses (*Golda Slept Here*). While *My Damascus* exhibits these similar themes through a focus on her Syrian lineage, it is her first text addressing the topic of slavery in the Levant.

The representation of journeys and homecomings of Amiry's family members necessarily involves a discussion of changing borders and political relations in the region. The traditional cultural mandates whereby women leave their childhood homes for their matrimonial homes mean that movement is not only influenced by geo-politics but also by class and gender. *My Damascus* records the multitude of journeys the Baroudi women make across the Levantine region which signal marriage and motherhood. Amiry's grandmother Teta leaves her childhood home in 'Arrabeh for Damascus to marry Jiddo in 1896. Decades later, Amiry's mother, Samia, leaves her family in Damascus to marry her husband and live in Jerusalem in the 1940s, before moving to Aman in the 1960s. In contrast, the enslaved women involuntarily arrive at Beit Jiddo and are bound there. The Levantine region has been immobilizing for slaves even though it was easier to move, as evidenced through Teta's and Samia's journeys, prior to the establishment of modern nation-states with borders and migration regimes. The relationship between the changing region and Amiry's representation of female mobility uncovers a particular depiction of Arab womanhood that is unique to the region and its time, but it also shows how the ancestral home is a locus to explore the national and cultural identities of the various inhabitants. Beit Jiddo contains multicultural facets of the surrounding region, revealing the plurality of the Levantine world. This plurality involves the trade of goods from the surrounding regions but, more importantly, the trade of people. At the same time, until it falls into ruin, the house is the family's centre of gravity. Although the text is primarily set after the fall of the Ottoman Empire, the legacy of the empire is depicted within the social hierarchies at the house itself. The long chronology of the text allows for a focus on the relation between older traditions and the changes that were taking place throughout the twentieth century. *My Damascus* illuminates the practice of slavery by depicting the lives of women of African descent held in bondage, and it also shows the ways in which racism and anti-blackness determined the place that enslaved or formerly enslaved women occupied in the household and in the narrative itself.

I argue that while Amiry attempts to redress the marginalization of enslaved African women in the Levant by including these subaltern narratives in her family history, she writes in a racialized tone that reveals entanglements between modernity, slavery, and racism. These enslaved women, Sajeda and Ghalia, are already othered due to their precarious and vulnerable position in the Baroudi household, yet they are further othered by how Amiry narrates their stories through her oftentimes callous depictions of them, such as focusing on their distinct physical features. Therefore, I suggest that the text performs a dual layer of othering. Amiry speaks and thus writes for Sajeda and Ghalia: they do not speak for themselves, which leads their representation to be seen through Amiry's racialized lens. In order to examine Amiry's enactment of othering, I also elucidate the enslaved women's lack of agency and mobility. Their stories illustrate their plural positionalities between Damascus and the wider Arab world, as well as their valued yet subservient relationship to Amiry's family. Within this context, Beit Jiddo is a site of exclusion and alienation for these two enslaved women as they are forcibly removed from their families to come and serve the Baroudi family.

While works on slavery remain sparce in Arab literary contexts, *Mashreq* (including the Levant) conversations on anti-blackness and racism and legacies of slavery are almost non-existent, as the few representations of Afro-Arab identity are from the *Maghreb* (North Africa). According to Sudanese-Egyptian writer Tarek El-Tayeb "*we* still deal with blacks in stereotypical ways, especially in film, *they* are always presented and associated with certain jobs" (Kareem, 2019). In addition, S.J. King states:

> There is an ambient racism across the contemporary Maghreb. Both native Blacks and black migrants are constantly subjected to verbal reactions by white Maghrebis that range from simple mockery to outright hostility, with the common sentiment of contempt towards black skin. [...] To attack the humanity of Black Maghrebis, the Arabic word for servant, *khadim* pl. *khuddam*, also became a common collective noun for black people, especially black women.
>
> (2021, 39)

El-Tayeb's and King's observations show us that anti-blackness persists in the Arab world with a clear separation between *us* and *them*, as *they* are relegated to certain roles of servitude. In light of this context, Afro-Arab writers have sought to tell their own stories. Sudanese writer Hammour Ziada's *The Longing of the Derwish* (2014) and Mauritanian writer Mohamed Bouya Bamba's *Outside Servitude* (2019) detail the long-lasting effects of slavery on

50 *Arththi Sathananthar*

the formerly enslaved protagonists. On the other hand, Saudi writer Mahmoud Trawri's *Maymouna* (2001) centres on an enslaved African individual which makes this text one of the most important literary representations of slavery in the Arab world. These Afro-Arab authors' works emerge out of a literary tradition that pre-dates the modern period:

> *Aghribat al-Arab*, "crows or ravens of the Arabs", was the name given a group of early Arabic poets who were of African or partly African parentage. [...] Originally, it apparently designated a small group of poets in pre-Islamic Arabia whose fathers were free and sometimes noble Arabs and whose mothers were African, probably Ethiopian, slaves [...] Both themes-servitude and blackness-occur in some of the verses ascribed to these poets and, in a sense, define their identity.
>
> (Lewis, 1985, 88)

However,

> [a]fter the eighth century, blackness as a poetic theme almost disappears from Arabic literature. [...] Few of the slaves were sufficiently assimilated to compose poetry in Arabic; while the few Arabic poets of African or part African ancestry were too assimilated to see themselves as black and therefore Other.
>
> (Lewis, 1985, 96)

The diminishment of Afro-Arab self-representations has opened up the gap for non-black authors like Amiry to write for these communities.

Compared to their American counterparts, representations or auto-narratives by enslaved individuals in the Ottoman and Muslim societies are close to non-existent. Whichever records that show the enslaved's voice are used to shape their employer's narrative:

> Slaves do appear in Ottoman texts, but these are mostly government and court records, where slaves made statements to judges and police investigators. These utterances were recorded by state officials, and are therefore at least once removed from genuine personal accounts. Thus, Ottoman slaves are indeed *"contained"* and *"represented"* by their masters or Other non-slaves in society.
>
> (Toledano, 2002, 59)

While *My Damascus* is primarily set in the early to the middle of the twentieth century, it details the Ottoman Levantine legacies of slavery. Amiry integrates the narratives of the enslaved women in the Baroudi household together with her female relatives to present a seemingly harmonious representation of Arab womanhood. Due to the socio-political backdrop that rendered enslaved people powerless, Amiry takes on the role of writing for them and "contains"

Re-writing the Other 51

their narratives within the illustrious Baroudi family history. In her seminal paper, *Venus in Two Acts* (2008), where she explores the limits of the archive concerning enslaved African women on the Transatlantic slave route, Saidiya Hartman argues,

> The loss of stories sharpens the hunger for them. So it is tempting to fill in the gaps and to provide closure where there is none. To create a space for mourning where it is prohibited. To fabricate a witness to a death not much noticed.
>
> (2008, 9)

Because narratives by enslaved people in the Ottoman and Muslim world are almost non-existent, the fact that Amiry's text provides a lens into the lives of two enslaved women shows a desire to fill in the gaps of these women's lives by giving them their voices back. Her inclusion of these marginalized voices highlights the role these two enslaved women play in Amiry's conceptualization of home and belonging in Beit Jiddo.

However, "The intention [...] isn't anything as miraculous as recovering the lives of the enslaved or redeeming the dead, but rather labouring to paint as full a picture of the lives of the captives as possible" (Hartman, 2008, 11). I contend that the picture that Amiry paints of the enslaved women's lives is problematic mainly due to her racialized tone. This tone she employs as a "white" Arab diminishes the merits of African representation in Arab literature. Amiry is not alone in poorly portraying African voices within the Arab literary scene. Mona Kareem notes that there is "a massive trend in contemporary Arabic literature to monetize 'minor groups,' whether Black-Arabs, African migrants, South and East Asian migrants, women, Assyrians and Yazidis, as well as Arab Jews" (2019). The publications of Jordanian author Samiha Khreis' *Slaves Peanuts* (2016) and *Pistachio Ebeid* (2017), and Libyan author Najwa bin Shatwan's *The Slave Pens* (2016) exemplify the monetization of African enslaved narratives for an Arabic readership as well as addressing the topic of slavery to this audience. *My Damascus* is situated within these works. While Khreis is a Levantine writer like Amiry, her two novels are set in Sudan. Amiry's text is unique in that it details the lives of enslaved African women in the Levant itself. Her writing exposes the racial biases and illuminates the social injustices which these enslaved women were subject to in Damascus such as Sajeda's father paying for two camels with his own daughter (37). However, by narrating Sajeda and Ghalia's stories, Amiry further creates a distance between the enslaved women's truths and thus cements a separation between their own histories and the history depicted in the text.

In order to explore the representation of nineteenth and twentieth century Arab institutions of slavery, I highlight the intersection between borders, socio-political ties, mobility and gender. The text locates multiple places across Damascus, 'Arrabeh, and Jerusalem to demonstrate the plurality of

52   *Arththi Sathananthar*

the Baroudi family's lives. However, it is important to note that the national distinctions between these cities are contemporary. Amiry aims to capture what it means to be Arab at a time before these national distinctions were constructed. She understands the Israeli occupation in Palestine and its effect on the surrounding region as a result of "the lack of contact with the Arab world. If you ask me today what is the end of the occupation for you, it is for us to be united again with our Arab culture" (2016b). Although she attempts to unify and represent the women in the text under a collective shared identity, Amiry renders these enslaved women as foreign in their adopted home.

The Institution of Slavery in the late Ottoman Empire

Before I analyse how the characters of African origin are represented in *My Damascus*, I will first provide an outline of the socio-historical context of how slavery, with particular regard to people of African descent, operated in the Ottoman Levant. The text sheds light on an obscured region of slavery, the Arab region in the early twentieth century. However, Amiry does not provide details of the socio-economic structures behind this institution of slavery. Interestingly, at the launch of her book, she notes that slavery is not discussed in the Arab world (2016b). Slavery is indeed rarely discussed, let alone portrayed in Arab literature. With the global momentum that the #BlackLivesMatter revolution gained in 2020, conversations on anti-blackness are finally beginning to take place. Therefore, Amiry's inclusion of Sajeda and Ghalia's narratives in her family history is important, even if her representations of them are problematic. While narratives of slavery in Arab literature remain far and few in-between, there have been many foremost scholars on the topic throughout the decades such as Ehud R. Toledano, and several recent publications.[2] Karamursel states:

> Slavery had long been a practice in the Mediterranean, one that was deeply rooted in customs shaped by the politics and economics of war, expansion, and commercial circulations. The existence of the practice preceded the formation of the Ottoman state itself, but in the later centuries, the latter's own politics and economics of war and expansion not only endorsed it but also built a bureaucratic system that relied heavily on slave recruits.
>
> (2016, 139)

Under the Ottoman Empire, there were four types of bondage: "(1) military-administrative, or *kul*, slavery, [...] (2) harem slavery, [...] (3) domestic slavery (*Ar. riqq, ' ubüdiyya*), [...] and (4) large-scale institutional slavery, ranging from agricultural slavery, [...] or political elites, to galley slavery" (Wilkins, 2013, 347). "Part of the problem is understanding that enslavement in the Ottoman, Iranian, and Arab societies of the Middle East and North Africa was driven by patronage, grounded in the family, and backed by *Shari'a* law and socio-cultural norms" (Toledano, 2017, 116; Toledano, 2002). In this context, the intersection between domesticity and slavery is important to understanding how this institution operated long after abolitionist movements in the Western world. In this chapter, I discuss domestic slavery in particular, as *My Damascus* is concerned with how the two enslaved women of African descent are closely bound up to Beit Jiddo. Despite these women's integral roles in maintaining the ancestral home, they are shown as not fully belonging in the Baroudi household, thus foregrounding their status as other.

For the Ottomans and Muslim societies during the sixteenth through the nineteenth centuries, the identities of African and slave were interchangeable (Toledano, 2002, 64–65). While enslaved people under the Ottoman Empire came from several parts of the world, such as the Caucasus lands and Georgia, the "overwhelming majority of slaves were female, African, and domestic" (Toledano, 1998, 6; Zilfi, 2004, 29). The Ottomans were unfamiliar with the African context and "tended to refer to all dark-skinned slaves as 'black' *(zenci),* despite the fact that there was a great variety within that group, and the only sub-group they recognized among Africans was that of Ethiopians" (Toledano, 2002, 71). Amiry regurgitates this anti-blackness and homogenization of people of African descent by referring to Sajeda as coming from "deep dark Africa" (2016a, 75). According to Toledano,

> Estimates of the total volume for the entire century from the Swahili coasts to the Ottoman Middle East and India are put at 313,000, across the Red Sea and the Gulf of Aden – 492,000, into Ottoman Egypt – 362,000, and into Ottoman North Africa (Algeria, Tunisia, and Libya) 350,000. If we exclude the numbers going to India, a rough estimate of this mass population movement would amount to more than 1.3 million people.
>
> (2017, 107–108)

These statistics reveal the dependence of the Ottoman Middle East on the trading of people from the African continent as well as the Ottoman Empire's power and dominance over this region. This mass migration demonstrates that these people were forcibly removed from their homelands to be rendered immobile subjects in their adopted lands, which means that this form of migration was not multidirectional.

Slavery in Muslim societies was supposedly "milder" because slaves were not systematically abused and subjugated like their counterparts in the Americas, the Caribbean and elsewhere. They were thought to be better integrated into Arab society, and this resulted in "the resistance to the abolition of slavery and the absence of abolitionist movements in many [Arab] societies" (Toledano, 1998, 16). In lieu of these abolitionist movements in the Arab region, gradual integration was the mode by which the institution of slavery supposedly ended through inter-racial relationships: "Exogamy and the passing of several generations ensured the social absorption of free

54 *Arththi Sathananthar*

children in cross-racial marriages, and the dilution of the gene pool affecting phenotypes led to the disappearance of dark-skinned Africans from the observer's 'gaze'" (Toledano, 2017, 108). This "dilution of the African gene pool" suggests a measure to integrate enslaved or formerly enslaved people as Arab, with the Arab identity in this sense being "white". This ethnic integration is evidenced by the joke that Amiry's mixed race uncle, Sami, makes about the woman he seeks to marry: "I shall marry the most blonde and blue-eyed woman in the world" (42). The joke turns to a prophecy as he goes on to marry three white women. His African mother's lineage fades away in the family as he deliberately chooses to marry three Caucasian women, thus exemplifying his separation from his African heritage and his pursuit of a "lighter" Arab gene pool.

There is a tension between scholars' claims on the integration of enslaved African people into Muslim society. While I have just outlined that Toledano argues that racial assimilation through sexual relationships wiped out the African ethnic identity, he also claims that "enslaved persons were absorbed into families, and diasporic communities of enslaved and manumitted persons preserved their origin cultures and produced hybridities with local brands of popular Islamic cultures" (2017, 106). Wilkins concurs on this social assimilation, "where slaves and other immigrants established durable human relationships, came to terms with the existing structures of power, and formed new affiliations and identities" (2013, 349). Therefore, there lies a paradox concerning the sense of belonging that enslaved and formerly enslaved individuals of African descent have in the Arab world. On the one hand, Arab racial superiority sought to wipe out and dilute the African race, but on the other hand, this superiority did not prevent simultaneous co-existence as a unified Arab society. *My Damascus* grapples with this tension as it attempts to highlight the social integration of the enslaved women into the Arab family, thus creating a hybrid and multicultural household. However, as I will demonstrate in the following section, this ideal is not successfully realized.

The issue of manumission is a contested one in the Arab region. Wilkins describes three forms of manumission under Islamic law:

> immediate or "pious" manumission (*'itq*) the grant of provisional manumission that takes effect after the death of the master (*tadbir*) and contractual manumission (*mukàtaba*), according to which the master grants the slave freedom in exchange for the rendering of money or labor. Thereafter, the manumitter and freed person were to remain in a relationship of patronage (*wala*), which included the entitlement of the patron (or his heirs) to a certain portion of the estate of the freed person.
>
> (2013, 367–368)

In the nineteenth century, in different parts of the world – Europe, the Americas and the West Indies – slavery ended at different times. Toledano states:

Re-writing the Other 55

In the Ottoman state which conquered its vast territories in the fifteenth and sixteenth centuries, slavery was legal, and the slave trade flourished until the collapse of the Empire during the First World War. But the traffic in slaves decreased dramatically toward the end of the nineteenth century, and the institution itself died out in the first decade of the twentieth century. In some of the successor states in Arabia, however, the practice lingered on well beyond the Second World War, and actual bondage in various forms continues to exist covertly even today.

(1998, 3; Toledano, 2017, 105–106)

This example illustrates the Ottoman state's reluctance to abolish slavery as it was so deeply ingrained into the backbone of Ottoman society. While the above passage states that slavery remained in Arabia, *My Damascus* shows how this is true for the Levantine states as well. According to Zilfi,

One can argue that slavery, like polygamy, which hovered around five per cent of the Ottoman population, was the practice of a small, privileged minority and as such scarcely reflected the experience of the majority. In fact, most families and households operated without slaves or servants of any kind.

(2004, 29)

Beit Jiddo is indeed a peculiar household. Although the women occupy the workplace (Amiry's mother and aunts were all teachers), the presence of the enslaved and of servants in the household indicates social and economic prestige, thus suggesting how slavery was perceived to be acceptable in affluent Damascene society. Based on a case study on slavery in Aleppo during the late Ottoman Empire, Wilkins claims, "The relatively large number of women manumitting female slaves reflects primarily women of high status; most notably, this pattern points to the practices of women grandees, who had at their disposal considerable wealth and sizeable entourages" (2013, 360). We might wonder if Amiry's aunts, who became the matriarchs of the household after the grandfather Jiddo's death, freed their slaves. To what extent are they really free if they still reside in Beit Jiddo and serve the family? There is no suggestion in the text that they are given any reparations or receive a salary; only that they continue to perform domestic labor for the Baroudi family. Therefore, Sajeda and Ghalia remain "covertly" in bondage. Wilkins remarks that some elite women were found to be generous to their slaves as seen through the deeds of Sitt Fatima who manumitted her Russian female slave and bestowed upon her material goods such as articles of clothing and kitchenware (2013, 373). Although the Baroudi women are affectionate and show tender care towards Sajeda and Ghalia, it is ambiguous whether this affection extends to material endowment to these enslaved women, thus further questioning whether or not they were manumitted. In the following section, I examine Amiry's representations of the enslaved African women. These women's lack

56 *Arththi Sathananthar*

of socio-economic mobility and their status as the foreign "other" in the household render them helpless in a patriarchal bourgeois society.

Beit Jiddo: A Site of Bondage

The text illustrates the journeys to and from Beit Jiddo made by the Baroudi women and by the domestic staff who leave the house at various points:

> seventy-year-old Ghalia's waning energy could only carry her from Beit Jiddo to Abu Rummaneh, the most fashionable residential neighbourhood in Damascus, where Aunt Is'af lived at that time. Only Sajeda was saved this sad farewell. She, who died a few years earlier, had already moved out of Beit Jiddo to live with her son Sami.
>
> (173)

Here, Ghalia and Sajeda are not able to return home to their ancestral place of origin but remain bound to their Arab employers. Although Amiry narrates the stories of Sajeda and Ghalia, the tone she writes in suggests a detachment from the representation of their narratives. This detachment offers a glimpse at the difference between the experience of these women from their employers due to both their ethnic and socio-economic backgrounds.

Sajeda is the most senior member of the household staff. Although Amiry makes no explicit mention that she is enslaved, the circumstances that brought her to the family suggest otherwise:

> 'Poor thing' was how Teta had referred to Sajeda ever since she had arrived at the Baroudi Mansion twenty-five years earlier. The "poor thing" was a reference to how Sajeda's widowed father had given her away at the age of twelve, after her mother died while giving birth to yet another baby girl. [...] Teta could not recall how, out of the blue, "the poor thing" arrived with Jiddo after one of his many business trips to al-Hijaz.
>
> (37)

Sajeda's history points to the cultural setting of girls being undervalued in families and being pawned away, which is evidence of another form of bondage. This exchange is reflective of Toledano's observation:

> Following universal abolition in the post-imperial nation-states of the Middle East and North Africa, the demand for domestic labor was being filled through a practice known in Ottoman societies as the recruitment of *besleme*. Poor families would offer their daughters (*besleme kız*), and sometimes sons, to elite and better-off urban and rural families, to be cared for and properly raised, in return for services in the household that included cleaning, cooking, caring for the children, and entertaining guests.
>
> (2017, 116)

Re-writing the Other 57

The repetition of "poor thing" to refer to Sajeda strips her of her humanity as she is objectified by Teta in a condescending tone. Sajeda is a victim of her own family as well as the Baroudi family. Not long after serving in Beit Jiddo, Jiddo impregnates her; Amiry does not reveal whether the relationship was consensual.

This form of subjugation of female slaves underlies a larger systematic oppression:

> while the Europeans paid a higher price for male slaves than females, the reverse was the case with the Arabs. [...] the Arabs saw profit in sexual satisfaction/reproductive potential. Offspring of the union between Islamic master and female slave was born free, out of respect of the child's Islamic paternity.
>
> (Pavlu, 2018)[3]

Given this cultural framework of the operation of enslavement, Jiddo is neither charged nor convicted of his rape, thus his crime is not perceived as an injustice towards Sajeda. Madeline Zilfi points out that "the court [of law] could not have interfered with owners' rights to their female slaves' services, of whatever kind. Nor, under ordinary circumstances, could the female slaves have complained about their employment even if it involved sexual relations" (2004, 28). Instead, Sajeda is punished by the Baroudi family for Jiddo's transgressions against her and is sent away from the mansion. The incident takes place at the beginning of the book and signifies the impact of this relationship on Amiry's grandmother, Teta (32–46). Rather than focus on Sajeda's vulnerable situation, Amiry foregrounds Teta and takes the angle that her husband has betrayed her, thus marginalizing Sajeda's experience. Zilfi adds, "Female slaves as models of servitude, servility, and sexual availability were a historical reality in the immediate pre-modern past" (2004, 29). Sajeda's story manifests this reality. However, Teta takes pity on her and requests that she be brought back to Beit Jiddo. Sajeda then gives birth to Sami.

Despite Sajeda and Sami continuing to reside in Beit Jiddo, they are heavily racialized and dehumanized in the house and the text. *My Damascus* is littered with racist undertones when describing Sajeda and her son:

> While chubby Sajeda, who originally came from deep dark Africa, had pronounced features, plump lips, a wide flat nose and wide hips, Ethiopian Ghalia had tiny features and a slim body.
>
> (74)

> all his features were large and pronounced: a big round head, big black droopy eyes, big flat nose, and big mouth with voluptuous lips.
>
> (40)

58   *Arththi Sathananthar*

> she [Samia] simply replaced her porcelain blonde doll, […] with her new animated black doll [Sami].
>
> (41)

> A magical bond developed between the two, between the innocent baby devil and the good-hearted old angel.
>
> (41)

Darkness and blackness are equated with servitude and subservience. Despite being Samia's half-brother, as an infant Sami is already placed in implicit bondage to her. He becomes her plaything due to his half-"African" lineage, itself represented homogenously without acknowledgment of the diversity of the "deep dark Africa" from where his mother had come. Operating within this framework of homogenization, the enslaved Africans' physical features were brought to the forefront, as noted by Toledano:

> in Ottoman and sources from earlier Muslim societies, there are regular references to certain parts of the slave's body and neglect of others. Thus, the head of the slave, mainly the eyes, hair and teeth, receive special attention, and authors also comment about build, for example whether the slave is slender, heavy, tall or short. […] But attention to the slave's body was not merely a matter of physical appearance and attraction. Rather, in large measure, it reflected deep concern for the slave's health, often not only linked to his or her ability to perform the chores intended for them, but affecting their actual survivability. High mortality on some of the routes, especially those originating in Africa, weeded out the weaker among the slaves.
>
> (2002, 68)

This fixation on physical appearance extends to contemporary times. As Kareem argues, "Arabs, like their western teachers, when discussing anti-black racism and black issues, seem fixated on skin colour, ideals of beauty, and visual representations; in a sense they express their own racial anxiety" (2019). Amiry does not mention where in the African region Sajeda originated from, but her text nonetheless relies on racialized descriptions of Sajeda's and Sami's features, all of which signals their othering from the rest of the Baroudi family who are presumably light skinned. Although this is not explicitly commented on in the text, it is well-established that elite Arab families such as the Baroudis were fair skinned due to the integration of Circassian and Georgian enslaved women into elite households as "potential concubines and future wives and mothers" (Toledano, 2002, 72). Moreover, the way in which darkness is contrasted with lightness and the equation of these terms with goodness and evil, respectively, indicate the role which skin colour played in the household precisely because of the way in which it marked the bodies of Sajeda and Sami as different. Although Amiry sheds light on an obscured topic in Arab discourse, she perpetuates and maintains a dark tone towards her own family member, her half-uncle Sami.

Ultimately, in the case of Sajeda and Sami, class overrules blood ties. Amiry portrays a façade whereby Sami bridges both the master and servant narrative, but Sajeda's position contradicts this:

> Running and falling, between the downstairs and upstairs spaces; between his mother's room in the servant's quarter and his father and Teta's bedroom, between the kitchen where his mother, Ghalia and Fatima spent most of their time, and the *liwan* and courtyard where Teta and his stepsisters and brother socialised, little Sami wove an unusual, unprecedented fabric of relationships, a fabric of equality between the upstairs and downstairs in the Baroudi Mansion.
>
> (42)

> Habits never changed in a place like Beit Jiddo, or for that matter in a city as ancient and archaic as Damascus. Neither did her [Sajeda] status in the household, even as the mother of a Baroudi child.
>
> (78)

Amiry stresses that the city was "ancient and archaic", a perception that reflects the archaic traditions of African female sexual servitude. The first passage claims that Sami wove "a fabric of equality" between his mother's and father's distinct class status, yet this is disputed in the second passage which details Sajeda's subservient position. Because Islamic law prevented the sale of pregnant women, the enslaved's pregnancy was seen as an "insurance policy" as it tied the mother to the father of the child (Toledano, 2002, 69). In the Baroudi household, this is not the case. Despite being impregnated by Jiddo, Sajeda remains in the servant quarters while it is only her son who is able to transgress the boundaries between the elite family and their domestic staff. Furthermore, Sajeda remains marginalized due to her ethnic identity which differentiates her from her Arab masters. According to Toledano,

> white slaves were relatively easily absorbed into elite society, whereas the Africans, also not infrequently joining urban and rural families, were incorporated into lower social classes. Thus ethnicity, once simply called race, more often than not determined the slave's type of employment and consequently her or his social placement.
>
> (2002, 72)

Therefore, Sajeda is not treated as equally as Sami due to her ethnicity. Had she been of a white background, she would be better integrated into the family. While the first passage suggests that Sami transcends class divisions and spaces, it also stresses the segregated spaces within the home that kept employer and servant apart. Toledano notes that "female slave labour was

60   *Arththi Sathananthar*

created by the desire to reduce the burden on free women" (1998, 14). This is evident in the separation between the kitchen and *liwan* where female labour is contrasted with female leisure, and where the white employer is separated from the black staff.

The enslaved women of African descent were lower in the social hierarchy than the other household staff, discriminated against and vulnerable to sexual exploitation. Despite these circumstances, they were integral to the household where they worked and lived. Therefore, the existing hierarchy does not rule out possibilities of integration as seen through the representation of Sami in Beit Jiddo who has the advantage of Arab blood. Amiry writes of Sami,

> He glowed like sunshine
> He felt like sunshine
> And, like sunshine, he radiated warmth and security
> He was his mother's sunshine
> His sixty-five year old father's sunshine
> Sunshine of all the downstairs staff
>
> (41)

Based on the various excerpts from the text, it would appear that Amiry tends to write in a contradicting tone; she dehumanizes a character in one instance while showing praise for the same character in the next. Here, Sami is seen in this positive light, his skin colour juxtaposed with the perception that others have of him due to the Arab patriarch being his biological father. Had Sajeda been impregnated by a man of African descent, Sami would be unlikely to receive the same treatment or be seen as the "sunshine" in the family. The status of a mixed-race child is complex because it brings into conflict conceptions of Arab superiority with those of African inferiority in a Muslim society where patrilineal descent is important. In earlier times, "The term commonly used by the ancient Arabs for the offspring of mixed unions was *hajin*, a word which, like the English 'mongrel' and 'half-breed,' was used both of animals and of human beings" (89). Amiry's representation of Sami as the "sunshine" in the family subverts archaic terminology on mixed-raced African children, but Sami nonetheless occupies a liminal status, which is reflected in how he is represented in the household, and how he might have been perceived in Arab society in earlier time periods.

On the other hand, Ghalia's story explicitly details her pronounced position as a slave. In the only subsection in the book that exclusively narrates her story, the heading titled "A Wedding Present" itself objectifies and dehumanizes her in the Baroudi family history. Amiry notes how the Friday family feasts affect Ghalia:

> It was not the exhaustion of a long day's work that brought Ghalia close to tears every time the Baroudi family gathered to celebrate La Grande

Re-writing the Other 61

Bouffe or any other family occasion. The truth was that family gatherings made Ghalia miss the family she never had.

(124)

Unlike Sajeda, who has her son, Ghalia is completely cut off from her family. Her story depicts the sobering reality of slave auctions and markets:

She may have had a faint memory of who her family was or where she came from, but all she recalled was the tragic day when she was separated from her two older brothers at the age of five. She was taken to the female slave market, while her seven-year-old twin brothers were dragged to the male section. It was her physical features that made her, and others, suspect that she was of Ethiopian or Nigerian origin. [...] no one ever bothered to ask Ghalia her story. "She was the wedding present that Baba got from his eldest sister Alia, when he went to visit her in Jeddah in 1896."

(124–125)

Compared to Sajeda, Ghalia does not take up much space in the text, but this passage speaks volumes for the predicament that brought her to the Baroudi family. "From Africa, slaves were run via Sahara Desert routes, the Ethiopian plateau, the Red Sea the Nile Valley, the Persian Gulf, and the pilgrimage routes to and from Arabia" (Toledano, 1998, 7). Jiddo acquires Ghalia and Sajeda in Jeddah and al-Hijaz respectively, major hubs for the commerce of slaves. Ghalia's and Sajeda's narratives underline the economic relations between the Levant and the Arabian Peninsula and how human trade from the African continent was a major source of income in these trade routes. The text highlights both the spatial and temporal dimensions of the institution of slavery. Ghalia arrives at Beit Jiddo long before slavery is outlawed in Ethiopia in 1935 (Pavlu, 2018; Bonacci and Meckelburg, 2017, 14). Unfortunately, her whole life is distilled to this: "Ghalia deeply resented that her life story had been reduced to two words: 'wedding present'" (125). During this time, many female slaves "entered the household as gifts rather than purchases", which highlights their lack of agency (Zilfi, 2004, 24; Wilkins, 2013, 358). Their mobility or lack thereof is dependent on the economic and political ties between the Levant and the African continent. The text contrasts the multiple journeys the Baroudi women, such as Teta and Samia, take of their own free will back and forth between their childhood homes against the involuntary journeys that Sajeda and Ghalia are subject to and how they end up in Beit Jiddo.

Furthermore, Ghalia's history is belittled by English Aunt Umaimah who thinks that she is fabricating her origins. She describes the following:

I don't know where she brings or invents these weird stories from. [...] Ghalia's are a bit racist and stereotypical [...] Who said you have to be

62   *Arththi Sathananthar*

white to be racist? Many blacks have internalised their white master's racism. […] If the stories she narrates to the kids are real, then they're too fictional. And if they are fiction, they could very well be real.

(125–126)

This scene is the only explicit discussion of race in the text. While Aunt Umaimah refers to the binary between white and black politics, as a white woman speaking to this topic she is ignorant of the racial politics of Arabs as masters of enslaved Africans. Interestingly, the last two sentences from her claim suggest an acknowledgement of Ghalia's history that dismantles her earlier attitudes on race. In this instance, the blurring of fact and fiction allows Ghalia's voice to be heard and taken seriously by her employers.

Conclusion

By telling the stories of these two figures, Amiry records their significance in the Baroudi household and the important roles they each play. Despite including them in her family's narrative, she depicts a hierarchical sense of community in the Baroudi mansion between employer and staff. The way in which the experiences of the enslaved are represented highlights their inferiority and vulnerability to the Baroudi family, and to a larger bourgeois Arab society. While Amiry foregrounds women's voices across different social classes, her problematic representation of the characters of African descent diminishes the merits of the text in telling their stories. The "African" voice is not adequately represented as she homogenizes, in particular, Sajeda's ethnic background. *My Damascus* is one of the few contemporary Arab literary texts that details the institution of slavery in the *Mashreq*. As this chapter demonstrates, anti-blackness and racism towards Black-Arabs and African migrants in the Arab region permeates contemporary society, which is reflected in racialized depictions of these communities in literature. My analysis of the entanglements between modernity, slavery and racism calls for culturally sensitive and politically aware literary representations of Black communities by non-black authors. It is not only important to include subaltern narratives in Arab literature, but to be critical of the ways in which these representations are manifested in such texts. By doing so, conversations on racism and anti-blackness within and beyond literary and cultural studies can be brought to the forefront with the aim of changing how we see and treat marginalized communities in the Levant and the wider Arab region.

Notes

1 Amiry has also published books in Italian, Se Questa E' Vita (2005), Niente Sesso in Citta' (2007), *Storia di un abito inglese e di una mucca ebrea* (2020) – *The Story of an English Suit and a Jewish Cow* – which is expected to be released in English. All her works have been translated into Italian and she has been awarded Italian literary

prizes – Viareggio-Versilia Prize 2004 and the Nonino Prize in 2014. Amiry's latest release is a historical novel set in Jaffa, *Mother of Strangers* (2022).

2 See W.G. Clarence-Smith (2020). *Islam and the Abolition of Slavery*. London: Hurst & Co.; M. Ennaji (2013) *Slavery, the State and Islam*. translated by Teresa Lavender Fagan. Cambridge: Cambridge University Press; M.C. Zilfi (2010). *Women and Slavery in the Late Ottoman Empire*. Cambridge: Cambridge University Press.

3 See also S. Abulhawa. (2013). Confronting Anti-Black Racism in the Arab World. [online] *Aljazeera*. [Viewed 21 May 2020] Available at: www.aljazeera.com/indepth/opinion/2013/06/201362472519107286.html

References

Abulhawa, S. (2013). Confronting Anti-Black Racism in the Arab World. [online] *Aljazeera*. [Viewed 21 May 2020] Available at: www.aljazeera.com/indepth/opinion/2013/06/201362472519107286.html

Amiry, S. (2003). *Sharon and My Mother-in-Law: Ramallah Diaries*. London: Granta.

———. (2010). *Nothing to Lose But Your Life: An 18-Hour Journey with Murad*. Doha: Bloomsbury Qatar Foundation Publishing.

———. (2010). *Menopausal Palestine: Women at the Edge*. New Delhi: Women Unlimited.

———. (2014). *Golda Slept Here: Palestine: The Presence of the Absent*. Doha: Bloomsbury Qatar Foundation Publishing.

———. (2016a). *My Damascus*. New Delhi: Women Unlimited.

———. (2016b). My Damascus, Suad Amiry Talks about Her New Book. [online] *YouTube*. [Viewed 31 October 2019] Available at: www.youtube.com/watch?v=wgEQ02v6EMA

Bawader (2020). Mobilizing against Anti-Black Racism in MENA: A Reader. [online] *Arab Reform Initiative*. [Viewed 3 March 2022] Available at: www.arab-reform.net/publication/mobilizing-against-anti-black-racism-in-mena-a-reader/

Blalack, J. (2019). Outside Servitude: A Novel Exploring Enslavement in Mauritania. [online] *ArabLit*. [Viewed 3 March 2022] Available at: https://arablit.org/2019/02/07/outside-servitude-a-novel-exploring-enslavement-in-mauritania/

Bonacci, G. and Meckelburg, A. (2017). Revisiting Slavery and the Slave Trade in Ethiopia. *Northeast African Studies*, 17(2), 3–30

Clarence-Smith, W. G. (2020). *Islam and the Abolition of Slavery*. London: Hurst & Co.

Ennaji, M. (2013). *Slavery, the State and Islam*, translated by Teresa Lavender Fagan. Cambridge: Cambridge University Press.

Hartman, S. (2008). Venus in Two Acts. *Small Axe: A Journal of Caribbean Criticism*, 26(26) 1–14.

Karamursel, C. (2016). The Uncertainties of Freedom: The Second Constitutional Era and the End of Slavery in the Late Ottoman Empire. *Journal of Women's History*, 28(3) 138–161.

Kareem, M. (2019). Arabic Literature and the African Other. [online] *Africa is a Country* [Viewed 2 March 2022] Available at: https://africasacountry.com/2019/05/how-do-arabs-talk-and-write-about-black-people

King, S.J. (2021). Black Arabs and African Migrants: Between Slavery and Racism in North Africa. *The Journal of North African Studies*, 26(1), 8–50.

Lewis, B. (1985). The Crows of the Arabs. *Critical Inquiry*, 12(1), 88–97.

64   *Arththi Sathananthar*

Osman, G. and Forbes, C. (2004). Representing the West in the Arabic Language: The Slave Narrative of Omar bin Said. *Journal of Islamic Studies*. 15(3), 331–343.

Pavlu, G. (2018). Recalling Africa's Harrowing Tale of its First Slavers – The Arabs – As UK Slave Trade Abolition is Commemorated. [online] *NewAfrican*. [Viewed 21 May 2020] Available at: https://newafricanmagazine.com/16616/

Qualey, M.L. (2020). Black Saudi Author Focuses on Neglected History of African Migration and Slavery. [online] *Al-Fanar Media*. [Viewed on 3 March 2022] Available at: www.al-fanarmedia.org/2020/07/a-black-saudi-author-focuses-on-a-neglected-history/

Shahadah, A. (2019). The History of Arab Slavery in Africa. [online] *African Holocaust*. [Viewed 2 March 2022] Available at: www.africanholocaust.net/arabsla vetrade/

Toledano, E.R. (1993). Late Ottoman Concepts of Slavery (1830s–1880s). *Poetics Today*, 14(3) 477–506.

———. (1998). Introduction: Ottoman Slavery and the Slave Trade. In *Slavery and Abolition in the Ottoman Middle East*. Washington: University of Washington Press. pp. 3–19.

———. (2002). Representing the Slave's Body in Ottoman Society. *Slavery & Abolition: A Journal of Slave and Post-Slave Studies*, 23(2) 57–74.

———. (2017). Enslavement and Freedom in Transition: MENA Societies from Empires to National States. *Journal of Global Slavery*, 2 100–121.

Wilkins, C.L. (2013). Slavery and Household Formation in Ottoman Aleppo, 1640 – 1700. *Journal of the Economic and Social History of the Orient*, 56(3) 345–391.

Yelibenwork, A. (2011). Slavery in Ethiopia. [online] *African Holocaust* [Viewed 2 March 2022] Available at: www.africanholocaust.net/slavery-in-ethiopia/

Zilfi, M.C. (2010). *Women and Slavery in the Late Ottoman Empire*. Cambridge, Cambridge University Press.

———. (2004). Servants, Slaves, and the Domestic Order in the Ottoman Middle East. *HAWWA: Journal of Women of the Middle East and the Islamic World*. 2(1) 1–33.

Part II

Ghurba in Narratives of Displacement

3　*The Woman from Tantoura*

Structural Marginalisation and the Re-Making of Home among Palestinian Refugees in Lebanon

Roba Al-Salibi

Introduction

After the 1948 expulsion of Palestinians from their homeland at the hands of the Israeli settler colonial project, an event known in Arabic as 'Al-nakba' (meaning catastrophe), a new form of Palestinian literature began to emerge, one that is primarily concerned with narrating the plight of Palestinian refugees and with highlighting the devastating conditions of exile and the everyday realities of refugee camps. One of the most prominent Palestinian writers, whose literary works were crucial in giving voice to the systematically silenced Palestinians, is Ghassan Kanafani. Kanafani was a rigorous advocate of a Palestinian literature that is directly engaged in resisting the Zionist colonisation of Palestine and exposing the multiple forms of epistemic and material violence that Palestinians inside and outside Palestine are subjected to. Kanafani coined the term 'resistance literature' to refer to the role of literary production in the context of Palestine and its function as a resistance strategy against historical amnesia and the structural silencing of Palestinians (Hamdi 2011). His framing of literature relies on his rigorous analysis of the cultural, the literary, and the artistic, as being embedded within and reflective of wider power relations, including the settler colonial relation and class relations.

Under the banner of resistance literature, Palestinian literature of exile emerged as a literary form that narrates the Nakba as a collective traumatic memory and as a spatial and temporal rupture that continues to define the Palestinian present. Preserving Palestinian memory and identity against continuous and systematic obliteration is central to Palestinian forms of literary and cultural production. Literary narratives of exile, in particular, are of great significance to the Palestinian struggle as they articulate the subjective experience of displacement that is shared collectively among refugees in their multiple exilic locations. The emotional and affective implications of displacement and the subsequent trauma of loss are the main existing premises that define this literature.

DOI: 10.4324/9781003301776-6

68 *Roba Al-Salibi*

In this chapter, I offer an analysis of Radwa Ashour's novel *Al-Tantouriya*, published in 2010 and translated into English by Kay Heikkinen as *The Woman from Tantoura* in 2014. The novel narrates Palestinian exilic lived experiences in Lebanon. It speaks of the trauma of exile as well as the subsequent traumas Palestinians in Lebanon experienced as they were cast as unwanted and excluded subjects. *The Woman from Tantoura* offers a powerful narration from the perspective of a Palestinian woman who witnessed the devastating impact of the Lebanese civil war on Palestinians and the forms of othering and structural marginalisation they were, and still are, subjected to. The novel constantly links the subjective with the collective, the structural with the everyday, and the emotional with the political.

The Woman from Tantoura offers a unique insight into Palestinians' realities in Lebanon from a subjective standpoint which is always collective and political. It articulates what usually goes missing from academic scholarship that is often fixated on meta-structures of power without considering the ways in which these structures are affectively experienced, negotiated, and resisted in the everyday. Moreover, Ashour's novel highlights the specificity of the historical experience of Palestinian refugees in Lebanon which, in comparison to other contexts in which Palestinian refugees are present, constitutes the most marginalised and rights-deprived case. In Lebanon, not only are Palestinians denied citizenship and the benefits associated with it, but they are also subject to forms of political oppression and social discrimination that are specific to the postcolonial nature of the modern Lebanese state.

The author, Radwa Ashour, was an acclaimed Egyptian novelist and literary critic whose writing is concerned with narrating an alternative history to official historical narratives and challenging their exclusions and epistemic violence. Although not Palestinian, Ashour was deeply preoccupied with the Palestinian question and saw it as the main cause that should concern every Arab intellectual. This belief was not unique to Ashour as many writers and intellectuals of her generation, especially leftists and committed intellectuals, also centred Palestine in their writing. Ashour had an intimate relationship to Palestine as she was married to the poet Mourid Barghouti, who himself was an exiled Palestinian. The author was Palestinian at heart, and her political commitment towards Palestine was translated into a literary commitment in which she exposed, through her creative writing, the violence of the Zionist colonisation of Palestine and the lived realities of Palestinian refugees away from their homeland. Ashour's literary works on Palestine sit squarely within the parameters that define the Palestinian literature that Kanafani advocated and which is fundamentally preoccupied with the Zionist colonisation of Palestine, Palestinian memory, exile, and identity. Palestinian literature, therefore, is not limited to the identity of the writer, but is rather defined by the articulation of these themes and issues. Since most Palestinian literary productions took place outside Palestine due to Al-Nakba and the subsequent exile, Refqa Abu-Remaileh (2021) maintains that Palestinian literature should 'transcend national identities and embrace a reality of open, multiple,

The Woman from Tantoura   69

and hybrid identities' (2021, 71). She further argues that Palestinian literature should include those who identify as Palestinians regardless of their legal status as well as non-Palestinian writers who made valuable contributions to Palestinian literature (2021, 71). Abu-Remaileh's conception of Palestinian literature offers a more expansive definition that recognises the forms of transnational solidarity with Palestine in the literary field, which many Arab writers contributed to, such as Radwa Ashour, Elias Khoury, and others.

The first section of this chapter's analysis attends to the structural forms of marginalisation, violence, and exclusion that Palestinian refugees in Lebanon were subjected to in the early years of their displacement and during the period of the Lebanese civil war (1975–1989). The second section focuses on memory as a tool used by Palestinian refugees in their practices of home remaking and in the spatial recreation of the homeland. Understood as both individual and collective, memory is analysed as a site that allows for a sense of continuity to be achieved following the rupture of exile. My analysis grounds memory in the rupture of exile and the trauma of Al-Nakba, but it also perceives memory as an emotional investment of exiled Palestinian subjects in building new localities, sites of intimacy and homes, even if these are considered symbolic and temporary until return is realised.

Background to the Novel

The Woman from Tantoura traces the life of Ruqayya, a Palestinian woman who, at the age of 13, was displaced from her village of Tantoura at the hands of the Zionist paramilitary forces. The novel follows Ruqayya's life in Lebanon as a refugee and her multiple journeys of migration as she becomes a mother and a grandmother. Tantoura is a Palestinian village located on the Mediterranean Sea to the south of Haifa city. It was completely obliterated during the violent events of Al-Nakba. The novel deals with questions of exile, memory, structural exclusion, and home in the everyday realities of Palestinian refugees in Lebanon. It narrates multiple and intergenerational stories of displacement and displaced Palestinians' relationship to Palestine, both as a spatial location under Israeli colonisation and as an imagined geography in exile. It is structured as a narration of memories by Ruqayya who has been asked by her son, Hassan, to write her memories of Al-Nakba and her experience as a Palestinian refugee in Lebanon for a Palestinian archiving project. In her narration, Ruqayya gives an account of life in Palestine before Al-Nakba and her childhood memories there, spent at the beach with her cousins and neighbours. These memories are then disrupted by the violent event of Al-Nakba, which constitutes the major rupture in Ruqayya's life trajectory and the beginning of her exilic journey. The trauma of Ruqayya's displacement is exacerbated by the loss of her father and two brothers who were killed while fighting for their village. The trauma of this double loss stays with her in the long years of her exile and haunts her in the multiple places she resides in. The novel takes place across different exilic locations between Sidon, Beirut,

70 *Roba Al-Salibi*

Abu Dhabi, and Alexandria as Ruqayya moves between these places either in search for an alternative home, or to escape from the violent years of the civil war in Lebanon where Palestinians were brutalised, massacred, and besieged. Ruqayya's story is one of trauma and grief as well as survival and resilience. It is a story that resembles that of many Palestinians who lived through the Nakba and its aftermath, and a story that demonstrates the structural continuity of Al-Nakba, what can be called *al-nakba al-mustamirra* or the continuous Nakba.

Existing scholarly treatments of the novel focus primarily on the trauma and memory associated with the Palestinian Nakba (Nashef 2021; Najm and Islam 2020). While the individual and collective trauma of Al-Nakba constitutes a major theme in the novel, the Palestinian refugee experience in Lebanon as narrated in the novel is not adequately examined in these existing works. Memory has also been taken up as a point of analysis and was approached as a mode of survival for Palestinian refugees in the camps. However, in my own approach to how memory is presented in the novel, I go beyond this notion into analysing how memory itself becomes a strategy through which a remaking of home in exile takes place. The collective memory of expulsion and the loss of the homeland bring Palestinian refugees together as a community and reduce their sense of *ghurba* through a sharing of their loss. Communal acts of remembering centre the lost homeland in the everyday navigation of the space of exile, thereby allowing for new meanings of home to be forged. Feminist scholar Sara Ahmed argues that the forming of communities among those who are seen as strangers through 'collective acts of remembering' makes possible a recreation of migrant selves and carving spaces of familiarity. She maintains that:

> The gap between memory and place in the very dislocation of migration allows communities to be formed: that gap becomes reworked as a site of bodily transformation, the potential to remake one's relation to what which appears as unfamiliar, to reinhabit spaces and places.
>
> (1999, 344)

I take Ahmed's observation in my analysis of the novel where I argue that the forming of a Palestinian community in Lebanon and the sharing of memories of Palestine becomes a terrain through which new meanings of home are created and new ways of inhabiting an unfamiliar place are produced.

Palestinian Refugees in Lebanon: Othering, Marginalisation, and Exclusion

In the aftermath of the violent expulsion of Palestinians from their homeland in 1948, around 110,000 Palestinians, particularly those living in the north of Palestine, sought refuge in Lebanon (Morris 1987; Khalili 2007). Most of those who became exiled in Lebanon had originated from the Galilee area and

The coastal cities colonised in 1948 (Sayigh 1998). The United Nations Relief and Works Agency (UNRWA) was founded to provide aid and employment for Palestinian refugees and set up fifteen refugee camps in Lebanon on lands either rented from the Lebanese state or purchased from landowners (Peteet 2005). The refugees who resided in the camps were overwhelmingly peasants, while those who came from Palestinian cities and small towns resided in urban Lebanese districts. Both UNRWA and the Lebanese state were the governing bodies of the refugee population before the Palestinian Liberation Organisation's (PLO) political parties held power inside the camps.

In Lebanon, the warm reception of Palestinian refugees soon turned into increased hostility that continues to define the Palestinian exilic experience until today. Throughout Ruqayya's narration, the structural marginalisation and othering of Palestinians emerge as central themes, beginning from the restrictions on Palestinians' movement inside Lebanon to the long and brutal years of the civil war and the Zionist invasion of Beirut. The political context of Lebanon in the post-independence era made the Palestinian presence there fraught with tension and the cause of divisions. The French imposed a sectarian political system in Lebanon that divided power between Christians and Muslims, so the coming of Palestinian refugees, most of whom were Muslims, raised concerns over the balance of power. This postcolonial formation has placed the Palestinians as a demographic threat and led them to be put under close surveillance by the Lebanese secret service throughout the 1950s and 1960s (Khalili 2007, 735). In addition to this fragile political system, other factors have led to the systematic oppression of Palestinians, such as the economic implications of large numbers of low-wage labour and fear of political organising inside Palestinian refugee camps which could challenge the sovereignty of the Lebanese state (Peteet 2005, 6). The production of the category of the Palestinian refugee in Lebanon was premised on 'exclusivist ethnoreligious state formation and the imposition of a bureaucratic-administrative regime' that represented and consolidated an image of the Palestinian refugee as an 'other' (Peteet 2005, 94). Palestinian refugees have been denied citizenship, which prevented them from obtaining civic rights that are only granted to people who hold the Lebanese nationality. In 1963, a decree was issued that categorised Palestinians as foreigners 'not holding documents from their original countries and residing in Lebanon' (UNHCR 2006). This decree barred Palestinian refugees from 'social and political rights beyond those secured by UNRWA' (Knudsen 2007, 4).

The living conditions and legal status of Palestinian refugees in the Arab world differ. In Jordan, for example, where the highest number of refugees outside Palestine reside, Palestinians were given citizenship rights but, as Sari Hanafi maintains, they were deprived of the 'possibility of political organising based on national origins' (Hanafi 2006, 151). Restrictions on political organising among Palestinian refugees were also implemented in Egypt, which received much smaller numbers of Palestinian refugees compared to Syria, Lebanon, and Jordan. Palestinians there could obtain citizenship and

72   *Roba Al-Salibi*

the rights available to citizens but 'they face tight restrictions on their access to education, to work, to own land or property, to benefit from government services' (El-Abed 2009, 1). In Syria, Palestinians 'were treated equally with Syrians in all areas except that of citizenship and voting rights while preserving their original nationality' (Chen 2009, 46). The Gulf states did not host Palestinians as refugees. Rather, they were there as 'important labour resources' (Chen 2009, 47). Iraq's invasion of Kuwait in 1990 had resulted in the expulsion of some 300,000 Palestinians due to Kuwaiti authorities' reprisals against the Palestinian community (ibid). In Europe, there has been a recent increase in the presence of Palestinian refugees, with the largest concentration of Palestinian communities being in Germany, the Scandinavian countries, Britain, and Spain (Shiblak 2005, 7).

Palestinian refugee communities are dispersed all over the globe. There are differences pertaining to their social, legal, economic, and political status depending on their country of residence. They are granted certain rights in some states more than others based on the host's policies towards them. Within the Arab states, Palestinians 'are granted very few benefits as a matter of *right*' and these benefits 'are at best understood as *privileges* for Palestinians and thus revocable at any time for any reason' (Akram 2002, 44). European states grant Palestinians a refugee status only when they prove that they have a well-founded fear of persecution in their last place of residence (Akram 2002, 44). Claims of persecution by Israel do not grant them a refugee status either because they are not Israeli nationals or Israel is not their last country of residence. These policies make the process of seeking asylum in Europe very complex and have placed Palestinian refugees under precarious legal and economic conditions. The marginalisation of Palestinians in Lebanon, therefore, should be situated within the larger marginalisation of Palestinian communities in the Arab world and Europe. However, there are unique aspects to their marginalisation and exclusion in Lebanon compared to other states, as their presence has been marked by extremely cruel living conditions enforced by Lebanese legislation and non-settlement policy, hence the significance of Ashour's depiction of how these conditions are experienced and navigated in *The Woman from Tantoura*.

Narrating Palestinian Exile in Lebanon

Ruqayya's family, like many other Palestinian families from northern Palestine, were displaced to Lebanon to escape an inevitable death with the hope that return will be very soon. Having lost her father and two brothers while defending their village against the Zionist military gangs, Ruqayya and her mother, the only surviving members of the family, join Ruqayya's uncle in Sidon where she would stay until she gets married to her cousin, has two children, and moves to Beirut. The first two decades of Palestinian refugees' presence in Lebanon, before Palestinian political organisations could secure control inside refugee camps, were characterised by extreme economic hardship

The Woman from Tantoura   73

and restrictions on movement and participation in the labour market imposed by the Lebanese state. These structural forms of oppression and exclusion further exacerbated the loss and trauma experienced by Palestinian refugees in the aftermath of the Nakba. In Ruqayya's narrative, we read multiple stories of the exclusion and surveillance refugees faced prior to the advent of the PLO in Lebanon when Palestinians were able to have a more powerful position inside the camps. For instance, Ruqayya narrates how refugees were obliged to obtain a permit from the Lebanese authorities if they needed to leave the camp, and how displaced Palestinians living in villages in the south outside the refugee camps were forced to move to the camps so that the state could control their presence and movement (90).

In addition to these structural procedures of containment, control and surveillance, Palestinian refugees in Lebanon also faced discrimination and othering in their daily interactions with Lebanese citizens affiliated with right-wing political parties, particularly Phalange supporters, who opposed their presence in the country. After Ruqayya moves to Beirut and her sons start going to school there, they encounter racism for being Palestinians and are pointed at as outsiders who threaten Lebanon and its security. Although Palestinians who lived outside the camps were not subjected to the same mechanisms of control and surveillance as those who lived in the camps, they still faced forms of othering. In a conversation between Ruqayya and her son, Abed, the latter points out to the fact that the Palestinian in Lebanon, whether inside the camp or not, is regarded with suspicion and hostility:

> The camp, whether you live inside or outside, it's your story and there's no getting away from it. Your classmate suddenly turns against you and you don't know what's angered him, only to discover a day or two later that he's found out you're Palestinian and that your existence, the very fact that you exist and that you are you and no other, is a provocation that arouses anger or indignation or, at the very least, disgust. It's as if you were an insect that unfortunately fell in a bowl of soup. And you've known, for a long time before that, the meaning of the 'Phalange' and the meaning of 'the Forces' and what's waiting for you at their hands, and that you are a son of the camp even if you are lucky and don't live in it!
>
> (60)

The emotions of disgust and anger that Abed describes are manifestations of a nationalist ethnoreligious politics that sets clear boundaries of inclusion and exclusion within the body of the nation-state. Palestinians are othered, excluded from citizenship, employment, and public services, and are put under constant surveillance because they are represented by state authorities as bodies that contaminate the 'purity' of the nation; bodies that evoke feelings of disgust. In *The Cultural Politics of Emotions*, Sara Ahmed discusses emotions without viewing them as grounded in individual phycological states. Rather, she argues for an analysis of emotions as 'social and

74   *Roba Al-Salibi*

cultural practices' and offers a reading of emotions as part of larger discursive and material structures of nation-states (2014, 9). Her argument does not suggest that emotions are located in either the individual or the collective, but 'produce the very surfaces and boundaries that allow the individual and the social to be delineated as if they are objects' (10). Emotions work to align some subjects together while constructing other subjects as outsiders, as 'others'. Ahmed's analysis of the feeling of disgust is suggestive here. She maintains that disgust is 'dependent upon contact: it involves a relationship of touch and proximity between the surfaces of bodies and objects' (2014, 85). Proximity of the unpleasant object is what gives rise to feelings of disgust through the 'registering of the proximity as an offence' (2014, 85). In the above quote, disgust and anger become the feelings that Abed encounters as soon as his Palestinian identity is revealed and he comes into close contact with those who see his existence as illegitimate and dangerous. These subjective feelings of disgust and anger are grounded in larger relations of power and reflect a nationalist discourse that deems the Palestinian as a threat that should be contained, if not expelled.

The early 1970s mark both the intensification of violence against Palestinians in refugee camps by the Phalange militias and the Lebanese Army, and the increasing power of Palestinian political factions inside the camps (Peteet 2005, 8). This has led to a 15-year civil war (1975–1990) between Right-wing Christian militates and the progressive forces in Lebanon known as the Lebanese National Movement (LNM), which was a political ally of the Palestinians. We follow the events of the civil war through Ruqayya who witnesses these events unfold from her flat in Beirut. Her narration of the civil war starts with the fear she felt for her sons who are repeatedly met with hostility and resentment at school:

> I'm afraid of the army's bullets, of the militias and the Phalange and their evil intentions toward us. I'm afraid of a clash at school that would result in the boy coming home with his blood flowing. I'm afraid of Beirut.
>
> (111)

The fear that Ruqayya expresses as a mother whose sons, by virtue of their Palestinian identity, could be killed at any moment, envelopes her in the early years of the civil war until her sons eventually leave Lebanon. Although she refuses to leave Beirut, she was insistent on her sons to leave, 'to travel to any place far away. Any place' (141). Her son Sadiq, like many other Palestinians during the civil war, migrates to the Gulf and finds a job in Abu Dhabi, while Hassan goes to Egypt to join a university there. Ruqayya remembers the years of the civil war as a continuous chain of wars and massacres where language fails to articulate the horror and devastation Palestinians lived during these years. In the middle of these horrors, Ruqayya finds solace in silence as a mechanism that would make her more resilient in the face of adversity. When her son Hassan asks her to document the events she witnessed as a Palestinian

The Woman from Tantoura   75

refugee beginning from Al-Nakba until the years of the civil war, she is reluctant to write down her memories as she questions the logic behind 'living through the details of the disaster twice' (183). Hassan handed her a notebook with 'al-tantouriya' (the woman from Tantoura) written on it, which tempts her to start writing her story, as she could hear the blank pages whispering to her saying: 'aren't you the Tantouriya?' The empty pages 'become the space on which her silence can live' (Nashef 2021,12) despite the pain that comes with remembering and reliving the traumas of exile and the violence inflicted on Palestinian refugees in Lebanon.

Insanity is the word Ruqayya chooses to describe the years of civil war and the Israeli invasion of Beirut in 1982, a sweeping violence and destruction coming from all directions, sea, land, and air, that can't be articulated through a coherent narrative or be made sense of. Ruqayya offers us an image of the city of Beirut, where she stayed throughout the years of the war, that is disintegrating and whose people are being annihilated and brutalised:

> Here, insanity overflows: shelling from airplanes, battleships, heavy artillery, bombs, charges that explode cars which just minutes before had seemed tame as sleeping cats, fires. The water is cut off, and the electricity. There's no bread. You go to look for it and the earth explodes beneath your feet. God's heaven is your enemy all day long, a siege from all six directions. Senseless bombs bring down buildings, which collapse on their residents and leave a deep ditch, before which all we can imagine of hell and its deepest pit seems small. Cluster bombs continue exploding, as if forever.
>
> (165)

Palestinians in refugee camps were subjected to the most horrifying massacres and long periods of siege by both the Phalange militias and the Israeli army during the civil war (Sayigh 1997; Hagopian 1985). The Maronite Phalange militias imposed a siege on the camp of Tal al-Za'tar in 1975/6 and killed around 3000 Palestinians with the complicity of Israel and Syria (Harris 1996, 165). In 1982, the camps of Sabra and Shatila were subjected to another massacre committed by the Phalange with the military support of Israel, which resulted in the death of hundreds of Palestinian and Lebanese civilians (Khalili 2007, 735). The 1982 Israeli invasion of Beirut ended Palestinian autonomy and institution-building inside refugee camps and eventually to the withdrawal of PLO forces and personnel from Lebanon, leaving the camps without protection (Peteet 2005, 9). Since 1982, Palestinian refugees in Lebanon have lacked a unified local leadership able to make political and social demands on their behalf. Additionally, a number of Lebanese decrees and laws were issued that have further deprived them from the most basic rights and subjected them to political and economic containment (Khalili 2007; Peteet 2005). Palestinians were blamed for the civil war by most of the Lebanese political factions and were subsequently denied of *towteen* (settlement) as part of the government's plan to encourage them to migrate and

76 *Roba Al-Salibi*

build a nationally pure Lebanon (Sayigh 1997). The post-civil war period increased the marginalisation of Palestinian refugees through different violent mechanisms of spatial confinement and institutional exclusion, which rendered their lives extremely precarious and filled them with uncertainty about their future. As Peteet argues, refugee camps in the post-civil war period, 'served most importantly as sites of incarceration and new techniques of boundary maintenance and control' (2005, 11).

Hostility towards Palestinian refugees in Lebanon and the forms of othering they were subjected to in the post-civil war period took both institutional and non-institutional forms. We read about the ramifications of the civil war on the daily lives of Palestinian refugees in Ruqayya's narration. In a chapter titled 'to Cross a Path', she gives an account of the forms of violence Palestinians are met with while contemplating the reasons behind her refusal to leave Beirut despite the continuous insistence of her elder son, Sadiq, to join him and his family in Abu Dhabi, and despite the daily harassments of Palestinians there:

> I wouldn't leave my home, I wouldn't leave Beirut. Stubbornness? ... Why? Why wouldn't I take my son and daughter and escape with them, far from this place that had come to say implicitly to us, 'Get out of the country, you're aliens'. Did I say implicitly? That's a mistake, they said it frankly every day. I saw it with my own eyes written on the walls. In the newspapers there were leaks about plans to reduce the number of Palestinians in Lebanon from half a million to fifty thousand. Did they want to throw us into the sea? ... Daily arrests, killing at the barricades, kidnapping, destruction of any wall built in the camp – how can people live in houses without walls? And strangulation: there was no work, there were no work permits. The men of the camp were killed or imprisoned or had left with the evacuation, and the few remaining were unemployed.
> (205)

Having lived the majority of her life in Lebanon, Ruqayya considers the place as her second home after Tantoura. The contradiction between her own emotional relationship to Lebanon and her socio-political positionality as a Palestinian who is cast as an unwanted alien becomes more evident in the post-war era. When Ruqayya agrees to move to Abu Dhabi and later to Alexandria, she does not feel at home in either of these places. She eventually returns to Lebanon despite the explicit forms of exclusion and othering that became more consolidated in the period after the civil war. The reasons behind Ruqayya's return vary, but perhaps the strongest one lies in the proximate distance between Beirut and Tantoura, the two places Ruqayya calls home:

> Perhaps I didn't want to go farther away, as if the shore of Beirut would lead me to the shore of our village, as if Shatila were one end of a street that I could follow, walking in a straight line, to arrive in Tantoura.
> (206)

Memory and Home-Remaking Among Palestinian Refugees in Lebanon

Palestinian refugee camps were not merely spaces of containment, marginality, and exclusion. They were also spaces where Palestinian refugees recreated a sense of place, identity, and home using the tools of memory, culture, and militancy (Peteet 2005, 1). In her book *Landscape of Hope and Despair*, Julie Peteet examines the contradictory meanings of refugee camps as both 'sites of poverty, marginality and terror as well as remarkable creativity' (2005, 1). Being in the space but not part of the state, Peteet argues that the Palestinian identity in Lebanon has been constructed through the navigation of a complex spaciotemporal framework that includes local and regional politics, the geographies of Palestine and Lebanon, and the temporalities of the past, present, and future (2005, 2). Here, I specifically consider the role that memory plays in the construction of a Palestinian identity in exile and in the making of a new locality through a literary analysis of our protagonist's narrative. I argue that memory takes a central position in the remaking of home for exiled Palestinians as it gives a sense of continuity following the violent rupture of displacement. In this sense, memory becomes an intimate site that connects Palestinians to each other in the present as well as to the past history of Palestine from which they were forcibly uprooted and dispossessed by the Zionist colonial project.

The contemporary Palestinian collective memory is rooted in Al-Nakba, which signifies the historical moment from which a new Palestinian identity and history have emerged (Doumani 1992; Khalidi 1997). Al-Nakba becomes what Pierre Nora calls a 'site of memory', which assumes the continuity of the past within the present (Nora 1998). Palestinian refugees' individual memories of Al-Nakba do not merely reflect psychological acts of remembering. Rather, they are situated within the larger social and political context of the Palestinian collective struggle. Laleh Khalili's conceptualisation of memory as a social practice in her study of Palestinian refugees' mnemonic narratives is highly suggestive here (2007, 732). She reminds us that memory, when viewed as a social practice, is both an individual and collective event (732). In the analysis that follows, I hope to elucidate the ways in which memory is used in the practical spatial recreation of the lost homeland and the re-making of home in the exilic present.

Laila Abu-Lughod and Ahmad Sa'di maintain that Palestinian memory is a 'dissident memory, a counter-memory' as Palestinians constantly struggle to preserve and reproduce it under the conditions of its silencing by the Zionist state and its allies (Sa'di and Abu-Lughod 2007, 6). Palestinian memory also presents a critique of the present conditions of violence, dispossession, and silencing that Palestinians are subjected to by hegemonic powers. Memories of Palestine before Al-Nakba and the violent events of dispossession take a central position in the novel at hand. In the exilic narrative told by Ruqayya, her story oscillates between the past and the present as interconnected

78   Roba Al-Salibi

temporalities, emphasising the continuity of Al-Nakba as a traumatic event that led to other traumas, such as the massacre of Sabra and Shatila. Memory is also emphasised as a tool that Palestinian refugees in Lebanon employ in their attempts at recreating their lost homes in exile and imposing new meanings of the camps as 'oppositional spaces' (Peteet 2005, 95). In the face of the deep-rooted sense of *ghurba* (estrangement) that characterises the Palestinian exile, 'only memory has been able to save them from alienation and self-estrangement' (Sa'di 2002, 183).

The place-making practices of Palestinian refugees in Lebanon through the work of memory are narrated in the novel from different perspectives. First, the generational transmission of memories of the Palestinian homeland before and during Al-Nakba is one site through which Palestine, both as an imagined and actual geography, asserts its presence as a home that intersects with the new places of displacement. Ruqayya tells us, for instance, how her uncle, Abu Amin, gathers the youth of Ain al-Hilweh camp to talk to them about his memories of Palestine and the major historical events he witnessed before the catastrophe of 1948. In another segment, Ruqayya narrates a recurring activity that takes place in their family where Abu Amin teaches his grandchildren the names of Palestinian cities and villages stolen by the Israeli settler state. Abu Amin would draw the Palestinian map and let the children write the names of cities and villages:

> Hasan would have distinguished Tantoura by writing its name in larger letters than he used for the names of Haifa or Jaffa or Jerusalem, marking its place with a large circle that he colored in red, as if Tantoura were the district capital and not Haifa. Abu Amin would scrutinize the details more closely, then scoot over and sit on the map, reaching out and taking the pencil from Hasan and adding towns and villages neither I nor Amin had ever heard of.
>
> (95–96)

A second aspect of the centrality of memory in the remaking of home is revealed through Ruqayya's encounters with the refugee women in Shatila camp. When Ruqayya starts volunteering in the camp, she listens to the women's memory narration of their lost homes and their lives in Palestine before the 1948 expulsion, with each woman hanging the key to her house in Palestine around her neck. These encounters create spaces of intimacy among Palestinian women in which they share their memories of their past lives and use them to cope with the harsh conditions of exile in Lebanon. Palestinian refugee women resort to memory as an arena of reclaiming a sense of home in their exilic present. As Ruqayya spends time in Shatila refugee camp, she makes a chosen family of women with whom she shares the memories of Palestine before exile, the memories of Nakba, and the years of displacement in Lebanon with the unfamiliarity and uncertainty they entailed:

The Woman from Tantoura   79

There I acquired a new extended family – children, girls, women of my own age, elderly women, each of them with the key of her house hung on a cord around her neck, like my mother. In Shatila I learned that the world of women is more compassionate than the world of men. I love to listen to their stories, even if they're sad at first, because the stories always began with 'there', with what happened when 'they took over the village and threw us out and we fled to Lebanon'. The story moves on, but sometimes not completely, because as it advances in time it goes back, and remembers. The stories resemble each other but also differ, like the faces that tell them.

(119)

Palestinian women's narratives of displacement and their telling of memories, as Ruba Salih maintains, 'express their subjective feelings, emphasising the primacy of the immediate realm of affective ties over ideological or abstract imaginaries' (Salih 2017, 757). Palestinian women's narratives of exile constitute a form of emotional knowledge that contests the limitations of the Palestinian nationalist discourse through their narration of the emotional and embodied impact of Israeli settler colonialism and exile. Palestinian nationalist narratives, as many Palestinian feminist scholars have shown, have often portrayed women as the reproducers of future generations, linked women's bodies to the land and represented the colonisation of Palestine as a sexual violation of women's bodies (e.g. Abdo 1994; Hasso 1998; Salih 2017). These nationalist representations of Palestinian women limited the space for their own forms of narration grounded in the affective and the emotional. Their memories of everyday life before Al-Nakba and those of their displacement and fragmentation not only provide us with a historical account of Palestine before and after Nakba, but they also convey how these events are lived and felt by those who experienced them. The sharing of individual memories serves in deepening a sense of belonging to a collective, which in turn renders the realities of exile less difficult to bear. Ruqayya's affective encounters with the women of Shatila refugee camp provide her with a sense of belonging to a group with whom she shares the memories of the past and the exilic experience of the present.

The 'here' and 'there', 'then', and 'now' are not neatly delineated times and spaces in the memories and narration of the Palestinian women in Shatila. Instead, their narration weaves these temporal and spatial entities together, centring the past in the present. Against the unfamiliarity and estrangement of the present, a collective sharing of memories and past histories becomes a site of intimacy and a coping strategy with the realities of exile. In 'Home and Away: Narratives of Migration and Estrangement', Sara Ahmed suggests that a reconfiguration of home does not take place through 'the heroic acts of an individual' (Ahmed 1999, 331). Rather, this reconfiguration happens 'through the forming of communities that create multiple identifications through acts of remembering in the absence of a shared knowledge or a familiar terrain'

80 *Roba Al-Salibi*

(331). The sharing of memories between Ruqayya and the women of Shatila allows for a new relationship of inhabitance to be formed in the place in which they are seen as strangers.

Memory for Palestinian refugees in Lebanon serves as a tool to preserve a collective Palestinian identity against the systematic fragmentation of Palestinians inside and outside Palestine (Peteet 2005, 111). The naming of areas inside the refugee camps in Lebanon after villages in Palestine is one way in which memory of Palestine before Al-Nakba continues to define the Palestinian presence in Lebanon. The symbolic recreation of parts of Palestine in the camp spaces charges them with political and social meanings. The Palestinian homeland thus intersects with the everyday experience of exilic places through memory, remembrance, and narration transmitted from one generation to the other. Despite the systematic forms of oppression and exclusion that Palestinian refugees face in Lebanon, new meanings of home are forged at the intersection of their everyday experience of the place and the memories of the lost Palestinian homeland.

The closing scene of the novel takes place at the border separating Lebanon and Palestine. Palestinians on both sides of the border come together as a collective to emphasise their right to return and to articulate a politics of refusal against their systematic fragmentation. The border turns into an affective space where Palestinians on both sides of the border engage in singing folk songs and talking about their home villages from which they were expelled during Al-nakba. Ruqayya joins the mass of Palestinian refugees coming from different refugee camps in Lebanon. There, she meets her son Hassan and his daughter who are at the other side of the border in colonised Palestine. Ruqayya hands Hassan's daughter the key to her family house in Palestine, the same key that her mother wore around her neck after they were exiled and until the day she passed away. The act of transmitting the key to her son's daughter reflects the centrality of Al-Nakba as a collective site of memory and Palestinian refugees' hope to return to their lost homes. The traumatic memories of Al-Nakba remain alive among the second and third Nakba generations who did not witness the uprooting of Palestinians in 1948 but continue to feel and live its continuous effect not as an event, but as a structure that still defines the Palestinian present.

Conclusion

Palestinian refugees' presence in Lebanon has been marked, since the beginning, by hostility and exclusion. The Lebanese postcolonial state divided along sectarian lines pushed the Palestinian refugees outside existing structures of citizenship and belonging. Fear of changing the demographic balance and the advent of the Palestinian Liberation Organisation to Lebanon were some of the main factors that led to the continuous exclusion and marginalisation of Palestinian refugees and their deprivation of the most basic rights. In this contribution, I attempted to highlight, through reading *The Woman from Tantoura*, the Palestinian experience in Lebanon from the viewpoint of a Palestinian woman who witnessed dispossession during Al-Nakba and the harsh realities of exile in Lebanon. The novel offers an expansive, rich and a highly emotional historical account of the 1948 expulsion and the subsequent long years of exile characterised by marginality as well as a continuous struggle to maintain a Palestinian identity and collectivity in the face of systematic obliteration. *The Woman from Tantoura* offers a reading of history from below; it foregrounds the ways in which Palestinian refugees experienced, felt, and resisted the violence inflicted on them. Ashour's unique contribution to literary narratives articulating the exilic experience of Palestinian refugees stems from her close attention to the working of power structures – the Lebanese state, right-wing militates and Israel – in producing unbearable living conditions for Palestinian refugees in the camps. Her contribution is made more powerful by her narration of the camp space not only as a space of containment and othering but also as a space where Palestinians re-created themselves politically and culturally through memory and community.

The novel represents a powerful narration of Al-Nakba as a site of memory that disrupts conventional understandings of temporality as linear and fixed. It foregrounds the ways in which Palestinians' individual memories of their expulsion are situated within the broader Palestinian collective memory. Furthermore, the novel highlights the central position that memory takes in giving exiled Palestinians a sense of continuity and identity in the face of the continuous oppression they endure in exile. The structural and the subjective are narrated as interconnected in the way they define the Palestinian exilic existence in Lebanon. *The Woman from Tantoura* proposes a counter-narrative to the hegemonic and imperial discourses that continue to suppress and silence Palestinians and their multiple narratives and lived experiences of settler colonialism and exile.

References

Abdo, N., 1994. Nationalism And Feminism: Palestinian Women And The Intifada – No Going Back?. Gender And National Identity. In: V. M. Moghadam, ed. *Gender and National Identity: Women and Politics in Muslim Societies*. London: Zed Books and Oxford University Press. pp. 148–170.

Abourahme, N., 2015. Assembling and Spilling-Over: Towards an 'Ethnography of Cement' in a Palestinian Refugee Camp: Ethnography of Cement in a Palestinian Refugee Camp. *International Journal of Urban and Regional Research*, 39(2), pp. 200–217.

Sa'di, Ahmad H., and Abu-Lughod, Lila, eds. 2007. *Nakba: Palestine, 1948, and the Claims of Memory*. s.l.:Columbia University Press.

Abu-Remaileh, R., 2021. Country of Words: Palestinian Literature in the Digital Age of the Refugee. *Journal of Arabic Literature* (52), pp. 68–96

82 Roba Al-Salibi

Ahmed, S., 1999. Home and away Narratives of Migration and Estrangement. *International journal of Cultural studies*, 2(3), pp. 329–347.

Ahmed, S., 2014. *The Cultural Politics of Emotions.* Edinburgh: Edinburgh University Press.

Akram, S., 2002. Palestinian Refugees and Their Legal Status: Rights, Politics, and Implications for a Just Solution. *Journal of Palestine Studies*, 31(3), pp. 36–51.

Chen, T., 2009. Palestinian Refugees in Arab Countries and Their Impacts. *Journal of Middle Eastern and Islamic Studies*, 3(3), pp. 42–56.

Doumani, B., 1992. Rediscovering Ottoman Palestine: Writing Palestinians into History. *Journal of Palestine Studies*, 22(2), pp. 5–28.

El-Abed, O., 2009. *Unprotected: Palestinians in Egypt since 1948.* Washington, DC Ottawa: the Institute for Palestine Studies and the International Development Research Centre.

Hagopian, E., 1985. *Amal and the Palestinians: Understanding the Battle of the Camps,* Belmont, MA: Association of Arab-American University Graduates.

Hamdi, T., 2011. Bearing Witness in Palestinian Resistance Literature. *Race $ Class*, 52(3), pp. 21–42.

Hanafi, S., 2006. Les réfugiés palestiniens, la citoyenneté et l'État-Nation. In: F. D. Bel-Air, ed. *Migration Et Politique Au Moyen-Orient.* Beyrouth: Presses de l'Ifpo, pp. 145–162.

Khalidi, R., 1997. *Palestinian Identity: The Construction of Modern National Consciousness.* New York: Columbia University Press.

Khalili, L., 2007. Heroic and Tragic Pasts: Mnemonic Narratives in the Palestinian Refugee Camps1. *Critical Sociology*, 33(4), pp. 731–759.

Knudsen, A., 2007. *The Law, the Loss and the Lives of Palestinian Refugees in Lebanon,* s.l.: Chr. Michelsen Institute.

Million, D., 2009. Felt Theory: An Indigenous Feminist Approach to Affect and History. *Wicazo Sa Review*, 24(2), pp. 53–76.

Morris, B., 1987. *The Birth of the Palestinian Refugee Problem, 1947–1949.* Cambridge: Cambridge University Press.

Najm, A. H. and Islam, S., 2020. The Impact of Traumatic Experiences on Identity formation in Radwa Ashour's Novel The Woman From Tantoura. *EEO*, 19(4), 2644–2650. doi: 10.17051/ilkonline.2020.04.764627

Nashef, H. A. M., 2021. Suppressed Nakba Memories in Palestinian female narratives. *Interventions*, 24(4), pp. 567–585.

Nora, P., 1998. Between Memory and History: Les lieux de mémoire. *Representations*, Issue 26, pp. 7–24.

Peteet, J., 2005. *Landscape of Hope and Despair: Palestinian Refugee Camps.* s.l.: University of Pennsylvania Press.

Ramdan, A., 2013. Spatialising the Refugee Camp: Spatialising the Refugee Camp. *Transactions of the institute of British Geographers*, 38(1), pp. 65–77.

Salih, R., 2017. Bodies That Walk, Bodies That Talk, Bodies That Love: Palestinian Women Refugees, Affectivity, and the Politics of the Ordinary. *Antipode*, 49(3), pp. 742–760.

Sayigh, R., 1998. Dis/Solving the 'Refugee Problem'. *Middle East Report*, 207, pp. 19–23.

Shiblak, A., 2005. *The Palestinian Diaspora In Europe: Challenges of Dual Identity and Adaptation.* s.l.: Palestinian Refugee and Diaspora Center and the Institute of Jerusalem Studies.

UNHCR, 2006. *US Committee for Refugees and Immigrants World Refugee Survey.* Lebanon: s.n.

4 Memory and Resistance in Susan Abulhawa's *Against the Loveless World*

Benay Blend

Introduction

In "Invention, Memory, and Place," the late Edward Said reflects on the question of collective memory: what is remembered, how, and in what form (2000, 175)? Elsewhere Said explains that what marks the current era is the "vast human migration attendant upon war, colonialism and decolonization" ("Introduction" 2002, xiv), and consequent uprooting that requires adaption to new surroundings. Therefore, the contemporary world, with its modern warfare, imperialism and totalitarian regimes, is marked as "the age of the refugee" (Said, "Reflections on Exile" 2002, 173), in part due to mass immigration on a level unknown before. This chapter explores Susan Abulhawa's *Against the Loveless World* (2020), particularly the strategies of survival and adaptation employed by the family in this book. Among the many displaced people from Palestine during the 1967 war, Abulhawa's fictional family endure the struggles that Palestinians faced as exiles in Kuwait. According to Said, literature is inherently the work of a single individual, but that person is "tangled up in circumstances" specific to time and place ("Introduction" 2002, xv). In this case, Abulhawa's novel reflects the specific experiences of a Palestinian family who are also part of the larger migrant population in Kuwait. Because they are a nationalistic people without a nation-state, due to Israel's refusal to grant them their legal right of return, the Palestinian presence in Kuwait differs from that of other migrants. The problem for the critic is "how to align these circumstances with the work, how to separate as well as incorporate them, how to read the work *and* its worldly situation" (Said, "Introduction" 2002, xv). By illustrating the ways that memories—individual and collective—are conceptualized to deal with trauma and assert resistance, this study contributes to a broader understanding of Palestinians who have been forced to flee to other Arabic-speaking countries.

"It is as if Ghurba has been so integral to the collective character of a nation," Ramzy Baroud explains, that it is "now a permanent tattoo on the heart and soul of the Palestinian people" (2021). Said concurs. Defined as "a condition legislated to deny dignity, to deny an identity to people" ("Reflections on Exile" 2002, 175), exile is "like death but without death's

DOI: 10.4324/9781003301776-7

Memory and Resistance 85

ultimate mercy" (Said, "Reflections on Exile" 2002, 174). If the writer does not have the luxury of permanent abode, there must be some form of compensation, a style marked with "a unique freight of anxiety, elaborateness, perhaps even overstatement" (Said, "Introduction" 2002, xv), exactly those traits not found among those with a long history on the land. In *Nakba: Palestine, 1948 and the Claims of Memory*, Ahmad Sa'di and Lila Abu-Lughod explain that memory is particularly important because "it struggles with and against" a past contested by Israeli propaganda that still impacts the present (2007, 2). For Abulhawa, her own life, she says, is bound by a common theme of displaced people trying to preserve indigenous traditions (Kirpal 2020). Accordingly, exile can be both a creative and traumatic experience (Said, "Reflections on Exile" 2002, 173). It is an "unhealable" situation that divides individuals from their homeland, the self from its "true home," and consequently that "essential sadness" can never be overcome (Said, "Reflections on Exile" 2002, 173). While there might be achievements, those efforts are always undermined by what was irretrievably left behind.

Abulhawa and the Art of Storytelling

In Abulhawa's case, there has always been such grief, but storytelling served her well. Although her own life has been defined by the destruction of her world as she once knew it, remembrance has served a purpose (Kirpal 2020). In her writing, she uses it as refugees do, as a tool to guard against erasure and extinction. Born to refugees of the Six Day War of 1967, when her family's land was seized as part of Israel's takeover of what remained of Palestine, Abulhawa learned early what it meant to be stateless, without papers or a passport to define her. Because her mother went to Kuwait, where Palestinians were welcomed as a source of labor, then to Saudi Arabia, Abulhawa was left to her own resources to survive. Before turning 16 she had lived in 21 different homes (Abulhawa 2012, 15), only two of them with parents, while the rest consisted of relatives, foster care, or public institutions. This left her feeling like "an abstraction" (2012, 11), a feeling that she would transfer to characters in her books. Eventually, she graduated with a degree in biomedical science, but later gave up that career to become a writer and human rights activist for Palestine. Her books include *Mornings in Jenin* (2010), *My Voice Sought the Wind* (2013), and *Blue Between Sky and Water* (2015). Her latest, *Against the Loveless World* (2020), won the Palestine Book Award and is the focus of this chapter. As a speaker, she participates in the campaign for Boycott, Divestment and Sanctions, and also Al Awda, the Right of Return Coalition. Finally, she is the founder of Playgrounds for Palestine, a children's nonprofit NGO that focuses on Palestinian children in the Occupied Territories and in refugee camps scattered around the world.

Her life is not what her grandfather thought he was leaving to his family. Despite being the descendant of a "long line of a huge clan of Palestinian farmers," she grew up alone, not able to claim her "birthright" (Abulhawa

86   *Benay Blend*

2021, 15). Perhaps because she lacked her family, Abulhawa bestows it on the characters in her books. Unable to truly experience "Ramadan in el Ghorba," Abulhawa, despite being known for solidarity work, takes no joy in living abroad. In this poem, included in *My Voice Sought the Wind* (2013), Abulhawa explains that "there is no solidarity" here, no collective sense of belonging (2013, 25). In particular, she finds no way to recreate traditional rituals without access to proper food. "The time is different, too," so she "will not do the exact thing / at the exact time" (2013, 25). Since "dusk … comes[s] unannounced" with no *adan* (Muslim call to prayer) to mark the end of fasting, she settles for "*shorabat freika*" (soup consumed during Ramadan) and a "pre-recorded *adan*" (2013, 25). With no "superhuman meal," no gathering of relatives "sitting on the floor around the feast," Abulhawa does the best she can while surviving without shared rituals and homeland (2013, 25).

Rituals of Survival: Palestinians in Kuwait

An internationally known writer, Abulhawa has travelled far, but her heart remained in Jerusalem, where all of her ancestors are buried (Abulhawa 2012, 14). If memory serves Palestinians well in exile, so does family, a theme that she centers in *Against the Loveless World*. This chapter focuses on certain patterns evident in this fictional family in order to understand the larger role that such networks play in exile. In *Palestinians in Kuwait: The Family and the Politics of Survival* (2019), Shafeeq Ghabra analyzes the ways that families, who were displaced in the 1948 and 1967 wars, employed strategies that enabled them to preserve their social bonds in the face of loss. By providing a support system, familial relationships ensured that the Palestinian community in Kuwait, which was the third largest in the diaspora, would play a crucial part in helping to sustain the collective identity of the group (1987, 93). While these tactics were common among all immigrants in Kuwait, what distinguished the Palestinian diaspora was that the Israeli state refused to grant them right of return, leaving them loyal to a homeland to which they could not go back. In Abulhawa's novel, it is the women in the family, the central character Nahr, her mother and grandmother, who provide emotional and material support. Gender roles began to change in the exiled generation as women became "symbols of sacrifice and courage" (Ghabra 1987, 50), in Nahr's case providing funds for her brother's education as well as for the survival of her family.

The transference of cultural specificity from one generation to the next reflects a common theme in Palestinian literature. In this way Abulhawa's work fits into a particular trope that focuses on memory and family as tools to resist erasure of the Palestinian voice. These accounts more often than not consist of the history of battles, dispossession and displacement. Told within the broad context of geopolitics, narratives written by men leave little room for domestic detail (Humphries and Khalili 2007, 207). While Abulhawa includes male characters, they are secondary voices who serve as foils for

Memory and Resistance 87

three generations of women who pass down tales from a distinctly female lens. Nahr's father, for example, dies in the arms of one of what appears to be a succession of various girlfriends. Her brother, who is charged with treason during the Iraqi invasion, suffers permanent disabilities after being tortured by Kuwaitis. According to Humphries and Khalili, the specificities of women's memories have only recently come to light as a topic of academic study (2007, 209). While their research relates solely to Nakba memories, their findings can be extended to this chapter by considering the ongoing nature of the catastrophe. For example, Nahr is born shortly after the Naksa, when the Six Day War first displaces her family. Her formative years are spent as a second-class citizen in Kuwait, a country that exploits the labor of Palestinians but refuses to give them rights. After the Iraqi invasion the family is uprooted again, this time to Jordan where there are even fewer possibilities for employment because of the surge of refugees who preceded them.

This chapter, then, provides an understanding of the ways in which gender, class, ethnicity and colonialism all contribute to the conditions that a specific family experiences as refugees in Kuwait. While her problems are shared by other Palestinians, Nahr's narrative is unique because it is seen through the prism of three generations of women in her family. While women's changing social roles have been acknowledged, their memories of the Nakba have been underplayed for years (Humphries and Khalili 2007, 207). This study, therefore, fills that void by looking at sexual identity and the roles of women through the literary lens of Abulhawa's pen. Abulhawa knows what it's like to be alone, without papers or familial support. Though she was "denied [her] home and heritage," she declares, she had the "great fortune to claim [her] inheritance of Attiyeh's [her grandfather] stubbornness and his attachment to and love of the land" (2012, 16). All of this she weaves into the stories of strong women who speak their mind to whoever wants to listen.

Through an exploration of gendered themes present in Nahr's narration, it is possible to reach new conclusions about women's experiences in Kuwait, and in particular how their perceptions differ from the more familiar male story. In their study of Palestinian women's narratives, Humphries and Khalili (2007, 209) found that the history of Palestine is more often written from a nationalist perspective, focusing more on geopolitical agendas rather than details of daily life. Women's memories, though, are influenced by structures of power as women are doubly marginalized because of their gender as well as ethnicity. In works of literature as well as scholarly texts, the dominant voices more often belong to politicians, military leaders, and those who received a Western education, and those voices usually belong to men. Moreover, Nahr's own experiences veer away from the typical female norm. Sitti (grandmother) Wasfiyeh's narratives (and by default Abulhawa's) illustrate not only the many voices of the Nakba but also contribute to our understanding of the ways that the catastrophe affected ordinary people. When Nahr's mother and grandmother reminisce about the Nakba, certain themes emerge. While each laments the loss of family ties and possessions, they also focus on their

88   Benay Blend

roles as protectors of their sons and daughters, marking time by the birth of children and highlighting their ability to protect them. Nahr's mother was pregnant with her, Nahr relates, when Israel made her a refugee again in 1967. Previously she had made a home in her mother-in-law's ancestral village, but this time she brought whatever she could carry and her family across the Allenby Bridge to safety (Abulhawa 2020, 19). Palestinian women's voices are "doubly marginalized" by virtue of their ethnicity as well as gender (Humphries and Khalili 2007, 209). If Palestinian voices are rarely heard outside of certain circles, women's voices are often silenced by the more popular nationalist narratives that extol the role of men. Often, too, women are not considered "reliable conduits of Nakba history and its devastation" (Humphries and Khalili 2007, 209).

The gendered division of labor, family and livelihood, domestic details, and the role of mothers who are protective of their families—all are part of memories transmitted to Nahr through women, who, she says, "are the keepers of our traditions and heritage" (Abulhawa 2020, 12). These everyday experiences are framed, at times, by patriarchal discourse (Humphries and Khalili 2007, 209), so that even Nahr, who tries very hard to break out of the bonds of patriarchy that control her, fails to find an autonomous space of freedom. After the upheaval in 1948, long-held values were undermined. For example, Ghabra writes that women who migrated to Kuwait began to play a more active role in their families as well as the larger world (1987, 51). Nevertheless, their "experiences and reproduction of memory" (were still shaped by patriarchal values, including marriage customs, family honor, and gendered division of labor Humphries and Khalili 2007, 224). This was certainly true for Nahr's family, though she struggled throughout the book to shed those norms herself.

While Palestinian perspectives have been overshadowed by Zionist versions of history, Palestinian women's memories are doubly silenced by men. Moreover, those women who do have a platform often come from more affluent classes, a circumstance that makes Abulhawa's novel even more unique. Indeed, while Nahr's family had some social standing in their homeland, Zionists took all of their belongings "right down to their furniture, books and bank accounts" (Abulhawa 2020, 13), so the stories they tell as refugees are not those of the elite.

In the end, Abulhawa is both a chronicler of the exiled and an exile herself enriching literature with her creativity. Into her novel she writes her own recollections of food prepared for large family gatherings—all the events that gave meaning to her life. In addition, perhaps the act of writing itself helped to process less pleasant memories that she weaves into her work, thereby aiding in the practice of "sorting through the trauma of never really getting a foothold anywhere else in the world" (Kirpal). "While the crushing weight of exile is not unique to Palestinians," Baroud explains, the situation for them is nevertheless inimitable. "Throughout the entire episode of Palestinian Ghurba, from the Nakba until today, there has been very little acknowledgement of the injustices that the people have endured" (2021). Abulhawa agrees. "Mine has been an un-Palestinian life," she explains, referring to her lack of having a large family close at hand. Nevertheless, her life, she says, represents the "most basic truth about what it means to be Palestinian—dispossessed, disinherited, and exiled" (2021, 14)—all of the experiences that she pours into her work.

From this life she has learned "what it ultimately means to resist" (2021, 14). By October 1948, nearly 900,000 Palestinians were forced to leave their homes, and some eventually settled in neighboring Arab states. To this day, they have not been given the right of return, thereby allowing the Israeli state to claim their property (Ghabra 1987, 25). In "Rewriting the Story of the Palestinian Radical," Rozina Ali outlines both the "hot and cold" violence perpetrated by the Israeli state that finds its way in Abulhawa's book. Hot violence, she explains, is characterized by bombs falling on the citizens of Gaza or soldiers shooting at Palestinians in the West Bank. What frames Abulhawa's work, she says, is the following question: when the law does not prevent evictions, redirected water supplies, hours spent at checkpoints, how should one seek justice (2021)? By calling into question the status quo, Abulhawa holds out hope for a reconstructed Palestine and a claim to the right of return.

Moreover, her "stories are the stuff of [her] intifada" (Abulhawa 2012, 14). Because she hopes that her audience will go on to act as witness, "every reader is part of [her] triumph" (Abulhawa 2012, 14), part of her ability to make Palestinian voices heard. The book is divided into seven sections, each one beginning with reflections from the Cube, a solitary prison cell equipped with all the trappings of the latest surveillance technology and human rights abuses. From there Nahr writes her story of displacement and survival often on scraps of paper and the wall.

Nationalism Without a Nation-State

Abulhawa's novel continues a certain tradition of Palestinian writing, but it also departs from various tropes and themes that are peculiar to other exiles seeking to make sense of their condition. According to Joe Cleary, all Palestinians, wherever they might be, are aware of oppressive conditions that produce a sense of identity but are made more difficult when the people are scattered around the world. Even within the bounds of historic Palestine, Israeli-imposed divisions have made it difficult but not impossible to imagine a unified national state. "To put it simply," Cleary writes, "the difficulty for Palestinian people is that while their stateless condition induces nationalism, their dispersal across so many states thwarts construction of a common nation-state" (2002, 186). It is in the context of this dilemma that the assessment of Abulhawa's novel should take place.

Some of the burdens of the Palestinian writer are the same as other colonized people around the world. First, the basic aim of the colonized is to refute the official story. In this novel, Abulhawa's narrator reiterates from her solitary cell that she is not the terrorist that the Western press has made

90   *Benay Blend*

her out to be. Instead, she is a resistance fighter in the struggle for liberation of her homeland. "One of the abiding objectives of the Palestinian narrative," explains Cleary, "is to challenge the suppression of the Palestinian version of events and to insert the Palestinian back into history" (Cleary 2002, 192). This Abulhawa does quite well. If history is thought to be written by the victors, then stories stemming from the Nakba form part of a counter-history, a narrative of what happened in the past but also what injustices should be corrected in the future. Palestine means for many, part elegy, part displacement and exile, but for others, it is known most commonly as "Israel," "an 'empty' land returned according to biblical fiat" (Said, "Introduction," 2002, xxxiii). Consequently, there is an "irreconcilable, antinomian conflict" that will forever be "embodied in the land" (Said, "Introduction" 2002, xxxiii). In *Against the Loveless World*, the past is a constant reminder of injustice. For Nahr's family, still refugees in Kuwait, still waiting to return, still concerned with strategies of survival, the past is not what happened long ago nor is it over. Writing is a "political act that not only represents the past" (Slyomovics 2007, 27), but also, within the context of the case of Palestine, shapes what readers are expected to believe. "Words determine what is remembered and what is forgotten" (Slyomovics 2007, 27), which is why Abulhawa's novel is important. After the Nakba, Palestinians were in no shape to counter the official story that was put forth by the Israeli state (Sa'di and Abu-Lughod 2007, 11).

Second, because so much Palestinian land has been lost to Israeli settlements, but also by re-naming villages and landscape features in the Hebrew language, much of Palestinian writing has been engaged in reclaiming lost landmarks. Accordingly, both Nahr's mother and grandmother call attention to their former towns and villages lost to them in the war of 1967. Finally, the last marker is that of coming to terms with the Nakba, the catastrophe of 1948. Because of the enormity of the trauma, it produces a "sense of individual and collective humiliation, frustration, recrimination, rage, anomie and despair" (Cleary 2002, 193), all modes of feeling that inflict Nahr and her family from time to time. But does she make sense of it, as Cleary claims is the last task of the Palestinian novel? Though Nahr joins the Palestinian resistance, she does not seem to get over her sense of being stateless, not belonging to a specific place or time. "Going from place to place," she says, "is just something exiles have to do" (Abulhawa 2020, 27). From the time that her expulsion from Kuwait cements her sense of not belonging, to the final scene when she is sent from prison back to Jordan, Nahr never feels that she truly has a home.

"The paradox" is that situations that encourage nationalist narratives are strongest in colonized populations where "social conditions make it most difficult to realize" (Cleary 2002, 194). In Nahr's case, it is her statelessness that contributes to her participation in the Palestinian resistance, but this same condition prevents the novel from reaching its logical conclusion—a free Palestine in which Nahr can feel at home. For Abulhawa's predecessor,

Memory and Resistance 91

Ghassan Kanafani, who also wrote a novel of exiles in Kuwait, the same is just as true. The "whole trajectory" (Cleary 2002, 197) of Kanafani's career was to create art that served the struggle. In *Men in the Sun*, three Palestinians are left to suffocate in an empty water tanker being smuggled by a fourth Palestinian across the Iraq/Kuwait border. For both writers, there is a contradiction between their political concerns and the setting of their novels. All of their characters, except for Abulhawa's Um Buraq, are Palestinian, and the problems they depict stem from Israeli rule. Yet, the setting for *Men in the Sun* is not Palestine, and Abulhawa's Nahr does not reach Palestine until two thirds through the book. She spends much more time in Kuwait, where she learns what it means not to have a home. Moreover, Kanafani's novel ends in a space that Cleary calls "no man's land," an area "between states that defy representation" (1999, 198). After Kuwait, much of Abulhawa's book takes place in The Cube, a solitary prison cell perhaps analogous to the water-tanker that leads to the three men's death. Cleary sees the absence of the land as a symbol of the Palestinian dilemma—"the difficulty of representing a land that has no official existence" (2002, 199).

At the conclusion of Kanafani's novel, the lorry driver takes his passengers to the desert where he disposes of their bodies. Frustrated by their deaths, which seem to make no sense, he asks "Why didn't you bang on the sides of the tank? Why? Why? Why" (1999, 74)?" His words relate, perhaps, to Cleary's notion that the trauma is so great that it produces only isolation and despair instead of answers. Abulhawa shares this problem. She holds on to a vision for liberation, expressed through Nahr's joining the resistance. Nevertheless, Nahr's efforts are in vain, resulting in her capture and imprisonment for many years. Still, she got further than Kanafani's men, so the vision itself is clear even if there is no strategy yet for getting there. In *After the Last Sky*, Edward Said declares: "Wherever we Palestinians are, we are not in our Palestine, which no longer exists" (1999, 11). Given that the overall condition of Palestinians is not to have a homeland, Cleary argues that the "condition of the refugee, banging against the iron walls of the state" remains "paradigmatic of Palestinian writing" (2002, 193). Change the iron walls of the water tanker for the iron bars of the Cube, and Abulhawa's novel fits quite well into this context. Yet for all its similarity, *Against the Loveless World* goes much farther as Nahr's insight into her condition spurs her to join the struggle.

Boom Years in Kuwait

Nahr's childhood in Kuwait coincided with the period when oil income resulted in economic modernization, but it also served to accentuate boundaries between Kuwaitis and all others, elites and other classes, and between the genders. Mary Ann Tetreault and Haya al-Mughni examine these social policies that impacted the positions of non-Kuwaiti women, such as Nahr, by denying them employment opportunities, entitlement programs and

92 Benay Blend

education (1995, 403). Prior to the coming of oil, Kuwait already had in place a hierarchal system based on gender and economic class. As Kuwait transitioned to an oil economy, the labor market attracted foreign workers like Nahr's family. By 1965, two years before the Six Day War, Kuwaitis made up only 47 percent of the population, a shift that undermined the old order in ways that caused the government concern. Beginning in 1962, it began to encourage Kuwaiti women to enter the work force in order to mitigate the rise in foreign workers. Despite these new restrictions, Nahr found work but it was so low paying that she held several jobs at once. Even so, her salary barely supported the family with nothing left over to provide for her brother's education. Further complicating her life was the Kuwaiti political system that was intertwined with the patriarchal state. According to Tetreault and al-Mughni, women were "not merely subordinate to men, but under their direct control" (1995, 406). This condition was reinforced for religious reasons, but it also served as a "metaphor" for "social control and community security" (1995, 406).

Allegiance to the patriarchal family was synonymous with loyalty to the ruling family (Tetreault and al-Mughni 1995, 407). Abulhawa highlights this situation in the book. Nahr understood that while Palestinians prospered and had a major role in the development of Kuwait, they remained an "underclass" whose contributions brought back little from the state. "I knew that" (Abulhawa 2020, 22), she explains, but it didn't matter. Indeed, she loved everything about Kuwait—the food, traditions, and, most of all, the dance. In eighth grade, Nahr was selected to dance with an official troupe that performed annually on Independence Day. The following year, she was not included, because people believed inclusion should be only for Kuwaitis (Abulhawa 2020, 23).

"My life began in a two-bedroom apartment in Hawalli," Nahr says, "a Kuwait ghetto where Palestinian refugees settled after the Nakba" (Abulhawa 2020, 12). By congregating together in a specific area of the city, the refugees recreated kinship and village ties that had been destroyed during the 1948 and 1967 wars. Palestinian networks that developed in Kuwait could be described as "stateless and family-oriented" (Ghabra 1987, 1). Before the Nakba, Nahr's family had been well-off, but the conquering forces confiscated their belongings and bank accounts, leaving them "penniless overnight" (Abulhawa 2020, 13). Though the government offered no more than temporary residency, some Palestinians prospered while helping to build Kuwait into a modern state (Abulhawa 2020, 22). While the Palestinians may have been the first after 1948 to aid in the development of Kuwait, they are the last to receive the benefits. Their ability to create sustainable communities did not earn them civil or political rights. Their position as a stateless population had led them to rely on the family as a means to survive the many crises that people face in exile (Ghabra 1987, 164). As refugees, Nahr's family would face both external and internal conflicts, but nothing was so momentous as to cause them to split apart. Though Palestinians established formal organizations to help them

Memory and Resistance 93

meet their needs (Ghabra 1987, 1), Abulhawa's book deals with more basic systems that contributed to the survival of Nahr's family. What prevented them from being assimilated into Kuwaiti society? What held the Palestinian networks together as a distinct subculture? By focusing on one of the most important institutions required for survival, the family, it's possible to trace the ways that social bonds contributed to the preservation of culture and identity.

In her study of "identity and belonging" issues among third generation migrants in Kuwait, Nadeen Dakkak notes that though many people return to their home countries after a few years, among those who stay their children face "experiences of liminality" (2021) both in the Gulf States and in their countries of origin. Nahr knew that the contributions of Palestinians to their adopted state had earned them very little, but for her, she said, "it didn't matter. I loved Kuwait," she recalled. "It was my home" (Abulhawa 2020, 22). Her parents and grandmother were not so willing to accept another homeland as their own. Most of the refugees who fled during the 1948 war took their right of return for granted, and would continue to yearn for home (1987, 27). Unlike Nahr, who only gradually found her roots, her mother and grandmother idealized the country that they had been forced to leave, so much so that they would always consider it their home. For example, Nahr's mother kept a box of photographs from her life in Haifa safely hidden under her bed. Even more devoted to the past, her paternal grandmother, Wasfiyeh Hajjeh Um Nabil, had "never really left her village in Palestine" (Abulhawa 2020, 13), though she lived with the family in Kuwait. For Nahr, Palestine remained the "old country, a distant place of [her] grandmother's generation" (Abulhawa 2020, 13). Though she grew up hearing stories, Nahr "didn't get the politics nor did she care to learn" (Abulhawa 2020, 13). It would be many years later, when she watched her mother making traditional embroidery, then went to Palestine on her own, that she finally understood her family's fierce attachment to their homeland.

As a young woman, Nahr believed what she was told, that her life would begin with marriage to Mhammad Jalal Abu Jabal when she was 17. "I fantasized about fairy-tale love and sex" (Abulhawa 2020, 18), she recalled, about having her own home and family. Two years later, after her husband left, she met Um Buraq, also an abandoned wife who offered her a chance to make money dancing for men at private parties. "Until I met Um Buraq," Nahr explains, "it never occurred to me that patriarchy was anything but the natural order of life" (Abulhawa 2020, 48). There was "something alluring," she believed, about "living on the margins" (Abulhawa 2020, 73). Offered an alternative to "the drudgery of respectability, the low-paying jobs, social pretenses [and] children," she appreciated having "some autonomy without a husband" (Abulhawa 2020, 73). The extra income also allowed her to escape being relegated to a permanent underclass in Kuwait. She could now be her family's "breadwinner, the powerful woman who took care of others" (Abulhawa 2020, 73). Despite the fact that the older woman exploited her,

94 *Benay Blend*

Nahr was attracted to the money she could make as well as Um Buraq's ability to live outside the norms. "I felt affection for this woman who had blackmailed and prostituted me," she admits. "More paradoxical," she continues, Nahr understood that while the older woman returned her love, at the same time she "used and exploited" (Abulhawa 2020, 67) her, a mirror, perhaps, of the Kuwaiti state that welcomed Palestinians as cheap labor but refused to give them rights that they deserved.

Exiles Once Again

In 1959, the government passed a citizenship law, further reinforcing boundaries between Kuwaitis and foreign workers. It defined Kuwaiti nationals as those persons and their families who had lived in Kuwait prior to 1920 and maintained residence until 1959 (Tetreault and al-Mughni 1995, 403). Because she was beginning to understand her precarious position Nahr felt that nothing in her life was stable. Her relationship with the country where she grew up shifted from day to day, reflecting, too, the patriarchal system that influenced her mother's relationship with her father. With Kuwait Nahr held a love/hate relationship that she said the country also felt for her. In turn, her mother, she believed, loved her father, despite his philandering ways, while he loved her, too, in his fashion.

Prior to August 2, 1990, when Iraq invaded Kuwait, there were approximately 400,000 Palestinian residents, a proportion that in relation to Kuwaitis foretold future problems. The Six Day War, which displaced many Palestinians, followed by civil strife in Jordan, led Kuwait to impose regulations aimed at controlling the entry of Palestinians and other foreigners. In 1968–1969, Kuwait introduced a system making residency dependent on a Kuwaiti employer, thereby making it impossible for non-Kuwaitis to stay in the country after retirement; moreover, their adult sons could not remain without an employer who could grant them residency. Since Palestinians had no right of return and their sons had no guarantee of admission to another country, Palestinians were under much more pressure than their Egyptian and Pakistani neighbors (Lesch 1991, 42, 43).

Just before Iraq's invasion of Kuwait, Palestinians listened carefully to Saddam Hussein's promise to confront Israel. The Palestine Liberation Organization (PLO) tried to present a balanced position by opposing the occupation of Iraq while denouncing American intervention. The Palestinian community within Kuwait was divided: some hoped that events would lead to a resolution of their own dilemma, while others joined Kuwaitis in their opposition to Iraq. They suffered the same economic and social disruptions as Kuwaitis, though, thus forcing more than half of the Palestinian population to leave. The remaining community welcomed liberation, but, in the following weeks, Palestinians became scapegoats for the PLO and other Arab leaders who had shifted toward Iraq. Unable to take out their revenge directly, many Kuwaitis retaliated against the most vulnerable groups at hand.

Memory and Resistance 95

In addition to the prospect of arrest, Palestinians experienced a new wave of government-issued restrictions intended to pressure them to leave. Even though many were willing, it was necessary to organize their financial affairs before departing, a task in which the new regulations created obstacles (Lesch 1991, 45, 46, 47, 50).

As long as the stateless have no legal standing, they are ripe to become "political scapegoats and international victims" (Ghabra 1987, 12). During the early days of the first Gulf War, Nahr predicted that "in one way or another Palestinians would have to pay" (Abulhawa 2020, 127). Some Palestinians collaborated with Iraq, but the problems stemmed from Palestinians being a "convenient proxy for vengeance against Saddam" (Abulhawa 2020, 93). The family fled again, this time to Amman, Jordan, where Nahr finally understood what it meant to be in exile. But because her neighbors from Kuwait went, too, the continuity of familiar family networks made life in Jordan almost "bearable" (Abulhawa 2020, 93), if not altogether pleasant. In Amman, the family recreated practices that helped them survive the hardships of displacement. The "unfolding trajectory of continuous dispossession and upheaval" due to actions of the Zionist state "reshap[ed] the space of collective narrative over time" (Jayyusi 2007, 109). Although the events of 1948 were not "the last collective site of trauma," it became the "foundational station in an unfolding saga" (Jayyusi 2007, 109) of repeated dispossession.

This refusal to forget the past enabled Palestinians like Nahr's family to layer each new episode in relation to the original rupture, an experience that resulted in generational trauma but also provided common ground that would bind a people scattered around the world. For many second and third generation migrants in Kuwait and the Gulf, their attachment to countries of origin are the consequence of stories told by parents and grandparents who "often maintain their dialects and cultural practices because the Gulf is mostly a place that discourages cultural assimilation" (Dakkak 2021). Many Palestinians of the Nakba generation repeated their stories to their children and to each other (Sa'di and Abu Lughod 2007, 11). Indeed, Nahr's grandmother, who "roamed Ein El-Sulta in her mind" (Abulhawa 2020, 14), was a prime example of ways that elders transmitted stories to their children, and in this way guarded against erasure of their culture. "She bored us with tales of her childhood and about people we didn't know," recalls Nahr. "She was sure we would return someday" (Abulhawa 2020, 14), thereby passing on, along with stories, hope for a reconstituted future. For the first time Nahr understands the meaning of what it is to be a refugee, a person who feels the land unsteady beneath one's feet, always "struggling to carry on" (Abulhawa 2020, 113). From being forced to flee to Jordan, she learned that the world can pivot at any moment, a reminder of the original trauma which began the oft-repeated saga of dispossession (Abulhawa 2020, 87). Displaced already several times, her parents and grandmother had a much easier time adjusting than did Nahr. They very quickly "settled into a routine," said Nahr, "as if their lives had not been excised and replanted elsewhere," with just "a dusting

96 *Benay Blend*

of grief" that they eventually "shook off before returning to the business of living" (Abulhawa 2020, 113). Because they were "experienced refugees," concluded Nahr, her family was "better equipped to handle recurring generational trauma" (Abulhawa 2020, 113).

Nahr's grandmother told her stories repeatedly to a captive audience, thereby ensuring that Palestinian identity would pass on. To this day, Palestinians have not been able to make their voices heard over the official story, the version framed by Israeli spokesmen who stress their cultural and political alliance with the West. In this regard, Abulhawa constructs her narrative outside of the Western frame of reference. Nahr's grandmother, for example, refuses to ask the Israelis for a passport that would allow her to "go home. I have underwear older than the Zionist entity" (Abulhawa 2020, 127). Abulhawa, writing in a fearless voice for an audience who wants to listen, refuses to censor attitudes that she writes into her story.

Settled once again, this time in Amman, Nahr's mother took on the role of providing for the family. Having found work with a local tailor, she soon received orders for traditional *tatreez*, embroidery that varied from village to village, telling the story of each through its patterns (Abulhawa 2020, 114). Such embroidered dresses were actually limited to peasant wear that has become symbolic for all of Palestine. This emphasis on village lives "corresponds to a nationalized image of the Palestinian peasant" who is considered "steadfast, strong and fertile" (Davis 2010, 70), and this focus results from Palestinian desires to claim land lost after the Nakba.

Watching her mother create these patterns, Nahr begins to appreciate how the dresses told a story of her past. In Kuwait, Nahr had resented being part of a community and economic class that was looked down on by most Kuwaitis. "To my young eyes," she recalled, "embroidered caftans belonged to another generation, and I foolishly thought them unrefined compared to modern European clothes" (Abulhawa 2020, 115). Eventually, Nahr comes to see her mother as "an extraordinary artist," not a simple seamstress but instead "a maker of beauty, and a brilliant custodian of culture and history" (Abulhawa 2020, 117). Moreover, her mother was now making embroidered wedding *thobes*, "the most delicate and expensive" (Abulhawa 2020, 117) of embroidered clothing. When her mother returned from a short trip to Palestine to renew her papers, she reported that the settlements and checkpoints had changed the familiar landscape. "I felt like a stranger in my own country" she lamented (Abulhawa 2020, 132). In the face of such overwhelming loss, her embroidery took on new significance as the custodian of local memories and experiences. Though her brother had "always felt his roots and longed for the home that was his birthright" (Abulhawa 2020, 199), Nahr's interest came much later. For the majority of Palestinians, it is their exile from their homeland coupled with denial of their legal right of return that proves the most frustrating aspect of *ghurba*. Symbolized by retention of the key to their homes and land deeds, this continued desire to return represents a need on their part to "officially exist" (Ghabra 1987, 167), to point to a place on the map where they belong, and to have a government equipped to deal with the many problems of life in diaspora.

"Here Is Where We Began": Challenging the Official Story

Nahr "mark[s] the act of return as a reclaiming of territory and history," essentially a declaration of "Palestinian-ness" (Kirpal). As she entered Palestine this time, Nahr recalled all the childhood trips and family stories that had not mattered much to her till now. All were "there to greet me," she affirmed, "enfolding me in the embrace of our collective dislocation" from this place where "all our stories go and return" (Abulhawa 2020, 152). '*Awda*, meaning return, is a "charged term [that] unites nostalgia for the homeland" and also "reversal of the traumatic dispersion" (Abu-Lughod 2007, 77) that led to displacement such as that experienced by Nahr's family. "Here is where we began," Nahr explains. "Where our songs were born, our ancestors buried" (Abulhawa 2020, 152).

For these reasons, Abulhawa, too, has "always had this longing to go back. And that's not abstract for me. It's very real and personal" (2012, 16). Because she has long been an activist, too, her insistence on the right of return is a demand to right an ethical wrong. Her writing, then, is also a demand that the Nakba and its consequences not be eclipsed by Israel's official story. Several years ago, Israeli officials denied Abulhawa entry to her homeland on the grounds that her visa was incomplete. Accordingly, Palestinian memory is particularly complex because it "struggles with and against a still much-contested present" (Sa'di and Abu-Lughod 2007, 3).

In this regard, Abulhawa's novel explores the juxtaposition between the reproduction of memory, history, and ethics. Reflecting on exile and return, Said argues that "exile can produce rancor and regret," but just as easily it results in "sharpened vision" ("Introduction 2002, xxxv). What has been lost can either be lamented, or it can be used to provide "a different set of lenses" (Said, "Introduction" 2002, xxxv). Through the prism of Nahr and her family, Abulhawa seeks to challenge the official story through recollections that render their life in exile not only bearable, but also keeps them connected to their homeland. Israel's "standard narrative" entails a kind of "glorious rebirth, a story of exile and return" (Sa'di 2007, 286). Carried out by "a people of memory and suffering," eventually "redeemed by belonging to their own modern nation state" (Sa'di 2007, 187), this version erases the reality that the original inhabitants were expelled from their homeland in order to make room for the newcomers. By making clear the suffering of Nahr's family, first in Kuwait then in Amman, Jordan, Abulhawa refuses to assign the moral upper hand to the Zionist state.

In Palestine she meets Bilal, her ex-husband's brother, who introduces her to a life of resistance but also love. There she witnesses first-hand what Rozina Ali calls "cold violence," consisting of a world of "checkpoints, raids, and arbitrary arrests" (2021). After participating in weapon smuggling, Nahr's

98 *Benay Blend*

arrest leads to solitary confinement in a cell she calls the Cube. After serving 16 years, she is finally released, perhaps because the Israelis hope she will lead them to Bilal. Despite her fragile health, the woman who returns to her family in Amman is not broken. Once there, her family and her memories sustain her just as they had done for years. Shortly after her return, Um Buraq shows up, too. A shadow of her former self, suffering from her time in a Kuwaiti prison as well as a terminal form of cancer, Um Buraq represents to Nahr a symbol of how the state will always "imprison those who are truly free, who do not accept social, economic, or political chains" (Abulhawa 2020, 360) that seek to bind them to its power.

As was true for others in Kuwait and Jordan, the institution of the family, along with memories that get passed down, will continue to serve Palestinians well by keeping their spirits and their communities intact. By keeping these networks alive no matter where they might land next, Palestinians refuse to be erased by official history. "Since almost by definition exile and memory go together," concludes Said, "it is what one remembers of the past and how one remembers that determines how one sees the future" (Said, "Introduction" 2002, xxxv). What distinguishes Palestinian exiles from others in Kuwait and elsewhere is their tenacious loyalty to a homeland that has been denied them since 1948. Under such conditions, Nahr partially recovers, a testament to the endurance of her people. In *Nakba: Palestine, 1948 and the Claims of Memory*, Sa'di and Abu-Lughod explain that Palestinian memory is, at its very core, political (2007, 3). Despite displacement, Palestinians continue to remember their history and understand their place in the world based on their own realities. Indeed, Baroud explains that commemoration of the Nakba Day (May 15) is the one event that brings all Palestinians together (Baroud 2020). It is the event that led to Abulhawa's family's displacement, and it is the catastrophe that she recreates in her books. In the end, her story is the only part of Nahr that Israel can't control, so she holds fast to her memories while in prison. Abulhawa's narrative is above all a love story, writes Rozina Ali. She qualifies, however, that it is "a love story that cannot escape its geography" (2021), and in that way it is uniquely Palestinian.

References

Abu-Lughod, Lila. 2007. "Return to Half-Ruins: Memory, Postmemory, and Living History in Palestine." In *Nakba: Palestine, 1948 and the Claims of Memory*, edited by Ahmad Sa'di and Lila Abu-Lughod, 77–107. New York: Columbia University Press.

Abulhawa, Susan. 2010. *Mornings in Jenin*. New York: Bloomsbury.

———. 2012. "Memories of an Un-Palestinian Story, in a Can of Tuna." In *Seeking Palestine: New Palestinian Writing on Exile and Home*, edited by Penny Johnson and Raja Shehadeh, 4–17. New Delhi: Women Unlimited.

———. 2013. "Ramadan in El Ghorba." In *My Voice Sought the Wind*, edited by Susan Abulhawa, 25–26. Virginia: Just World Books.

———. 2015. *The Blue Between Sky and Water*. New York: Bloomsbury.

———. 2020. *Against the Loveless World*. New York: Simon and Schuster.

———. Interview by Philip Weiss. "Susan Abulhawa on her novel *Against the Loveless World.*" *Mondoweiss.* December 3, 2020. Accessed December 5, 2020. https://mondoweiss.net/2020/12/abulhawa-on-her-palestinian-epic-its-really-important-to-me-for-palestinian-characters-and-literature-to-speak-their-truth-without-apology/.

Ali, Rozina. "Rewriting the Story of the Palestinian Radical." *The New Yorker.* April 14, 2021. Accessed, April 21, 2021. www.newyorker.com/books/under-review/rewriting-the-story-of-the-palestinian-radical.

Baroud, Ramzy. "Imagining Palestine: On Barghouti, Darwish, Kanafani, and the Language of Exile." *Politics for the People.* February 24, 2021. www.ramzybaroud.net/imagining-palestine-on-barghouti-darwish-kanafani-and-the-language-of-exile/.

———. "Why Israel Fears the Nakba: How Memory Became Israel's Greatest Weapon." *Middle East Monitor.* May 19, 2020. Accessed April 20, 2020. www.middleeastmonitor.com/20200519-why-israel-fears-the-nakba-how-memory-became-palestines-greatest-weapon/.

Cleary, Joe. 2002. *Literature, Partition, and the Nation State: Culture and Conflict in Ireland, Israel and* Cambridge: Cambridge University Press.

Dakkak, Nadeen. "The Absent Voices of Second-Generation Migrants in the Gulf States." *Migrant-Rights.Org.* June 27, 2020. Accessed July 30, 2020. www.migrant-rights.org/2020/06/the-absent-voices-of-second-generation-migrants-in-the-gulf-states/.

Davis, Rochelle. 2007. "Mapping the Past, Re-creating the Homeland: Memories of Village Places in Pre-1948 Palestine." In *Nakba: Palestine, 1948 and the Claims of Memory*, edited by Ahmad Sa'di and Lila Abu-Lughod, 53–74. New York: Columbia University Press.

Ghabra, Shafeeq. 1987. *Palestinians in Kuwait: The Family and the Politics of Survival.* London and New York: Routledge.

Humphries, Isabelle and Laleh Khalili. 2007. "Gender of Nakba Memory." In *Nakba: Palestine, 1948 and the Claims of Memory*, edited by Ahmad Sa'di and Lila Abu-Lughod, 207–229. New York: Columbia University Press.,

Jayyusi, Lena. 2007. "The Relational Figures of Palestinian Memory." In *Nakba: Palestine, 1948 and the Claims Of Memory*, edited by Ahmad Sa'di and Lila Abu-Lughod, 107–135. New York: Columbia University Press.

Kanafani, Ghassan. 1999. *Men in the Sun and Other Palestinian Stories.* Boulder: Lynne Rienner Publishers.

Kirpal, Neha. 2020. "Susan Abulhawa: Daring to Lift the Veil." *The New Indian Express*, July 26, 2020. Accessed August 1, 2020. www.newindianexpress.com/lifestyle/books/2020/jul/26/susan-abulhawa-daring-to-lift-the-veil-2173929.html.

Lesch, Ann M. 1991. "Palestinians in Kuwait." *Journal of Palestine Studies* xx, no. 4: 42–55.

Said, Edward W. 1991. *After the Last Sky: Palestine Lives.* New York: Columbia University Press.

———. "Introduction." 2002. In *Reflections on Exile and Other Essays*, edited by Edward W. Said, xi–xxxv). Cambridge: Harvard University Press.

———. 2000. "Invention, Memory, and Place." *Critical Inquiry* 26, no. 2: 175–192. www.jstor.org/stable/1344120.

100 *Benay Blend*

————. "Reflections on Exile." 2002. In *Reflections on Exile and Other Essays*, edited by Edward W. Said, 165–173. Cambridge: Harvard University Press.

Sa'di, Ahmad. 2007. "Afterward: Reflections on Representations, History and Moral Accountability." In *Nakba: Palestine, 1948 and the Claims of Memory*, edited by Ahmad Sa'di and Lila Abu-Lughod, 285–315. New York: Columbia University Press.

Sa'di, Ahmad and Lila Abu-Lughod. 2007. "Introduction: The Claims of Memory." In *Nakba: Palestine, 1948 and the Claims of Memory*, edited by Ahmad Sa'di and Lila Abu-Lughod, 1–27. New York: Columbia University Press.

Slyomovics, Susan. 2007. "The Rape of Gula, a Destroyed Palestinian Village." In *Nakba: Palestine, 1948 and the Claims of Memory*, edited by Ahmad Sa'di and Lila Abu-Lughod, 27–53. New York: Columbia University Press.

Tetreault, Mary Ann and Haya al-Mughni. 1995. "Modernization and its Discontents: State and Gender in Kuwait." *The Middle East Journal* 49, no. 3: 403–418.

5 The Refugee as a "Russian Doll"

Haitham Hussein's Readings of *Ghurba* and Exile at the Time of the Global "Migration Crisis"

Annamaria Bianco

Introduction

Migration stands out as one of the central topics of Modern and Contemporary Arabic Literature. Nonetheless, much has changed since the very first departures of the Nahda and Mahjar eras, both in the modes of displacement and in their literary representations. At the end of the nineteenth century, the memory of the East–West "Enchanted Encounters" was erased by colonial domination through its mechanisms of coercion and exclusion (El-Enany 2006), which worsened during the Nakba of 1948 and the Arab struggles for independence. The newborn freedom was affected by the emergence of authoritarian regimes, whose brutal repression of any form of political dissent led to the departure of many committed intellectuals who found themselves exiled, along with the first Palestinian refugees. Their lives were intertwined under the sign of *ghurba*: a feeling of disarray, alienation, and loneliness which Isabella Camera d'Afflitto compared to the Portuguese *saudade*, in its most melancholic expressions (2010, 212). This intimate sense of alterity had both social and political implications and became the main theme of the emerging literature of exile (*adab al-manfa*). Yet, nostalgic attachment to the homeland and the pan-Arab commitment of the time were quickly erased by the 1967 defeat against Israel. A consistent part of the disappointed Arab youth started leaving less reluctantly to the West or the Gulf countries, which had become a popular destination following the discovery of oil. Those people were searching for fortune and purpose, but they only found misery and marginalization, as attested by novels centered on their urban ghettoization and exclusion from community life (Elayyan 2016; Dakkak 2019).

Since then, an unbroken chain of geopolitical events has swept through the Arab world, provoking a massive diaspora movement across the region and beyond. Although most displaced people from Iraq, Palestine, Sudan, and Syria are still in the Middle East (UNHCR 2021a), many others have made their way to Europe and contributed to generating what the Commissioner for Migration, Dimítris Avramópoulos, defined in 2015 as "the worst refugee crisis since the Second World War."[1] Among them were several authors who

DOI: 10.4324/9781003301776-8

102 *Annamaria Bianco*

eventually translated their traumatic experiences into fiction, enriching a recent body of literature on forced displacement that Johanna B. Sellman named "*adab al-tahjir*." The expression brings together all those writings that foreground the perspectives of undocumented migrants, such as the North African *harraga* and Middle Eastern asylum seekers, on experiences of flight, border-crossing, and resettlement since the beginning of the post-Cold War era (Sellman 2013, 3).

Taking Sellman's research as a starting point, I argue that this ongoing migration process of escape from a destroyed or disowned homeland has been shaping a new trend in contemporary Arabic writing, grounded on a genuine aesthetic of "refugeedom."[2] The theme of the quest for shelter and security has in fact undeniably slid to the heart of both prose and poetry produced over the last decade, by overtaking the previous *leitmotif* of "romantic exile." As I point out elsewhere, novels especially show a new generation of Arab migrants, where intellectuals and students have been replaced by all sorts of characters fleeing wars, persecution, and natural disasters such as epidemics and desertification, while interacting with the ambiguous international humanitarian system (Bianco 2023). This particularly applies to Syrian writers, whose country has become the first source of refugees in the world (UNHCR 2021a). Their literary productions even seem to constitute a self-standing genre in Arabic literature, to which some critics started referring as "literature of asylum" (*adab al-luju'*) (Jarmaqany 2017).

The present chapter calls for the need to further investigate such an imaginative breakthrough by examining the aesthetic shifts that occurred in current representations of *ghurba* and exile. My study will particularly underline the loss of their "literary halo" (Fischione 2018, 236), offset by more pragmatic concerns, such as coping, recovering, and belonging at the time of the global "Refugee Crisis." These interconnections between literature and socio-political issues will be explored in detail through my analysis of Haytham Husayn's (b. 1978; in the following Haitham Hussein) trajectory as a Syrian-Kurdish writer who fled Damascus to Edinburgh after the beginning of the 2011 Revolution. To serve my purpose, I will draw on an extra-literary archive, made up of interviews and statements released by the author, but also on some literary excerpts selected from his fifth novel,[3] *Qad la yabqa ahad, aghatha kristy … ta'aly aqul laki kayfa a'iysh* (*No One May Remain. Agatha Christie, Come, I'll Tell You How I Live*, 2018).[4] This work of pseudo-fiction, based on Hussein's real journey to Europe through the Middle East, portrays the refugee as a "Russian doll" that repeatedly relives its tragedy at each stage of its relocation, tracing a continuity between the first experience of shelter in the neighboring countries and its extension in the West. Eventually, the text will prove to be highly critical of mainstream migration discourses within both Eastern and Western traditions of hospitality, thus innovating canonical Arab writing on longing and exile.

Contemporary Shifts in Arab Migration Writings: The State of Research and Critical Debates on "Refugeeism"

The study of forced migration is a relatively new phenomenon that gained recognition as a legitimate academic field only in the 1980s. At first, scholars conducted research on refugees merely from a legal and economic perspective in the context of post-WWII Europe. Attention to the socio-cultural aspects of dislocation arose soon after, developing from the pioneer writings of Hannah Arendt (Stonebridge 2019). Later, scholars increasingly broadened their gaze to the realities of the Global South and gradually brought attention to other displaced voices in order to make them resonate worldwide and to push for decolonial perspectives in migration studies (Mayblin and Turner 2020). Recent approaches that centralize experiences of displacement in the Global South have been crucial to exposing the process of "invisibilization" undergone by refugees and asylum seekers within their host communities, as detected by anthropologists such as David Farrier. Farrier considers them to fit the definition of "new subalterns" postulated by Gayatri C. Spivak, criticizing the behavior of both the international humanitarian apparatus and local governments, which grant these people shelter and security at the expense of their agency and right of opinion (Farrier 2013, 5). These policies are then interiorized by the various host societies, which often reduce the refugees to being passive victims of their own condition, to be looked at with pity and treated in a patronizing way.

This flattened, infantilized understanding of the refugee figure, often combined with a securitarian rhetoric against the threat posed by the foreigner, has been quickly dismantled by the Arabic literature of forced migration as part of a larger global trend where authors traditionally considered to be "minoritarian" manage to speak out to a wider audience,[5] expressing a renewed literary commitment to human rights and freedom of mobility (Gallien 2018). More specifically, these writers have been questioning the practices of in-/hospitality and biopower (Foucault 1998 [1976]) recently implemented on migrants (Agamben 1998 [1995]) by both Western and Eastern societies, while sparing no criticism of the process of granting asylum, based on what is judged to be an unfair differentiated model, depending more on the origins of the applicants than on their motivations to flee the home country.

For its part, the expression *adab al-luju'* was forged around 2016 in response to the media boom which erupted around Syrian refugee writing in Germany. In a very specific study, "Adab al-luju' al-sury: al-shatat wa-l-ta'bir al-adaby" (Syrian literature of asylum: diaspora and literary expression, 2018), Muhammad al-Sallum attempts to describe this new production by defining it as a literature freed from the oppression of political power. According to him, this production aims to show the flaws of the Western reception system through an "epic narration" (*malhamiyya*) of the "emigration experience"

104 *Annamaria Bianco*

(*taghriba*) endured by Syrians and other displaced peoples, as well as to unmask the hypocrisies of neighboring countries whose governments boast of an Arab-Islamic solidarity that is rarely implemented in their welcoming practices (al-Sallum 2018). However, his definition is questioned by several intellectuals who point out that the works of Palestinian refugees and Iraqi defectors written in the past have never been treated as an isolated body from the canonical *adab al-manfa* (Hamza 2019). This different approach would then be the result of a "fashion wave" – or worse, a "label" imposed by the West to "satisfy its Orientalist fantasies" (Odoy 2020). In a similar vein, Mahmud Khity even warned against the risks of "falling into the trap of the emigrant literature revolution" ('Umran 2018). Some journalists have also tried to make reports on this topic by inviting various representatives of the Arab cultural world into their TV studios.[6] Not to mention the fact that many institutions are now funding works of art produced by Arab refugees in Europe and in their other host countries across the Middle East, instigating a process of "*NGO-ization* of culture," as Simon Dubois calls it, referring to the flourishing of the Syrian theatre of the diaspora (Dubois 2019, 160).

Haitham Hussein's memoir has been funded by one of these very associations, the Syrian *Ettijahat – Independent Culture*, established in Lebanon at the end of 2011, as well as by the German *Goethe – Institute*. The two of them are now well known for having been co-sponsoring several cultural initiatives for and in support of refugee artists across the world since 2015. The author is also an active member of other organizations for writers in distress, such as the English branch of *PEN International*, through which he carries out his own path of political engagement. As a rather prominent personality among displaced Syrian writers, he was personally asked by Al Jazeera about the debate opposing the brand new *adab al-luju'* to *adab al-manfa*. Hussein's answers, based on his multiple experiences of displacement in and outside Syria, stressed the differences between "asylum" and "exile" and, subsequently, their aesthetic readings. In particular, he affirmed that the refugee constantly lives in an "emergency phase" (*marhala tary'a*), "a nightmare" (*kabus*) from which he struggles to wake up, waiting for a "miracle" (*mu'ajaza*) that might bring him back to his previous reality. His peculiar *ghurba* is therefore rooted in the persistent impact of the experienced trauma on every aspect of his daily life,[7] thus interfering with the recovery process and his adaptation to a new reality of relative safety. People in exile have instead passed this coping stage and are able to try reflecting on their condition, while dealing with it more peacefully. Hussein thinks then that the latter definition better applies to his current situation (Hamza 2019). In this sense, his words seem to evoke what Edward Said already postulated in his *Reflections On Exile* (2001):

> Although it is true that anyone prevented from returning home is an exile, some distinctions can be made among exiles, refugees, expatriates, and émigrés. ... The word "refugee" has become a political one, suggesting

The Refugee as a "Russian Doll" 105

large herds of innocent and bewildered people requiring urgent international assistance, whereas "exile" carries with it, I think, a touch of solitude and spirituality.

(Said 2001, 178)

Precisely because of these structural differences, Hussein believes that the new literature produced by refugees will sooner or later fall into some framework, as "asylum has become a *pressing global issue*, and there are millions of refugees around the world, *everywhere*, who deserve to be heard" (Hamza 2019, my emphasis). His position thus seems to be in favor of devising new critical categories, challenging the more conservative and reticent bangs of Arab intellectuals who look at "refugeeism" – understood as a phenomenon of enhanced visibility of the refugees' issues in the public arena – as a potential danger to literary authenticity. "Europeans are deeply interested in the politics of the Middle East, in asylum and immigration, among other things, and readers look for political and cultural components and are eager for Middle Eastern literature," as stated by Stephan Milich and quoted in Yassin Hassan 2021. But, if it is true that this interest can lead Arab writers to produce some "instant literature," which rides the trends of the moment, it is also true that books are much more than anthropological documents to be used for deciphering societies. Time alone will determine which of these authors will keep writing, raising the right questions and experimenting with language and literary texts, as several intellectuals in the diaspora have already started doing, orienting the interests and tastes of the international editorial market to high quality productions (Lang 2021).

Haitham Hussein's Life-Path: Trapped into Homeland, Boundless in Exile?[8]

As already mentioned, Haitham Hussein is a Syrian Kurd novelist, a well-known critic and reviewer. He has been working for major Arab newspapers such as *al-Hayat*, *Assafir*, *al-Bayan*, and *al-Quds al-'araby*, gaining a prominent position in the transnational Arab cultural field, without betraying his Kurdish roots. Additionally, he has recently started running his own website on contemporary Arabic literature, *Alriwaya.net*, enriching the critical public debate.

The author was born in 1978 in Amuda and, after graduating in literature in 1998, he was appointed to teach Arabic in one of the remote villages on the Iraqi-Turkish borders where he spent a year before he was conscripted into the Syrian army. Back then, the author was badly injured in a fire, suffering third degree burns which left him with both psychological and physical scars. He was discharged after more than two years, but he couldn't return to teaching because standing on his feet was very painful. He managed then to settle into administrative work in his hometown. This immobility was interrupted in 2003, a year that boosted his writing career: he met one of his best friends and

106 *Annamaria Bianco*

colleagues, the lawyer and director Hassan Draei (Hassan Dara'i), and they co-wrote the script of *Amoudah is Burning*. The film was about the shocking fire that gutted Amuda Cinema on November 13, 1960, killing more than 200 Kurdish children and leaving another more than 200 injured and disabled; an arson that remains unsolved (Mémoire créative de la révolution syrienne, 2018). Three of Hussein's cousins were also among the victims, while his mother and uncle had left before the fire started.

This sorrowful experience stimulated Hussein to write about the Baathist persecution against his people by publishing his first novel, *Aram: salil al-awjai' al-mukabara* (Aram: The Descendant of Unspoken Pain, 2006), where he addresses the issue of Kurdish forced migration to Europe.[9] The author shows the same commitment in his second book, *Raha'in al-khati'ya* (Hostages of Sin, 2009), centralizing the issue of Kurdish diaspora in order to analyze the impact of displacement on women's lives. The deepest roots of this discrimination lie in the fact that the Kurds of Syria, who are victims of the ideological unanimity of the Baath, were never considered an ethnic minority despite their numerical importance – almost one and a half million people in 2004, or 8.1% of the population. Since Arab nationalism has become a central element of Syrian political culture, the exclusion of "Kurdishness" had indeed become a principle of the official doctrine of the State (Gunter 2014, Donati 2009, 305–307), and a reason for Kurds to leave the country.

This state of affairs prompted Hussein to take his analysis of social injustice to a broader level, and he decided to explore the issue of violence and corruption in the whole Arab world by publishing a third book with the title of *Ibrat al-ru'b* (The Needle of Horror, 2009). The absurd atmosphere of the novel and a kind of magical realism creeping into its background both suggest the influence of Salim Barakat (b.1951)[10] on this work, although the author also draws inspiration from many Western writers, especially for his critical reflections. For instance, he wrote the first of his five literary essays one year later, *al-Riwaya bayn al-talghim wa-l-talghiz* (The Novel as Mine and Puzzle, 2010), moving from Milan Kundera's announcement of "the death of the novel" (Kundera 2003 [1986]) to affirm that this genre will die only if it does not break the silence of oppression or uncover unspoken pain. This attitude attracted the attention of the Mukhabarat, the General Intelligence Services, which exerted pressure on him to give up his literary activity. According to Hussein, the regime had "maliciously ruined readers' tastes" by distorting their understandings, and "writers fighting corruption, injustice, dictatorship, and repression faced a [huge] challenge: the narration of a story kept in the dark, consigned to oblivion" (Hussein 2021). In fact, once he refused to give up his pen, the Intelligence assigned him teaching in a remote area near Tel Tamir, more than 80 km away from his city. He remained there until the beginning of the revolt against Bashar al-Assad in 2011. It was then that the Mukhabarat ordered his return to ease tensions in the rebellious Kurdish area – a sort of political pawn to cool off opposition in the directorate: although the regime had adopted a coercive policy towards the Kurds since its rise to power, it

The Refugee as a "Russian Doll" 107

tried its very best to rally them with a clientelist policy, trying to take advantage of their fragmented reality (Donati 2009, 305–306).

Thus, Hussein chose to move to Damascus, where his parents were staying in one of the capital's suburbs in East Ghouta. Within six months, their apartment was bombarded by the Syrian Fighters, and the family fled back to Amuda. The following repression against the Kurds, who eventually joined the insurrections against the central government (Gunter 2013, 442, 447), forced the writer to leave the country for good with his pregnant wife and daughter, in 2012. They headed to the United Arab Emirates (UAE) via Lebanon, where "bribes opened doors that were shut before" (Hussein, Qualey, and Fares 2021, 31). Then, they moved to Cairo only to discover that in Egypt as well, despite the absence of any political bias, prejudices against the Kurds were not lacking. For example, people there used to say "pulling a Kurd on me" when they accused someone of trying to trick them or take them for fools (98). Meanwhile, Hussein's younger brother and sister had already fled to Turkey, where he eventually joined them, later deciding to apply for asylum in Europe, disappointed by his experience of refuge in the Middle East. While in Istanbul, in particular, it seemed that everyone could get "their private city" (112), this did not apply to the author, who found himself faced with the contradiction of living in the cosmopolitan capital of a country that certainly did not boast a history of peaceful coexistence with its Kurdish minority and was not even welcoming to displaced Arab Syrians.[11] In this regard, the dialogue between Hussein and another Kurd he met in Batman,[12] whose family had emigrated from his own village in Syria years earlier, turns out to be extremely illustrative of the bond that unites persecuted and fleeing populations beyond time and space:

> I see the war grinding you down, and those fleeing it are drowning in the depths of this dark sea. A few days ago, a boat with dozens of you sank. … Young men in their prime, fleeing to Europe, dreaming of salvation, devoured by the sea monster. I swear I cried for them, and I still cry every time I remember them. It's as if we were destined to be the fuel that others burn in their wars. We pay the fees with the souls of our young and the future of our children. … I cry for them as I cry for my house, my village, and my children. It seems the curse of massacres (*la'nat mazajir*) will never leave us.
>
> (115)

Through his empathy, the man acknowledged a continuity between the history of the Kurds and today's refugee tragedy, thus prompting the author to reflect on his condition of "permanent diaspora" (116) once he reached England in 2014. In fact, things were not easier for him there either: his application for asylum was accepted only after a long stay in a refugee camp that reminded him of his months of captivity in Syria (14–15). Hussein experienced, again, strong alienation, exacerbated by the diversity of the cultural context, only

108   *Annamaria Bianco*

managing to settle down after the reunification with his wife and daughters. Once a new form of stability was achieved, the author went back to writing and published his fourth novel, '*Ushba darra fi-l-fardus* (A Weed in Paradise, 2017). The book, dedicated to the forgotten memory of the 2004 Qamishli riots,[13] aimed at retracing the events that led his community to flee Syria and scatter across the world. But it also laid the groundwork for his following autobiography, which saw the light in 2018. Indeed, in *No One May Remain*, Hussein finally tells his own "silenced story" and comes to terms with his experience as an outcast in Syria, going to the very roots of his feeling of out-of-placeness, sprouted in the heart of his homeland. The novel then becomes an attempt to reconcile his past as an "inconvenient intellectual," ostracized by the Baathist political regime,[14] with his present as a refugee, subject to controversial judgments and obligations in a society other than his own, and that shift with each relocation. The writing does not follow a precise chronological order, but rather assumes the fragmented characteristics of a collection of memories and reflections, thus resulting in a literary work halfway between reality and fiction. This is because the objective of the author is to lay bare and find a remedy to the mindset of anger, pain, and emptiness that still overflows his daily life, despite the security achieved by leaving a country in turmoil. In this perspective of self-analysis, the "limbo experience" lived by Hussein as a restless wanderer across the Middle East turns out to be a crucial interim phase in his search for a (safe) place in the world. Metaphorically speaking, we can therefore describe this stage of his path as a "transnational gateway,"[15] necessary to recognize, understand, and eventually overcome the different challenges of his European resettlement.

New Boundaries of *Ghurba:* "Otherness" and "Belonging" within the Asylum Regime

No One May Remain. Agatha Christie, Come, I'll Tell You How I Live was conceived as the first part of a planned trilogy, dealing with the notion of the self and its image in the mirror of the other, and this is not only with respect to the host/stranger dynamics intrinsic to every migration process. Hussein rather moves from a more implicit assumption: that "otherness" begins long before any journey, especially for those who belong to minorities or marginal communities in their own homeland. Before becoming an actual foreigner in the UK, Hussein was already considered an alien in Syria, as well as in the Middle Eastern countries he crossed during his flight. Thus, he had also already started developing his unconscious strategy of coping with the darkest sides of deracination to which this text provides a systematic literary framework before a larger audience, thanks to the English translation. In fact, the volume was imagined precisely for this purpose by its sponsors, allowing the author to vivisect his persistent feeling of *ghurba* while rediscovering the values of diversity among human beings. Besides, witnessing the impact and peculiarity of creativity through its reflections in the eyes of others, as well

The Refugee as a "Russian Doll" 109

as the ways in which it is received, is "one of the most important tests that have contributed to deepening the recent changes that occurred in Syrian narratives of diaspora" (Yassin Hassan 2021). These narratives are now much more concerned with the emergence of new issues such as integration, the uncertain future, and processing the aftermath of trauma.

No One May Remain's full title is a throwback to Agatha Christie's (1890–1976) most famous mystery novel *And Then There Were None* (1939), better known as *Ten Little Niggers*, but it is also a reference to a chapter of her memoir, *Come, Tell Me How You Live* (1946), which she wrote when she was living right in Amuda in the 1930s with her husband and archaeologist Max Mallowan. Christie describes the diary as a "very little book," full of everyday doings and happenings, "where little effort is made to educate the reader in the ancient history of the places that are being excavated" (Hussein, Qualey, and Fares 2021, 4). Instead, she paints a vivid picture of the human side of their expeditions and the personalities involved. The local population is presented in a sympathetic manner and Hussein finds himself so impressed by those descriptions that he chooses to start his novel with a letter addressed to the English woman; a fictional pretext to draw a parallel between the Orientalist's life in the East and the reality of refugees in the West, while justifying the pressing need to write about his own experience (7–9):

> My dear Agatha, were you happy here [in England]? Were you happy there [in Syria]? Were you happy in your life? … You point out that you began writing your non-chronological diaries before the [Second World] war, but that, four years after the war ended, your thoughts kept carrying you back to the days you spent in Syria. . … You say it is good to remember such days and places – and, in that precise moment, the marigold hill bloomed, and old men with white beards walked behind their donkeys, perhaps entirely aware that a war went on. So, I ask you these questions about happiness that I am sometimes asked as well: Were you happy to be there? Were you happy in Edinburgh? Were you happy to have made it to Britain and saved yourself and family from war? Were you happy in your life?
>
> (6–8)

From the answers provided to these first questions, we immediately understand that the issue of happiness is of great importance in Hussein's writing, where it seems to be the ultimate goal to reach; the "man's impossible dream" (8) of healing from the wounds of his past. Rather than wallowing in the sad awareness of being faced with the illusions of return, and thus giving into melancholy, the author seeks to keep himself busy in the endless cycle of "life and its surprises" (9), while peacefully settling for brief moments of "relative happiness" (10) in his new country. This image clashes with the gloomy picture of exile formerly provided by the Arab writing tradition, where it was classically featured as "a place of negation" (Sellman 2013, 38).

110   *Annamaria Bianco*

Although the terms *ghurba* and *manfa* are both still used in Arabic to translate this notion, it must be stressed that their different roots refer to distinct semantic connotations. The root GH-R-B originally designates what is "far, rare," in the sense of a distancing from one's self, but it especially indicates something "foreign," "unfamiliar." Related to the West, which is understood as a geographical and symbolic space (i.e., the place where the sun disappears), the term refers to an experience "of otherness" with both potential positive and negative connotations (Lory 2011, 202). On the other hand, the root N-F-A has the literary meaning of "expelling," "excluding," and "banning," so the word *manfa* represents a condition of exclusion from the nation or any other form of collectivity (Casini 2008, 7), which inevitably implies a "loss" or an "erasure." While using both terms, Hussein predominantly employs the first within this text, where it recurs 20 times more than the other (25:5 ratio), enriched with new implications and interpretations, as it is dictated by the peculiarities of his state of refuge. Asylum, unlike canonical exile, does not in fact place the author in a condition of banishment, but rather embodies an emergency exit from "the inferno of death in its many forms" (Hussein 2021, 11). It namely entails an idea of salvation, a will to survive the violence of war, even if this implies the abandonment of one's land, habits, and affections, as well as the exposure to new forms of marginalization and abuse which are nonetheless preferable to death.

Paradoxically, in his first search for a sanctuary, the author considered himself neither a "refugee" nor "an immigrant, an exiled or an expatriate" (12–13). Despite the fact that the Middle Eastern countries where he found himself living were (and still are) not signatories of the 1951 Refugee Convention,[16] and that Hussein and his family had experienced some forms of racism and discrimination, although they were not part of any special aid program,[17] the surrounding cultural context was not alienating for the writer. At least these are the retrospective considerations he makes in *No One May Remain*, published after relocating to the West; a shift that he describes as deeply disorienting, not only for himself, but also for the other migrants he met over the years and whose testimonies intervene to enrich the text. This is probably due to the fact that Hussein's departure from the region made him look at his past wanderings in a different light. At that time, the author thought of his experience as temporary and lived it as such, considering himself much more a "travelling guest" than a "foreigner," as in the Islamic tradition of hospitality (Siddiqui 2015, 10). Arriving in UK, instead, marked for him the impossibility of returning to Syria and the inevitability of a destiny of exile. Once he landed at Heathrow airport and asked for international protection, the author thus became "the other *par excellence*," the "stateless refugee" who now embodies the paradigm of our century, according to the philosopher Giorgio Agamben (Agamben 2000 [1996], 20). Since that precise moment, he had to face a different kind of strangeness, which transcended the socio-political Syrian frame of exclusion to which he was accustomed as a Kurdish intellectual, as well as the mistrust shown towards his ethnicity in other Arab

The Refugee as a "Russian Doll" 111

countries. This strangeness soaked all the new, everyday-life aspects on his path of integration, starting with the basis of communication:

> The refugee faces the dilemma of defining himself *to himself,* as well as *to those around him.* If he sees himself as an immigrant (*muhajir*), his new country will never become a homeland (*watan*), nor will it replace his previous country. And if he continues to see himself as an immigrant, he will soon erect borders to separate himself from his surroundings and his new world, and will remain distanced, late to integrate or perhaps never desiring integration. ... Attempts to integrate aren't limited to the desire to learn a country's language, but also encompass the refugee's effort to convey an appropriate image of his culture and people, so that his new country sees him as an asset and not a burden.
>
> (11, 18, my emphasis)

The key to this reflection lies in the fact that refugees are perceived by the author as absolute strangers in the host society. Obtaining international protection, or having their previously violated rights respected, do not ensure their immediate participation in the life of the community, since they *must* demonstrate that they want to be a part of it, taking on a clear and precise identity, while acting as the spokesmen for all their other fellow displaced. In fact, refugees are considered to be "bad until proven otherwise" (17) and are seen as a problem to be solved or a threat to be contained. They need to be put "under some sort of observation until [they] prove [their] competence and ability to coexist and accept others, to look at the country as [their] own rather than as a waypoint that doesn't concern [them]" (17). In other words, they live in a sort of "suspended life," as stated by Zygmunt Bauman (4), where time goes slow, punctuating the wait for a new ID, a new job, and a new routine attesting his ultimate new belonging. Having to constantly relate to the Other from the "position of the accused" is precisely what binds the different attempts of seeking refuge. This creates a vicious cycle of suffering, which seems particularly difficult to break without a process of redrawing the boundaries of *ghurba*:

> Refugee life has become a Russian doll that restores its ordeal and mutilated copies, replicating the same successive tragedies, again and again. ... In exile (*ghurba*), one question persists on our minds – the question of homeland (*watan*). The sense of belonging (*intima'*) we seek and the security (*aman*) we dream about. *In escaping our homeland, we may end up finding it.* Exile (*ghurba*) introduces us to *a belonging to the self and to others,* to a distance that becomes a way to get closer to others, become more familiar. *Sometimes, the homeland becomes a veil, and exile (ghurba) becomes a mirror and a way home.* A real homeland is wherever one finds a moment of peace, a sincere smile, a deep sleep, a comfortable bed, a longing for tomorrow that replaces fear, the shiver of a lover, and

112 *Annamaria Bianco*

> an eagerness to see a loved one. Such simple details build a true home-land. For us refugees, longing for home (*al-shawq lil-watan*) is key. ... *We used to miss belonging to a stolen homeland, but now we miss ourselves and draw strength from our opaque future.*
>
> (6–7, my emphasis)

In this passage, the author namely suggests re-interrogating the sense of belonging to the lost homeland in order to find in oneself and in the confrontation with the Other a way to recompose the pieces of a fragmented identity. In other terms, the *ghurba* becomes a pretext to "come out of one's self," dismiss previous traumas and beliefs, and seek another form of *aman*: the serenity that comes from the acceptance of one's own condition. Along these lines, the experience of forced displacement seems to constitute a "privileged site" to reflect on the meanings of words such as "homeland," "citizenship," and "community," despite the attempts at forced assimilation made by hosting governments who would like refugees to leave their past behind as soon as possible. In fact, most of the "welcoming programs" focus more on the pragmatic integration of migrants into society than on their mental or emotional health. Insisting mainly on the first aspect is dangerous and counterproductive in the eyes of the writer, and it also represents one of the great paradoxes of the Asylum Regime, which does not really prepare people for the encounter with alterity and advocates the opening of borders without raising the necessary awareness on the causes of contemporary mass displacement (38). This is a serious contradiction within the frame of reception strategies, affected by the exasperated do-gooderism of the "Humanitarian Reason" (Fassin 2011), as well as by the common belief spread in both Western and Eastern societies that refugees should find their fulfillment in the simple fact of being alive, showing eternal and blind gratitude to the countries who welcome them. As evident in Hussein's writing, this framework has a strong impact not only on social encounters but also on the refugees' perception of themselves and the place where they live. Political and social structures play a major role in facilitating feelings of alienation that can lead the displaced subject to a violent as well as counterproductive denial of his current condition. It is therefore up to the individual to find and put into practice all possible strategies to avoid being caught in the depressive vortex of the dream of an impossible return to the homeland. The refugee is in fact neither an exile nor a migrant, as Hussein himself came to understand at the end of his long journey, and he cannot cope with reality if he is stuck in a limbo of waiting. According to the author, this applies to all kinds of people for whom the geographical nature of the place of refuge does not seem to affect the most intimate essence of their experience. He draws these conclusions precisely from his bumpy path between the Middle East and Europe:

> I have met, and continue to meet, many people from both the East and the West who moved from their homelands to other countries and are *obsessed*

with a hope of return. They believe that their stays in these new cities, which for some have stretched to years, are only temporary, and that it won't be much longer before they will, surely, go back to their homelands. This presumed inevitability reflects an unintended fallacy, a deceit of the self, because time does not wait for one to complete his projects or meet his goals, nor for him to fulfill his dreams and accomplishments before returning him to his permanent life back home. ... By then, time will have exhausted the man and kept him on the edge of life until he realizes that *he has been the permanent resident of the place he saw as temporary*. He has become a prisoner of his habits, a prisoner of a novel kind of alienation (*ghurba*) that he created to fool himself into believing he would move back, away from this diaspora (*ghurba*) that clings to him like seawater, in which he will forever swim.

(33, my emphasis)

The only way to prevent this scenario is by fully inhabiting one's own diaspora, since "asylum (*luju'*) unveils the facts of people's personalities": "[t]his new life will force people to rip off the masks they have grown so used to wearing" (21) and turn their look to the future, however uncertain. If the feeling of exile encloses the subject within a quantum foam fueled by his mournful attachment to the past, taking refuge allows him instead to venture into a new territory and to explore it as soon as the urgency of the danger is overcome, and physical security is achieved. Dealing with the effects of trauma thus means trying to get out of one's shell and coming to terms with his own image – inevitably changed by events – before the mirror of reality. In this way, Hussein brings the *ghurba* back to its original literary meaning, additionally assigning it virtuous connotations. Due to the colonial and post-colonial contexts of the last two centuries, these had in fact been completely obscured by the canonical Arab production on emigration, in which the tragic epilogue of al-Tayyib Salih's *Season of Migration to the North* (1967) is surely the most emblematic and notorious case of the failed encounter with the Other (El Enany 2006, 106–108). However, the latest introduction of the globalized realities of contemporary forced migration into Arab literature started featuring increasingly complex and broad representations of these dynamics of social interaction (Sellman 2013, 9). One of the major outcomes of this evolution is that literary texts are in fact no longer limited to staging a dichotomous confrontation between East and West, but they rather show a more multifaceted reality, not neglecting the contradictions intrinsic to the fragmented Arab world.

According to Hussein, focusing on "positive ways to see this terrible displacement" (6) provides a tool for helping refugees cope with their status, by shifting the paradigm of belonging from the realm of geopolitics to that of individual ethics and needs of safety. His reasoning fits into a context in which several intellectuals and researchers have begun to speculate on the changing notions of exile in the transnational Arab community. His remarks on homeland and diaspora stand in continuity with El Khachab's statements on the achievement

114   *Annamaria Bianco*

of a "modern post-national Arab subjectivity" (Khachab 2010). This latter result from the investment of an "ethnoscape," a virtual space of people on the move, who – as theorized by the anthropologist Arjun Appadurai – constitute the essential feature of our shifting world, transcending national boundaries. Even more so, tourists, immigrants, refugees, exiles, guest workers, and other groups of displaced individuals appear to affect the politics of nations to a hitherto unprecedented degree. In this framework, Arab asylum seekers form an "ethnically distinct subject" (Khachab 2010) which, based on my above analysis, gets to be the bearer of very precise claims of justice and equality. Through his particular experience, Hussein thus comes to further expand and embrace this paradigm, transcending his Arab-Kurdish identity in order to answer the universal macro question of our age: "How do you turn exile into a home, when your old home has turned itself into an exile?" (18).

Conclusion

Ghurba and *manfa* are words to which the study of Arab intellectual and artistic production has inevitably accustomed us. Nevertheless, with the changing geopolitical structure of the Arab world and, in particular, with the phenomena of mass dispersion that plunged us into the new millennium, these two terms have both undergone profound changes. Their meanings have embraced different semantic fields, assuming new connotations, linked to the remodeling of the notions of homeland, citizenship and belonging at the time of the so-called global refugee crisis.

The recent fiction of forced displacement and the critical debate it provoked stand as witnesses to this ongoing process, which produces new senses and readings at the crossroads of aesthetic and political languages. With *No One May Remain*, Haitham Hussein inscribes himself precisely in the wake of these new trends, raising many questions about refugeedom and refugeeism that do not always find a precise answer. The book is configured as a journey through the memories and thoughts of its author, halfway between essay and novel. As we have seen, Hussein moves from his personal background, as a Syrian-Kurdish writer fleeing a country in chaos, to develop more universal reflections on the aftermath of trauma and flight. In doing so, he manages to speak both to Arab and Western readers of a problem that is becoming increasingly topical before our eyes, using literary references and images that are familiar to the two audiences in order to raise awareness. The English translation and distribution of the book further serves his purpose, contributing to broadening the current socio-political debate on welcoming and hospitality, and to reflecting on the question of otherness and the place of minorities in the future of new communities to come.

Indeed, the intertwining of the old Kurdish issue with the Syrian refugee question, currently in the world's spotlight, adds a further degree of complexity to Hussein's work. He demonstrates that, for many displaced people, the feelings of *ghurba*, alienation, and out-of-placeness precede their experience of being a foreigner in other neighboring countries and Europe, painting the homeland as a "prison" and the whole Middle East as a "limbo gateway" on the road to salvation. In this sense, exile is freed of its classical negative connotations, configuring itself as a place of possibility and opportunity, if migrants do not allow themselves to be crushed and accept that the temporary has become permanent. The result is a novel reading of *ghurba*, understood as that "venturing into the unknown" related to the original sense of the term, which leads to the (re)discovery of one's own self and to a truthful encounter with the other. Only in this manner can refugees hope to escape the "Curse of the Russian Doll," breaking the cycle of their endless ordeal and turning asylum into a true haven of peace.

Introducing these new topics and imagery in the Arabic tradition of fiction of forced displacement, Hussein opens important spaces of discussion in the transnational Arab cultural field, shaking it from the inside with his critique of the fluctuating inter-Islamic solidarity. Moreover, in a global context where these kinds of literary productions are more and more widespread, his work brings new perspectives to studies analyzing the development of refugee writings worldwide, helping to multiply the hitherto unheard voices of the Global South.

Notes

1 The sentence has been reported worldwide by diverse media outlets. In 2015 more than 1,000 refugees arrived at the European Union's southern borders and another 3,771 people died in the same attempt (UNHCR 2021b).
2 This English word is the translation of a term first coined by the Russian-Jewish scholar Avram Kirzhnits during the First World War: *bezhenstvo*. This definition is worth reviving in the field of Refugee Studies because it does not only direct attention to the "experience of refuge" itself (which we might refer to in Arabic as *"luju'iyya"* or *"halat al-luju'"*), but also "encompasses the process of labelling and categorization," stressing an existential and psychical human condition which Hannah Arendt understood as universal. See: Gatrell 2020, 21, 30–31.
3 For reasons of space, the excerpts will be provided only in their 2021 English translation. A few keywords will still be included in the original Arabic.
4 *Qad la yabqa ahad* is Hussein's first volume to be entirely translated into English, thanks to the work of Nicole Fares (Hussein, Qualey, and Fares 2021). From now on, I will refer to the book using its translated title.
5 On the access of postcolonial literatures to the Olympus of contemporary world literature and its sociological implications, see: Graham, Niblett, and Deckard 2012.
6 See, for example, the emissions "Ma al-farq bayn adab al-luju' wa adab al-mahjar?" (What is the difference between Literature of Asylum and Literature of Emigration?) in the Jordanian program *Orient Radio*, broadcast on 25/01/2019 (online at: https:// youtu. be/sTYPsqWOzMY, last accessed July 6, 2021) and "Adab al-luju' al-sury bayn ma'ana sh'ab wa tanawwu' al-tajarib al-fardiyya" (Syrian Asylum Literature between the Suffering of a People and the Diversity of Individual Experiences) from *Syria TV* on October 21 of the same year (online at: https://youtu.be/hg3u9thi fmw, last accessed July 6, 2021).

116 *Annamaria Bianco*

7 On the so-called "insistent return" of the traumatic event in the memory of the traumatized subject, see: Caruth 1995, 5.

8 Most of the biographical information mentioned in this paragraph comes from Hussein 2012.

9 According to a report by the Council of Europe, the Kurds living in Western Europe at the time of publication of this novel were approximately 1.3 million. See: Russell-Johnston, David. 2006.

10 Another Syrian author of Kurdish origin, who has marked the history of contemporary Arabic literature. He is currently based in Sweden. To further explore the production of Kurds writing in languages other than Kurdish, often banned by different regimes, and the intellectual debate regarding this issue, see: Ahmadzadeh 2007, 585.

11 On these points see, respectively: Saraçoğlu 2011 and Eder, Özkul 2016.

12 A province in the Southeast Anatolia region of Turkey with Kurdish majority, which has been a site of bloody clashes between the Kurdistan Workers' Party (PKK) and the Turkish central government in the last decade.

13 The Qamishli riots were a great uprising led by Syrian Kurds in the north-eastern city of Qamishli in March 2004, generated during a football match. At least 30 of them were killed by the Baathist military and, as a result of the crackdown, thousands of others chose to flee to Iraqi Kurdistan. See: Brandon 2007, Donati 2009, 305.

14 A fate he shares with several contemporary Arab writers, as evidenced in Günther, Milich 2016.

15 I refer here to April Shemak's reading of the theories of Wilson Harris on the movements of asylum seekers across the Caribbean, "hung by law, suspended between civil identities and national spaces" (Shemak 2011, 20).

16 On the refugee status in Islam, see: Shoukri 2010.

17 As previously noted, the situation of refugees in Arab countries is not necessarily one of easy integration. In addition to the Turkish case that I gave as an example, we must not forget that Syrians and Palestinians in Lebanon, as well as in Jordan to a lesser extent, have long been subjected to xenophobic attitudes and structural marginalization. For more details on the representations of this phenomenon in contemporary Arab novels, see: Qutait 2020.

Reference list

Abdallah, Umran. 2018. "Rasa'il al-manfa … al-hijra wa-l-luju' bayn al-adabayn al filastiny wa-l-sury." *Aljazeera.net*, December 14, www.aljaze era.net/news/cultur eandart/2018/12/14/الهجرة-واللجوء-بين-الأدبين-الفلسطيني (last accessed July 6, 2021).

Agamben, Giorgio. 1998 (1995). *Homo Sacer: Sovereign Power and Bare Life*, trans. D. Heller Roazen. Stanford: Stanford University Press.

———. 2000 (1996). *Means without End: Notes on Politics*, trans. V. Binetti. C. Casarino. Minneapolis: University of Minnesota Press.

Ahmadzadeh, Hashem. 2007. "In Search of a Kurdish Novel that Tells Us Who the Kurds Are." *Iranian Studies*, Vol. 40, 5, 579–592.

Bianco, Annamaria. 2023. "Les gardiens de l'air: une généalogie romanesque de l'exil en Syrie" in Dahdah, Assaf, David Lagarde, and Norig Neveu (ed.). *Réseaux, trajectoires et représentations des migrations.* Beyrouth: Presses de l'IFPO and Open Edition Books.

Brandon, James. 2007. "The PKK and Syria's Kurds." *Terrorism Monitor*, Vol. 5, 3, online https://web.archive.org/web/20080917223313/http://www.jamestown.org/terrorism/news/article.php?articleid=2370250.

Camera d'Afflitto, Isabella. 2010. *Letteratura araba contemporanea: dalla nahdah a oggi.* Rome: Carocci Editore.

Caruth, Cathy (ed.). 1995. *Trauma. Explorations in Memory.* Baltimore/London: The Johns Hopkins University Press

Casini, Lorenzo. 2008. "Beyond Occidentalism: Europe and the Self in Present-day Arabic Narrative Discourse." *EUI Working Papers*, RSCAS 2008/30, 1 – 21.

Christie, Agatha. November 1939. *Ten Little Niggers.* London: Collins Crime Club.

Christie, Agatha. 1946. Come, Tell Me How You Live. New York: Dodd, Mead and Company.

Dakkak, Nadeen. 2019. "Migrant Labour, Immobility and Invisibility in Literature on the Arab Gulf States," Aguiar, Marian, Mathieson, Charlotte, and Lynne Pearce (eds.) *Mobilities, Literature, Culture.* Cham: Palgrave Macmillan, 189–210.

Donati, Caroline. 2009. *L'exception syrienne: Entre modernisation et résistance.* Paris: La Découverte.

Dubois, Simon. 2019. "A Field in Exile: The Syrian Theatre Scene in Movement" in Jacquemond, Richard and Lang, Felix (ed.), *Culture and Crisis in the Arab World: Production and Practice in Conflict*, London: I.B. Tauris, 169–192.

Eder, Mine, Özkul, Derya. 2016. "Editors' introduction: Precarious Lives and Syrian Refugees in Turkey." *New Perspectives on Turkey*, Vol. 54, 1–8.

Elayyan, Hani. 2016. "Three Arabic Novels of Expatriation in the Arabian Gulf Region: Ibrāhīm Naṣrallāh's Prairies of Fever, Ibrāhīm ʿAbdalmagīd's The Other Place, and Saʿūd al-Sanʿūsī's Bamboo Stalk." *Journal of Arabic and Islamic Studies*, Vol. 16, 85–98.

El-Enany, Rashid. 2006. *Arab Representations of the Occident. East–West Encounters in Arabic fiction.* New York: Routledge.

Fassin, Didier. 2011. *Humanitarian Reason: A Moral History of the Present.* Berkeley and Los Angeles: University of California Press.

Farrier, David. 2013. *Postcolonial Asylum: Seeking Sanctuary Before the Law.* Liverpool: Liverpool University Press.

Fischione, Fernanda. 2018. "Building a Homeland upon the Ruins of Literature: al-Bukā' 'alā al-aṭlāl by Ghālib Halasā as a Case Study." *Altre Modernità*, Vol. 2, 234–247.

Foucault, Michel. 1998 (1976); *The History of Sexuality, Vol. 1: The Will to Knowledge.* London: Penguin Modern Classics.

Gallien, Claire. 2018. "Forcing Displacement: The Postcolonial Interventions of Refugee Literature and Arts." *Journal of Postcolonial Writing: Special Issue on Refugee Literature*, Vol. 54, 6, 735–750.

Gatrell, Peter. 2020. "Refugees in Modern World History" in Cox, E., Durrant, Sam, Farrier, David, Stonebridge, Lyndsey, and Woolley Agnes (eds.). *Refugee Imaginaries: Research Across the Humanities.* Edinburgh: Edinburgh University Press Ltd, 18–35.

Graham, James, Michael Niblett, and Sharae Deckard. 2012. Special Issue "Postcolonial Studies and World Literature." *Postcolonial Studies*, Vol. 48, 5, 2012, 465–471.

118 *Annamaria Bianco*

Gunter, Michael. 2014. *Out of Nowhere: The Kurds of Syria in Peace and War*. London: Hurst & Company.

———. 2013. "The Kurdish Spring." *Third World Quarterly*. Vol. 34, 3, 441–457.

Günther, Sebastian, Milich, Stephan (eds.). 2016. *Representations and Visions of Homeland in Modern Arabic Literature*. Hildesheim: Olms Verlag.

Hamza, 'Arif. 2019. "Adab al-luju' aw al-manfa? Mawjat al-kitaba al-jadida ba'd al-rabi' al-'araby." *Aljazeera.net*, 5 November, www.aljazeera.net/news/cultureandart/ 2019/11/5/العراق-سوريا-المهجر-أدب-العربي-الربيع (last accessed July 6, 2021).

Husayn, Haytham. 2018. *Qad la yabqa ahad, aghatha kristy… ta'aly aqul laki kayfa a'iysh*. Damascus: Dar Mahmud 'Adwan lil-nashr wa-l-tawzi'.

Hussein, Abdullah Mezar. 2012. "Haitham Hussein: The Continuing Story of a Syrian Kurd Novelist." *Kurdistan Tribune*, December 1, https://kurdistantribune. com/haitham-hussein-continuing-story-of-syrian-kurd-novelist/ (last accessed April 1, 2021).

Hussein, Haitham. 2021. "The Syrian Novel: Enlightenment in the Face of Darkness. Writing against Tyranny in Assad's Syria." *Syria Untold*. February 23, https://syri auntold.com/2021/02/23/the-syrian-novel-enlightenment-in-the-face-of-darkness/ (last accessed July 6, 2021).

Hussein, Haitham, Qualey, Marcia Lynx, and Fares, Nicole. 2021. *No One May Remain. Agatha Christie, Come, I'll Tell You How I Live*. London: Dar Adab.

Jarmaqany, Rana. 2017. "Almanya … nahw hadina li-adab al-luju'." *Qantara.de*, 2 January, https://ar.qantara.de/content/ليست-اللاجئين-حكايات-اللجوء-أدب-ـل-حاضنة-نحو-ألمانيا آدابهم-ترجمة-عن-بديلًا (last accessed July 6, 2021).

Khachab, Walid El. 2010. "Sufis on Exile and Ghorba: Conceptualizing Displacement and Modern Subjectivity." *Comparative Studies of South Asia, Africa and the Middle East*, Vol. 30, 1, 58–68.

Kundera, Milan. 2003 (1986). *The Art of the Novel*. London and New York: Harper Perennial Modern Classics.

Lang, Felix. 2021. "Transformations of the 'Syrian' Literary Field Since 2011" in Ouaissa, Rachid, Pannewick, Friederike, and Alena Strohmaier (eds.), *Re-Configurations, Contextualising Transformation Processes and Lasting Crises in the Middle East and North Africa*, Wiesbaden: Springer VS, 261–275.

Lory, Pierre. 2011. "L'expatriation dans la pensée musulmane classique" in Avon, Dominique and Messaoudi, Alain (ed.), *De l'Atlas à l'Orient musulman: Contributions en hommage à Daniel Rivet*. Paris: Karthala, 201–204.

Mayblin, Lucy and Turner, Joe. 2020. *Migration Studies and Colonialism*. Cambridge: Polity Press.

Mémoire créative de la révolution syrienne. 2018. "Amouda." *Chroniques de la révolte syrienne: Des lieux et des hommes 2011–2015*, online at http://books.openedition. org/ifpo/12819.

Odoy, Mari. 2020. "On the 'Boom' of Syrian Literature in Berlin." *Arablit.com*, 30 September, https://arablit.org/2020/09/30/on-the-boom-of-syrian-literature-in-ber lin/ (last accessed July 6, 2021).

Qutait, Tasnim. 2020. "'All of Them Had Been Forgotten': Wasted Life as Literary Symbol in the Arab World" in Allon, Fiona, Barcan, Ruth, and Eddison-Cogan, Karma (ed.) *The Temporalities of Waste: Out of Sight, Out of Time*. New York: Routledge, 107–121.

Russell-Johnston, David. 2006. "The cultural situation of the Kurds, A report by Lord Russell-Johnston." *Council of Europe*, Retrieved on January 11, 2015, http://assem bly.coe.int/nw/xml/XRef/X2H-Xref-ViewHTML.asp?FileID=11316&lang=en (last accessed July 6, 2021).

Said, Edward. 2001. *Reflections On Exile and Other Literary and Cultural Essays.* New York: Granta Books.

Salih, Tayeb. 1969. Season of Migration to the North (D. Johnson-Davies, Trans.). London: Heinemann. (Original work published 1967)

al-Sallum, Muhammad. 2018. "Adab al-luju' al-sury: al-shatat wa-l-ta'bir al-adaby." *Harmoon Center for Contemporary Studies*, January 31, https://harmoon.org/wp-content/uploads/2018/01/Literature-of-Syrian-asylum-diaspora-and-literary-exp ression.pdf (last accessed July 6, 2021).

Saraçoğlu, Cenk. 2011. *Kurds of Modern Turkey: Migration, Neoliberalism and Exclusion in Turkish Society*. London: I.B. Tauris.

Sellman, Johanna B. 2013. *The Bio-Politics of Belonging: Europe in Post-Cold War Arabic Literature of Migration*. PhD Thesis. Austin: The University of Texas, online at: http://repositories.lib.utexas.edu/bitstream/handle/2152/21155/SELL MAN-DISSERTATION-2013.pdf?sequence=1 (last accessed April 1, 2021).

Shemak, April. 2011. *Asylum Speakers: Caribbean Refugees and Testimonial Discourse.* New York: Fordham University.

Siddiqui Mona, *Hospitality and Islam. Welcoming in God's Name*. New Haven and London: Yale University Press, 2015.

Shoukri, Arafat M. 2010. *Refugee Status in Islam: Concepts of Protection in Islamic Tradition and International Law*. London: Bloomsbury Publishing.

Stonebridge, Lisa. 2018. *Placeless People: Writings, Rights, and Refugees*. Oxford: Oxford University Press.

UNHCR. 2021a. "Figures at glance." *UNHCR Data Portal*, 18 June, www.unhcr.org/ figures-at-a-glance.html (last accessed July 6, 2021).

———. 2021b. "Refugee Situations: Demography of Mediterranean sea arrivals (2015)." *UNHCR Data Portal*, www.unhcr.org/figures-at-a-glance.html (last accessed April 1, 2021).

Yassin Hassan, Rosa. 2021. "What Did Exile Change in Our Narratives? Syrian Narratives in the Eyes of Others." *Syria Untold*, January 26, https://syriaunt old.com/2021/01/26/what-did-exile-change-in-our-narratives/ (last accessed July 6, 2021).

Part III
Religious Spaces of *Ghurba* and Belonging

6 *Ghurba* and the Emergence of a Gendered Pious Consciousness in Popular Religious Novels by Arab Women

Hawraa Al-Hassan

Background and Contextualization

This chapter argues that modern religious fiction by Shia Muslim women in the Arab world emerges directly as a result of the isolation and marginalization experienced by their communities during the decades of state-led nationalist secularization projects, especially those directed at women. In particular, didactic novels with an Islamic "flavor" produced in Iraq or by Iraqi women in diaspora, and consumed mainly in Lebanon and the Gulf, represent a political expression of *ghurba* in their attempts to build solidarity among believing female readers. In so doing, texts enact and shape a symbolic process whereby traditional religious spaces (the mosque, and in the case of Shia Islam, also the *husayniya*, a kind of religious community center) encroach into the public sphere as an indication of a growing popular religious consciousness. The texts included in this chapter are located at two ends of the history of modern secularism in Iraq. Amina al-Sadr, a female writer from a Shia clerical family, wrote the extremely popular *al-Fadila tantasir* (Virtue Prevails), which was published in 1969, at the zenith of the Ba'th Party's secular nationalist program of modernization, and Khawla al-Qazwini, a Kuwaiti author of mixed Iraqi and Kuwaiti origins, published her most famous novel *'Indama yufakkir al-rajul* (When a Man Thinks) in 1993, when religious discourses were ascendant in the Arab world, both by the state and its opponents. This chapter explores various iterations of *ghurba* in these two novels as the impetus for metaphorically expanding the religious space and overcoming the feeling of "not belonging" in one's own homeland.

The rise of Islam as a political force and a more visible social reality in the modern Arab world is the subject of complex historical and sociological enquiry. According to Gilbert Achcar, the third quarter of the twentieth century witnessed a shift from a hegemonic socialism, exemplified by Nasserism in Egypt, to what he termed the "Saudi Era" in the 1970s, where certain reactionary religious discourses were being supported by the United States as a result of cold war politics and the fear of the spread of communism (qtd. in al-Azmeh 2020, 1647). In Iraq, the ruling party, the Ba'th (1968–2003), crushed

DOI: 10.4324/9781003301776-10

124   *Hawraa Al-Hassan*

one of the largest communist parties in the Arab world, not through recourse to a religious discourse, however, but a nationalist one that accompanied state violence. Saddam Hussein's opportunistic and notorious "religious turn" would in fact come later, triggered by the Iranian Revolution of 1979 and the ensuing Iran/Iraq War, which lasted eight years (Bengio 1998, 190).

What its proponents termed the "sahwa" or religious awakening was experienced in diverse ways in communities across the Arab and Muslim world. For women, this often meant that outward signs of piety were adopted, such as the donning of the veil and other forms of traditional dress. Achcar notes that

> Veiled women had by the 1980s – Arabia excluded – come to be commonly regarded as an embarrassing anachronism in the broadest of social circles. In subsequent decades veiling gained social admissibility in most milieux and became indeed a token of conformist respectability.
> (qtd. in al-Azmeh 2020, 1649)

Pockets of religious communities, like Amina al-Sadr's family and the Shia clerical elite in Iraq, had by and large resisted some of the broad sweeping changes brought about by the secular state, such as the opening of state schools for girls. Amina herself was educated at home but convinced clerical authorities to fund her religious primary schools for girls, the first of their kind in Iraq (Wiley 2001, 154). For this community, deemed an embarrassment and publicly ridiculed for wearing the abaya for women and traditional robes and turbans for clerics, feelings of *ghurba* were acute.

The outward appearance of the "New Woman" in Iraq served as a visual signifier of progressiveness according to the Ba'th Party, whose publications for women featured western-style dress and hair in the 1960s and 1970s. According to Achim Rohde: "eroticised pictures of women highlighted contempt for religious sensibilities in the early days of the Ba'th" (2014, 76). Commenting on Iran's Shah Mohammed Reza Pahlavi's ban on the headscarf in 1936 as part of a broader plan to liberalize the country, Alex Shams writes that millions of conservative Iranian women were pushed into their homes and were practically barred from public spaces (2020). In Iraq, there was no outright ban on the hijab, but the donning of both the hijab and the abaya were explicitly discouraged by the General Federation of Iraqi Women, the female arm of the Ba'th Party (Helfont 2018, 60). This meant that women who dressed conservatively experienced the discomfort of out of place-ness in public spaces, and often opted to stay at home rather than compromise certain beliefs, such as gender segregation. This unease is often expressed as *ghurbat al-watan* (feeling out of place in one's own homeland), an expression that is often used in popular Arab culture and discourse but is given a moral dimension by pious female authors in Iraq. Religious fiction by Shia Muslim women suggests that, by imitating western values and norms in dress and social interactions, Arab countries have become unrecognizable by their

Ghurba *in Popular Religious Novels* 125

own native inhabitants. The result is a devastating kind of alienation that can only be countered, according to both Amina al-Sadr and Khawla al-Qazwini, through an active presence of devout men in the public space, and to a much lesser extent women, who are seen as less immune to the onslaught of western style modernization. In Shia Islam, being a *gharib* or an outsider/stranger acquires a deeper significance and has an almost sacred quality, as it is associated with the third imam in Shi'ism, al-Husayn ibn Ali, grandson of the Prophet Muhammad. Betrayed and killed in the foreign land of Karbala in 680 AD, al-Husayn's story is the ultimate personification of *ghurba*. As such, a character identified as a *gharib* would elicit intense sympathy and would resonate with Shia audiences at a subconscious level. Interestingly, novels written by female Shia authors in the Arab world, including the two novels examined in this chapter, rarely expressed any sect-based identity due to a combination of factors, including fear of state censorship, but most likely because it made no sense to privilege sect-based affiliation at a time when Islam as a whole was perceived to be under threat. However, the texts remain infused with a sense of nobility in isolation that gains more significance when situated within the context of a broader Shia religious consciousness.

The discursive battle over the identity of the public space at the height of Iraq's secular state project in the 1960s and 1970s was transposed onto the realm of cultural production. The novel has long been deemed a secular genre by literary historians, intimately linked to the rise of various modernizing processes, such as the development of printing presses and the formation of nationalist ideologies (Anderson 1983, 24). Whether the novel (or any genre for that matter) is inherently secular or otherwise when extricated from the material processes from which it is produced is important, because although secular in its genesis, the novel has expanded to include Islamic religious sensibilities in the Arab world. The emergence of a literate public was an instrumental factor in the emergence of fictional book production in the Arab world generally, and in Iraq specifically. The religious novel spearheaded by female writers was an unintentional result of the Ba'th's almost total eradication of illiteracy amongst women in Iraq by the beginning of the 1980s, a campaign aimed at better mobilizing women in the workforce (first in support of the Ba'th's national socialist ideology and later in its war effort), rather than empowering them for their own sake (Rohde 2014, 13). That the genre should be espoused by women first is, therefore, not coincidental. Reading is a solitary activity in comparison to poetry and other forms of traditional Arab storytelling. Individual rather than community centered, reading was thereby perceived as individualistic in outlook. Female religious authors expressed a fear of this furtive pleasure indulged in by teenage girls who were cutting their teeth on publications that were available to readers for the first time in Arab literary history: translated popular romances and foreign crime fiction, as well as lifestyle magazines specifically tailored towards women, often produced by the state itself. This deluge of written materials represented to religious authors an invasion of young minds and an assault on family values. They

126   *Hawraa Al-Hassan*

considered the new generation of women and young girls as gatekeepers of public morality; at once the ficklest members of society and the most impactful, which is why it was crucial to win them over to the Islamic cause (Al-Hassan 2020, 109).

Amina al-Sadr and the First Religious Novel

The politicization of religious spaces as potential hotbeds of dissent came to a head in 1977, when Saddam Hussein denied Shia faithful their visitation rights to the graves of al-Husayn ibn Ali and his companions in Karbala, which escalated into the Shia Uprising in the month of Safar (the second month of the lunar calendar). This galvanized the novelist and activist Amina al-Sadr (1937–1980), known by her penname Bint al-Huda (the daughter of righteous guidance), along with her brother Ayatollah Muhammad Baqir al-Sadr, and ultimately led to their arrest, torture, and execution. Al-Sadr is credited as the first writer of religious novels in Iraq, and her influence on a generation of pious female writers both within and outside Iraq is considerable. As mentioned previously, she came from a family of clerics and was home-schooled her entire life. When she came of age, al-Sadr wrote sermon style didactic tracts and short articles for *al-Adwa* (The Lights), a religious publication supported by Shia clergy. Al-Sadr anticipated the growing popularity of the novel and feared its potential to corrupt the minds of the young, particularly young women, and thus began writing a series of didactic novels in the late 1960s, which she believed would provide an antidote to translations of trashy popular romances from the West and local narrative production which she deemed equally corruptive. Her first and most popular novel, *al-Fadila tantasir* (Virtue Prevails), was published in 1969 and is a domestic drama detailing the clash between the value systems of two female cousins: Naqa (purity) and Suad (lucky or happy) who represent virtue and vice respectively, with the former ultimately triumphing. Naqa is represented as ultimately immune to the onslaught of foreign ideas voiced by Suad and even succeeds in reforming Suad's wayward husband Mahmud, taking him "from darkness to light" (Bint al-Huda 1980, 210), an expression lifted directly from the Quran.[1] In many ways, the novel expresses a struggle between competing versions of womanhood, on the one hand the "New Woman" envisioned by the Ba'th to be liberal and loyal, and on the other, traditional but quietly revolutionary.

The novel begins in the living room of Naqa's home where her cousin has come to visit; she is 16, engaged to be married to an upright man from a good family named Ibrahim and Suad has come to congratulate her. However, tensions arise when Suad begins to attack Naqa's life choices: who she is marrying, her lack of desire to learn to drive or to go to university (she enrolls in a vocational college for women to learn sewing instead), and most of all, the fact that she rarely leaves the house or socializes normally: "and is this pathetic lifestyle you love and the isolation you have imposed on yourself part

Ghurba *in Popular Religious Novels*   127

of your personal faith?" Naqa is mild tempered and replies good naturedly that she has her own society of "innocent relationships and pure friendships" in a politely veiled critique of the kind of company her cousin keeps (39). Suad responds by exclaiming: "What is [this] society? Why can't we see them publicly, these millions, who share your views?" (Bint al-Huda 1980, 45). Naqa's social group is not visible to Suad because the circles which the latter operates in are public ones; she is rarely in the home and spends her days in beauty salons and mixed swimming pools and her nights in clubs, bars and parties. Suad confidently expresses the voice of authority and the majority of Iraq's Muslim citizens, be they Shia or Sunni, when she admonishes Naqa's isolationism. This is because, as Aziz al-Azmeh notes, before the mid-seventies: "religious culture and its authority were concealed in pockets of society and secular culture prevailed publicly" (2020, 1891). What the novel ultimately shows us is that all but a small minority of Iraqi society experienced and participated in a secular public culture. Naqa's cousin Suad is also presumably Shia by social identity, even if she is not a practicing Muslim. Her integration into the new modern society encouraged by the Ba'thist state in Iraq and its vision of an ideal New Woman to symbolize it is indicative of the prevalence of secular culture and the resulting feelings of alienation by religious women in the public space.

Connecting feelings of *ghurba* in one's homeland to ideology, and in particular to religion, results in a spatial expansion in the worldview of the text and the formation of bonds beyond national borders. *Ghurba* is essential for the religious awakening of individuals in the texts; it isolates the individual both emotionally and physically from what she deems a morally bankrupt and corrupt society. In *Virtue Prevails*, Naqa refuses to attend Suad's mixed birthday party and does not frequent the salons, cinemas, public pools or clubs her cousin visits, nor attends the mixed parties she holds in her home. The fear of contamination due to physical proximity to places or people of sin is a recurring theme in religious novels, as space and individuals are not considered separate entities. This is taken to extremes when Ibrahim asks Naqa to tear a picture of herself and Suad, thereby symbolically severing the links between the two cousins.

In religious novels, spaces acquire a life of their own, a spirit and identity that either support or hinder individual growth. They are not neutral spaces, rather they are colored or shaped by the actions and behaviors of human beings; places like bars and clubs are deemed inherently sinful and according to religious authors, have been deliberately and intentionally established and supported by the state to corrupt the youth. With the extension of religious spaces metaphorically into the public space in Bint al-Huda's work comes a specific framework through which the world is understood. This framework has its own rules regarding dress and comportment, for example, as well as spatial limitations according to what it considers permissible in terms of gender mixing, but it also envisions an expansive collective imaginary by connecting believers beyond national borders. As a domestic drama, *Virtue*

128   *Hawraa Al-Hassan*

Prevails is local in outlook; however, in her short story collection *Laytani Kuntu A'lam* (*If Only I Had Known*), published in 1977, the author expresses solidarity with Palestinian freedom fighters in the short story "The Last Gift," written from the perspective of a wife awaiting the return of her husband from the battlefield (Bint al-Huda 1977, 33–37). Like *Virtue Prevails*, there are designated roles deemed fit for the members of each sex, with women ideally residing in the marital home raising righteous children, and men being successful propagators of Islamic values in the profession of their choice and supporting their families financially, or in the case of the Palestinian husband in "The Last Gift," as martyrs for faith and homeland.

In the same way that the boundaries between mosque and street are rendered ambiguous, local color is also bled out of didactic texts written by religious women in Iraq, rendering them unidentifiable in terms of location. Ambiguity of spatial context was deemed key to avoid government censorship but was also used to elevate texts to parable status in line with the conventions of religious genres. Ba'thism is an Arab nationalist socialist ideology that inspired the formation of political parties carrying its name. These parties ruled Iraq and Syria, making the Iraqi and Syrian contexts similar enough to be used interchangeably by Bint al-Huda in *Virtue Prevails*. For example, the narrator mentions the Ummayyad Mosque in Damascus in passing as a signal to censors, perhaps, that this novel is not set in Iraq and therefore not politically threatening. Moreover, modern standard Arabic rather than dialect is used in order to further obfuscate the geographical context. In a key episode in the novel, and one of the very few instances where the protagonist ventures outside the home, Naqa visits the conveniently named "Park of the Republic." She takes the letters sent by her fiancé and a novel by Victor Hugo to read in order to remain in a state of meditative isolation in public and in order to not attract the attention of the opposite sex. At this moment, Naqa is accosted by Mahmud, Suad's husband, who is tricked by his wife into believing that she is a woman of outward piety who is easily seduced. Suad deliberately wants to see Naqa's fall from grace as a form of revenge against Ibrahim, who had previously rejected her advances. However, Naqa transforms the Park of the Republic, a space maintained by and named after the secular state (Bint al-Huda 1980, 145), into a site of making *da'wa* (literally meaning to invite people to the word of God). Although there was a public blackout on the use of the word due to its association with the name of the largest Shia opposition party in Iraq (Hizb al-Da'wa, established in 1957), it would have been clear to the reader that Naqa was engaging in *da'wa*; countering the seductive advances of her cousin's husband Mahmud by inviting him to mend his wayward ways and hedonistic lifestyle, and replace it with a religious one. Naqa recommends books and presents arguments against a worldview that puts pleasure and money before principles. "She felt that she had something to say (to him) before she left … to make him understand that the daughters of Islam were not seduced by money" (Bint al-Huda 1980, 129–130).

Ghurba *in Popular Religious Novels*   129

Naqa extends the teachings of the mosque into the public space through her comportment as well as her dress. An example of how the religious spirit of forgiveness, trustworthiness and generosity is diffused through the public space is the earring incident in the park. Naqa drops a diamond earring, and it is stolen by a beggar woman she had just given money moments before. When Mahmoud exposes the thief in order to win Naqa over, she instead gives the beggar woman the other earring in order to spare her embarrassment and says that she had actually gifted them to her. This episode has two narrative purposes: it has a transformative effect on Mahmud and becomes a catalyst for change in him, leading to repentance and reform. He later tells Naqa:

> I saw you give up your diamond earrings out of mercy and goodness so that you would not expose a poor beggar woman. Since that day, there has been no doubt in my mind that you are a pure angel in human form.
>
> (Bint al-Huda 1980, 143–148)

Indeed, the second function of the episode is to re-emphasize the symbolic role of Naqa as a kind of walking mosque and personification of religious ideals.

Naqa is not a well-rounded character, but a symbol and an ideal to be emulated. Maintaining her faultlessness is often at the expense of the author's claims of realism which, as she states in the prologue to the text, was the main reason behind writing *Virtue Prevails*:

> I am not a novelist or story writer; I have never tried before this to write a story. Rather, what I present to you ... is merely one of many pictures of the society in which we live, and an example from real life.
>
> (Bint al-Huda 1980, 7)

If the author's intention is to achieve *waqi'iiya*, then her moralistic outlook makes this unrealistic, as the coherence of plot and characterization in the novel are sometimes sacrificed for ideological purposes. For example, on Naqa's first visit to the park, when she is accosted by Mahmud, she was accompanied by her father but walks alone to one side while her father speaks to his friends out of modesty and maintaining gender segregation in public (Bint al-Huda 1980, 145–146). That she should meet Mahmud in the presence of a male guardian and have extended conversations with him without her father noticing seems to be implausible. Naqa's guilt at speaking with a man who is not a blood relative without her fiancé's knowledge may explain the author's eagerness to provide loopholes justifying Naqa's behavior and ensuring that she is beyond reproach.

Ghurba is an isolating and lonely experience, but in religious novels it galvanizes individuals into social and political activism and resistance while engaging in alternate forms of community building beyond state imperatives and structures. According to Joyce Wiley, Bint al-Huda's voice was one of

130 *Hawraa Al-Hassan*

moderation for her time, striking a balance between the erroneous practices attributed to Islam by reactionary currents in Iraqi society, and the complete westernization advocated by the ba'thist state (Wiley 2001, 54). Moreover, she actively encouraged the economic betterment of women, especially working-class women, by supporting projects to teach handicrafts and other skills to help uneducated women achieve financial independence. For all her extolling of the values of marriage and staying at home for women, Bint al-Huda herself never married and worked to gain the support of the religious establishment to allow girls from conservative families to attend state schools. Seen from this perspective, "the confinement of almost all Bint al-Huda's fictional characters to the home seems to be a symbol of the isolation of conservative Shia communities from the wider, more secularized Iraqi society, rather than an explicit command not to work or study" (Al-Hassan 2020, 125). The question of whether or not the narrator's voice is distinct from the author's perspective in religious novels is further complexified when female characters are used as symbols in proxy discussions about morality and ideology in a political environment stifled by censorship. According to Zahra al-Ali, "Shia Islamicization with its gender norms (hijab and sexual morality) and religious rituals (Arba'in, 'Ashura) became tools to resist the Ba'th" (2018, 83). What ultimately emerges from even the seemingly most reactionary of religiously inspired texts is that the female voice is an assured one, and that devout female authors did not allow themselves to be marginalized in spite of and due to their chastity and modesty.

Both texts included in this chapter exhibit an overflow of religiosity that blurs the boundaries between private religious practice and public life which had been established in Iraq and other Arab nation states. This explains the rarity in which religious spaces appear; instead of providing containment for devout characters, places of worship metaphorically dissolve into the universities, streets and parks of the imagined world of the texts, where every space can be transformed into a religious one, so long as it is inhabited by those who are faithful to the cause. Early religious novels like *Virtue Prevails* show that the good Muslim can transform spaces and people. The home, for example, becomes a sacred sanctuary that protects individuals, especially women, from the onslaught of foreign ideas. It is a microcosm of the mosque, or the *husayniya* with its forbidden public rituals that are disdained and ridiculed for being old-fashioned. These physical boundaries are all means of protecting devout women especially and preventing them from unnecessary engagement with a corrupt world. As gatekeepers of public morality, the job of devout women is to protect themselves and the family unit from the secularizing forces of the state by building an imaginary fortress around the home. However, emboldened by an increase in religiosity, devout men and women emerge as more active participants in public life, including the cultural and political scene in Iraq. By writing novels, albeit under pseudonym, the home-schooled and unmarried Amina al-Sadr set a precedent for religious women that it was not only acceptable, but also admirable to write fiction. However,

Ghurba *in Popular Religious Novels* 131

al-Sadr's arrest, torture and execution for her political activities sent shock waves in the Shia community as the violation of the female body in such a way ensured that no other female figure from within the religious establishment ever emerged under Saddam Hussein's rule to take on her mobilizing role for the betterment of the lives of devout women.

Ghurba and Political Freedom in Khawla al-Qazwini's *When a Man Thinks*

Lack of political freedom and stifling oppression are directly connected to the protagonist's feelings of *ghurba* in Khawla al-Qazwini's (1955–) *'Indama yufakkir al-rajul* (When a Man Thinks), which was set in the 1980s and banned in Kuwait when it was first published in 1993. Claiming direct inspiration from Bint al-Huda, al-Qazwini, a Kuwaiti author of mixed Iraqi and Kuwaiti origins before borders between the two countries were fully demarcated, wrote at the peak of the ascendancy of political Islam and remains the most well-known of contemporary female religious authors. For the protagonist of her novel, Muhammad, a politically active university student, the inability to mobilize others politically due to government restraints (rather than just the day-to-day challenges of being a practicing Muslim) are at the heart of his feelings of *ghurba*. The novel emphasizes that personal and political corruption are two sides of the same coin and advocates for a committed political Islam as the only ideology capable of adequately addressing the perceived ills of society.

As with other religious novels by Arab women, Khawla al-Qazwini does not locate the novel in a specific locale in order to elevate the story to a level of parable. It is more expansive in its outlook than *Virtue Prevails*, perhaps owing to it being written after the Shia intifada in 1991, which was brutally crushed by the state and led to the mass exodus of Iraqis of all backgrounds and the gradual formation of Iraqi diaspora communities abroad. Muhammad also leaves his country to escape political oppression and threats to his life: "His road was full of spikes, full of boulders ... alone, with a sickle in his hand, trying to find a way through all these obstacles, transforming the path into a path of flowers and sweet-smelling herbs" (Al-Qazwini 1993, 18). Like his namesake the Prophet of Islam, the protagonist of *When a Man Thinks* (no surname to emphasize that he is merely "a" Muhammad among others) lost his father at a young age and is inclined towards solitude. He is also a loving brother and a humble and obedient son, sacrificing his own happiness to please his elderly mother by marrying the bride she has chosen for him: his incompatible cousin Manal.

The stage is set for the novel's central conflict in the opening chapter, which starts at a university in an unknown Arab country, and where a student named Ali, a budding poet and friend of the protagonist Muhammad, has just been expelled after publishing a scathing critique of the university's policies. In his article, Ali describes the university management as wild wolves preying on the students, whom he describes as frail lambs. The reasons behind

132 *Hawraa Al-Hassan*

Ali's discontent are ambiguous, but it seems that they are political in nature. He decides to leave the country to study in Cairo and pursue his political activities in relative freedom, but is worried about being alone, of feeling the weight of *ghurba* on him. Muhammad suggests that his sister Fatima would make Ali the perfect wife and would be able to support him through all the difficulties he may face abroad (26). When his mother objects to Ali being still a student with no financial means to support himself or her daughter, Muhammad insists that "in his *ghurba*, he [Ali] will need a wife to find peace and comfort with" (Al-Qazwini 1993, 29). What Muhammad calls "an ugly compromise" (Al-Qazwini 1993, 43) is then made whereby he agrees to marry the bride chosen by his mother, his maternal cousin Manal, in exchange for his mother's permission for Ali and Fatima's marriage. Manal is depicted as shallow, materialistic and almost completely incompatible with Muhammad. She forms a sharp contrast to Fatima, who is represented in the most positive terms as a self-sacrificing, humble and pious wife, dedicated to "the cause," an ambiguous term used in a large number of Shia religious works of fiction. The goals of the Islamic movement are never explicitly stated in *When a Man Thinks*, perhaps to avoid political controversy and to maintain focus on themes that would be more attractive to young girls, such as marital problems.

The conflation of Woman and nation is not unique to the Arab literary and cultural context. In her seminal book *Gender and Nation*, Nira Yuval-Davis notes that "gendered bodies and sexuality play pivotal roles as territories, markers and reproducers of the narratives of the nation and other collectivities" (2008, 39). In *When a Man Thinks* and other religious texts, a pious woman, and by extension the family which she carries literally and figuratively, functions as a sanctuary in the midst of *ghurba*. An uncommitted wife, on the other hand, heightens a protagonist's *ghurba* even if he does not leave his home country. An aspiring journalist, Muhammad accepts a job at a local newspaper in order to support his new family (and especially, to meet the financial needs of his demanding wife Manal), despite having radically different political opinions to its editors. Clashes over editorial policy and journalistic freedom snowball into a fully fledged conspiracy to discredit him and the Islamic inspired movement to which he belongs. He is sent to Russia to cover a story accompanied by a female secretary Suzanne, who is charged with seducing him, but instead of acquiescing, Muhammad rebuffs and attacks her for the way she dresses and behaves, saying that she is wrong to sexualize herself in order to please men. Because women function symbolically in religious novels, female characters show very little psychological complexity and are either extolled or completely demonized as if they only embody the polarized ideas they are meant to represent. Suzanne represents a type of *ghurba* that emanates from the West *gharb*; she is divorced from the supposedly authentic values of tradition, and her feelings of alienation push her to suicide. Interestingly, Manal is not overtly westernized in appearance like Suzanne, but nonetheless represents an intellectual *ghurba* in the form of

Ghurba *in Popular Religious Novels*   133

an assimilated petty capitalism, far more insidious than the *ghurba* represented by Suzanne. She is preoccupied with the material symbols of wealth and prestige and expects her husband to constantly shower her with expensive gifts. When Muhammad is blamed for Suzanne's suicide and rumors are spread by unknown enemies affirming that the two were in a relationship, Manal refuses to support her husband and, when he is later imprisoned and tortured for his political activities, she divorces him and takes his son.

Because the geographical plane of *When a Man Thinks* covers both East and West, *ghurba* represents a place and a sentiment, unlike in *Virtue Prevails* where the action of the novel is localized. Naqa is the only main character who has not visited the West in the latter text, and her fiancé Ibrahim who travels abroad often tells her: "if Europe was a pure place with a genuine, authentic culture I would have taken you there." Whereas in earlier religious novels, the West appears as a monolithic source of pollution, of "poisonous germs," as Ibrahim describes it (Bint al-Huda 1969, 29), in *When a Man Thinks*, it is a potential sanctuary that allows for the formation of supranationalist bonds and the actualization of an ideal Muslim *umma*. Following his release from prison, Muhammad is stripped of his citizenship and leaves for the United Kingdom to work for a London based Islamic newspaper. He meets Kawthar, a devout and politically engaged Palestinian researcher and marries her, but their happiness doesn't last long as he is assassinated in a Paris hotel by unknown gunmen while on a conference trip. The prospect that one's *ghurba* can provide respite from political oppression is thus shattered, but the novel ends on a hopeful note as Kawthar, now a pregnant widow, exclaims: "They killed Muhammad, but in his place, there are a thousand Muhammads!" (Al-Qazwini 1993, 392).

While on his ill-fated trip to Russia, Muhammad visits a Russian Muslim community and notes how the women all wear the hijab. He turns to Suzanne and adds: "while western women have begun to become more chaste and to dress modestly, Muslim women have begun to do the opposite and to dress provocatively" (Al-Qazwini 1993, 188). The idea that the Arab world is a land of Muslims without Islam, and that the West is a space where the values of Islam flourish and are implemented without Muslims has become a standard trope of encounter narratives since it was introduced by Muhammad 'Abdu on his visit to Paris in 1881. However, in *When a Man Thinks*, positive depictions of the West as a sanctuary from one's homeland and its unrelenting westernization and political oppression are undercut by a pervading sense of conspiracy and paranoia, of being watched by the intelligence services of unnamed countries for the crime of merely being devout. Although banned in Kuwait when it was first published for its political content, *When a Man Thinks* is strangely ambiguous concerning what the actual political activities of Muhammad and his friends are; there is no mention of political parties or ideological affiliation beyond the very broad allegiance to Islam. Muhammad also laments the fact that the West is the primary beneficiary of the flight of human capital from the Arab world and writes an essay entitled "the Arab

134 *Hawraa Al-Hassan*

Brain Drain to the West." Depicted as a sanctuary in spite of its role in destabilizing Muslim societies abroad, the novel sees the potential of the West as a homeland for Muslim communities where they are free from social pressures and government censorship. Complex depictions like al-Qazwini's in *When a Man Thinks* form a marked contrast to representations of the West that are found in earlier religious novels and pave the way for more positive views of the West as a space of growth and community in her later works, notably her novel *Mudhakarat Mughtariba* (1995), or *Memoirs of a Student Abroad*. In this novel, a gifted religious teenager is sent to the United States to study on a scholarship program and experiences immense emotional, spiritual and intellectual growth; she engages in debates with students of all faiths (and none) and even falls in love with a widowed Lebanese man, even though she is not permitted to marry him by her family back home.

Etymologically and historically, the concept of *ghurba* is inextricable from associations with the West, *gharb*. As a feeling, it connotes strangeness and outside-ness, similar, but not identical to the French *depayesment*. However, increased contact and encounters with Europe, as well as migratory movements from the Arab world westwards, have meant that *ghurba* acquired a spatial meaning and being a *mughtarib* (someone who lives outside the homeland) is sometimes treated as a type of identity. The two meanings, one emotive and the other physical, are now equated despite the broader connotations of homesickness that the term has now acquired regardless of geography. Oxymorons like *ghurbat al-dar* (out of place-ness in one's home) and *ghurbat al-ahil* (isolation amidst one's family/people) fuse the two meanings of *ghurba*: isolation as a result of foreignness and alienation as a result of not belonging. Ultimately, not only does the implementation of western values bring the *gharb* (and hence *ghurba*) to the Arab world, but generational clashes also heighten an individual's sense of alienation, like the dilemma Muhammad experiences when his mother pressures him to marry his incompatible cousin, thereby placing filial reverence and duty to one's parents at the expense of one's own happiness.

Conclusion

Modern literary criticism in the post-structuralist vein has long declared the "Death of the Author" (Barthes 1967) with the inception of her text, dismissing literary analyses that view works as "reflections" of their creators. The relationship between author and text is certainly psychologically and creatively complex; however, in the case of the didactic novels in this chapter, the explicit claims of their authors as to the ideological function of their characters and the raison d'être of their texts are crucial considerations if we are to understand the ways in which *ghurba* functions in religious fiction by women. The two texts analyzed in this chapter are the most well-known and popular examples of religious fiction by Shia women; by 1980, the year of her execution by the Ba'th, Amina al-Sadr's *Virtue Prevails* was already in its sixth

Ghurba *in Popular Religious Novels* 135

edition, and its popularity continued at least to the end of the twentieth century. As for al-Qazwini's *When a Man Thinks*, despite its initial ban in Kuwait where the author resides, it has now been reprinted three times, the last of which was in 2009. Both texts were often the first point of exposure to novel reading for generations of Shia girls and women. Moreover, they represented "vehicles through which Arab Shia women were able to bond together and establish a common foundation of cultural references and moral values that went beyond geographic borders" (Al-Hassan 2020, 144).

Ghurba is a key means of expressing the alienation felt by religious authors and by extension their characters; it fuels a desire to create a counter public that could claim ownership of the public spaces from which they were often excluded. Alienated individuals in religious texts are galvanized into action and attempt to enact change upon their environment, their social and religious obligations extending beyond the mosque. Despite being primarily homebound and gender segregated, female characters function as religious guides for other women, and sometimes even for men. Devout male characters, on the other hand, are predictably depicted as politically active and self-sacrificing. The inverse relationship between *ghurba* and the ascendancy of a more religiously laden discourse has meant that the sense of alienation in earlier novels by pious authors written or set in the seventies and eighties is decidedly stronger than in the ones produced in the late nineties and beyond. Feeling that their traditional values were under threat by the rise of secular Arab states, the discourse of clerics and religious elites reveals heightened levels of anxiety and hypervigilance, but also a sense of defiance and revolutionary zeal towards establishing a set of (Islamic) values which they believed society should ideally follow.

The deep sense of *ghurba* felt by religious protagonists in novels written before the high tide of the religious revival or *sahwa* in the Arab world is driven by an anxiety rooted in a fear of marginalization, of being outnumbered and alien, and of a way of life being eroded. In the case of Shia Islam where there exists a clerical class, there is the additional fear that sacred knowledge could potentially be lost, or that the task of educating the young might be wrested from the hands of religious men and their institutions. In this context, women function as both symbols and guardians of a way of life that is perceived to be under threat and deliberately targeted by the intense secularizing policies of Iraq and other Arab states in over three decades from the 1950s to the 1970s. For this reason, the tone of religious novels is perhaps expectedly solemn and grave, but never hopeless, as there is an awareness that the tide is turning in favor of political Islam. In *When a Man Thinks*, Muhammad receives a letter from his brother-in-law Ali, where he narrates an incident that took place at his university in Egypt. A female student had been physically forced to remove her niqab by the dean of his university, but the male students came to her rescue and beat him, then held demonstrations in the university to protest the discrimination faced by pious women. This episode encapsulates the heart of discourses in religious fiction: the conflation of morality and outward signs

136 *Hawraa Al-Hassan*

of piety, the debate surrounding who has the right to inhabit the public space and in what manner, and the symbolic use of women as political statements. It also points to a religious consciousness and solidarity that is inclusive, rather than centered on sect (Shia Muslim women rarely wear the niqab) and thus privileges affiliation to Islam over its smaller derivative identities.

Ultimately, I would argue that *ghurba* is impossible to understand in the context of religious fiction in Iraq without considering the role of women as signifiers of the nation, as mobile homelands that defy the spatial constraints of geography and locale. Moreover, women inhabit the discursive frontlines of nation and religion, blurring the boundaries between private and public spaces. Religious novels by Arab women highlight the transformative power of women to diffuse a religious consciousness beyond the traditional spaces of the home and mosque in order to combat the sense of *ghurba* experienced by devout characters in a hostile secular world. What is sacrificed, however, in the endeavor to combat *ghurba* in Islamic religious fiction is artistic nuance and ambiguity. The lack of plot coherence and psychological depth of characters did not hinder the popularity of the novels for the politically engaged readers of the Shia *sahwa* after the Iranian revolution of 1979, but it is a popularity that is unlikely to be sustained. Nowadays, Shia religious novels are rarely published, in part due to the quality of competing literary texts produced during the boom in the Arabic novel in the last 20 years but also due to the weakening (if not collapse) of the ideological framework that made earlier audiences so receptive to their messages.

Note

1 All translations of the texts are my own.

References

Al-Ali, Nadje Sadig. 2007. *Iraqi Women: Untold Stories from 1948 to the Present.* London: Zed Books.

Al-Ali, Nadje Sadig. 2005. "Reconstructing Gender: Iraqi Women between Dictatorship, War, Sanctions and Occupation," *Third World Quarterly* 26(4/5) (2005): 739–758.

Al-Azmeh, Aziz. 2020. *Secularism in the Arab World: Contexts, Ideas and Consequences.* Edinburgh: Edinburgh University Press.

Al-Hassan, Hawraa. 2020. *Women, Writing and the Iraqi Ba'thist State: Contending Discourses of Resistance and Collaboration (1968–2003).* Edinburgh: Edinburgh University Press.

Al-Hassan Golley, Nawar (ed). 2007. *Arab Women's Lives Retold: Exploring Identity through Writing.* Syracuse, NY: Syracuse University Press.

Ali, Zahra. 2018. *Women and Gender in Iraq: Between Nation-building and Fragmentation.* Cambridge: Cambridge University Press.

Al-Qazwini, Khawla. 1993.*'Indama yufakkir al-rajul.* Bayrut: dar al-ṣafwa.

Al-Qazwini, Khawla. 2006. *Mudhakkarat mughtariba.* Bayrut: dar al-ṣafwa.

Ghurba *in Popular Religious Novels* 137

Anderson, Benedict. 1991. *Imagined Communities*. London: Verso.

Ashour, Radwa, Ferial Ghazoul and Hasna Reda-Mekdashi (eds). 2008. *Arab Women Writers: a Critical Reference Guide 1873–1999*. New York: American University in Cairo.

Barthes, Roland. 1979. "From Work to Text" in Harari, Josué V. (ed.) *Textual Strategies: Perspectives in Post-Structuralist Criticism*. Ithaca, NY: Cornell University Press. 72–83.

Barthes, Roland.1977. "The Death of the Author" in *Image, Music, Text*. New York: Hill and Wang. 142–148.

Bengio. Ofra. 1998. *Saddam's Word: Political Discourse in Iraq*. Oxford: Oxford University Press.

Bint al-Huda. 1980. *Al-Fadila tantaṣir*. Bayrut: Dar al-taʿaruf.

Cooke, Miriam. 2001. *Women Claim Islam: Creating Islamic Feminism Through Literature*. New York: Routledge.

Hafez, Sabry. 2015. "Islam in Arabic Literature: the Struggle for Symbolic Power" in Abir Hamdar and Lindsey Moore (eds.) *Islamism and Cultural Expression in the Arab World.* London: Routledge. 31–59.

Helfont, Samuel. 2018. *Compulsion in Religion: Saddam Hussein, Islam and the Roots of Insurgencies in Iraq.* New York: Oxford University Press.

Rohde, Achim. 2014. *State–Society Relations in Baʿthist Iraq: Facing Dictatorship.* London: Routledge.

Shabout, Nada. 2010. "Images and Status: Visualising Iraqi Women" in Faegheh Shirazi (ed.) *Muslim Women in War and Crisis: Representation and Reality*. Austin, TX: University of Texas Press. 149–164.

Shams, Alex. 2019. "If Not for the Revolution: How Higher Education Became an 'Islamic Right' for Religious Iranian Women" in Goli M. Rezai-Rashti, Golnar Mehran and Shirin Abdmolaei (eds.) *Women, Islam and Education in Iran.* New York: Routledge. 103–121.

Wedeen, Lisa. 1999. *Ambiguities of Domination: Politics, Rhetoric and Symbols in Contemporary Syria*. Chicago, IL: Chicago University Press.

Wiley, Joyce. 2001. "Alima Bint al-Huda, Women's Advocate" in Walbridge, Linda S. (ed.) *The Most Learned of the Shia: The Institution of Marja Taqlid.* New York: Oxford University Press. 149–160.

Yuval-Davis, Nira, 1997. *Gender and Nation*. London: Sage.

7 Can the Qazani Speak?

Nineteenth Century Naqshbandi Migrants and Translators in Mecca during the Age of Print

Mariam Elashmawy

Shadows of great men fall across the pages of Naqshbandi literature, recurring time and again in their discursive heritage. These "ideal-heros" of Sufi *tariqa*s are the medium through which the history of mystical Islam is narrated. Over the very same pages of such a history, another meager shadow casts its outline along the page, a silhouette often obscured by the towering figures in historiography. Thus, a more thorough examination of the men in history whose intellectual labor and aspirations brought to us the texts and stories of the Naqshbandi heritage is due. The parables, histories, and teachings of the great Sufi masters would not have taken root within the collective memory of Sufi networks had it not been for the innumerable obscure disciples, editors, and translators. Such "inconsequential" men had operated along the outskirts of the Muslim world, or often, within the very heart of it, recognizing the call for maintaining and circulating the Naqshbandi tradition in spirit, and in print.

This chapter looks at how Sufi networks traversed spatial and temporal nodal points through the life and works of Muhammad Murad al-Qazani (d. 1352/1935). Al-Qazani, an immigrant and scholar from the Volga-Ural region, translated two seminal Naqshbandi books for publishing during the late nineteenth and early twentieth centuries: *Rashahat 'ayn al-hayat* (Beads of Dew from the Fountain of Life, 1886), and *Maktubat Imam al-Rabbani Ahmad al-Sirhindi* (The Letters and Correspondences of Ahmad al-Sirhindi, 1889) in Mecca. I particularly examine the printing and translation history of *Rashahat 'ayn al-hayat* by Fakhr al-Din 'Ali (d. 940/1533), a volume on the biographies of the Naqshbandiyya masters of Timurid Iran. Translated from Persian into Turkish, Arabic, Uzbek, and Urdu, the *Rashahat* experienced a multilingual journey through the publishing houses of the Islamicate world. Throughout the chapter, I demonstrate the role of diasporic Sufi networks in Mecca through the story of al-Qazani's migration to the Hijaz, and show how Sufi brotherhoods contributed to the development of print culture through transregional networks in the region. During al-Qazani's time in Mecca, he experienced episodes of psychological turmoil and homesickness. Hence, I examine how migrant Sufi spaces of religious learning and the publishing scene became a source of solace for al-Qazani during his emotional plight.

DOI: 10.4324/9781003301776-11

I do that by examining his relationship with the text that both joined him with his Sufi brethren and served as his companion during the death of his master and bouts of loneliness. The chapter thus argues that (i) al-Qazani's efforts were central in disseminating Arabic translations of the *tariqa*'s texts in the modern period; (ii) some interventions of al-Qazani into the body of the text illuminates how this religious text served as both religious and emotional solace for its translator; and (iii) the textual mapping of Mecca, as seen and experienced by al-Qazani in his writings on religious spaces and migrant communities, points to a melting pot of diasporic Sufi brotherhoods, teachers, and publishers, whose efforts spurred the Meccan publishing scene during the late nineteenth and early twentieth centuries.

Al-Qazani is our guide in this discursive multilingual journey that is constituted through texts, print, and language. What was his spiritual and intellectual upbringing like? What role did Ural-Volga Sufi intellectuals have in Islamicate networks, broadly, and in printing Muslim texts in the Arabophone world, specifically? The paratexts of the printed editions reveal much about individuals like al-Qazani and the role of publishing initiatives by diasporic Muslim communities. We find in the scholarship that the history of Muslim printing is often-times a story of a select group of reformers from the Arabophone printing centers of Cairo and the Levant. Consequently, the *Rashahat* is a particularly interesting episode in Sufi history in general, and book history in specific, for illuminating the importance of translation and print networks by non-Arab, immigrant Muslims.

It is not easy to follow the intellectual trails of a man who lived in humble quarters, leading a life so similar to hundreds of other migrants who settled in the Hijaz, for in the words of Jonathan Strauss:

> To write the history of translation in the Ottoman Empire, one must be a bit of a sleuth and a spy, searching for clues wherever they might exist, listening through the keyholes of title pages and colophons and other texts, and at times making imaginative (if evidence-based!) connections.
>
> (Booth 2019, 57)

The clues collected from al-Qazani's autobiography, what his contemporaries thought of his work, as well as the main operations of the *tariqa* transport us to various locales but particularly that of the Hijaz. The dominant reductive image of Mecca in scholarship during nineteenth-century historiography, such as in the ethnographic study of Christiaan Snouck Hurgronje (d. 1936), painted a polarized Muslim community – divided between Arabs and migrants, fundamentalists and Sufis – that is fundamental against modernity and European penetration, encapsulated in such a view:

> Mecca had become, in the eyes of European colonial powers with Muslim subjects, a safe haven for fundamentalist activities ('Muslim fanatics' as they were called). The city was seen as a place from where pan-Islamic

140   *Mariam Elashmawy*

ideas could radiate all over the Muslim world, a large part of which was by then governed by European nations – the hated unbelievers.

(2019, xiv)

I aim to provide an image of Mecca that showcases how the intellectual heritage had been preserved and interacted with as a result of the networks established by residents in the Hijaz, and through the impetus of editors and patrons of the publishing scene. Moving from the reductive scholarship on Mecca, I aim to acknowledge its intellectual heritage during the nineteenth century as a melting pot of spiritual groups and intellectual networks. In her book *A History of Jeddah: The Gate to Mecca in the Nineteenth and Twentieth Centuries*, Ulrike Freitag brings attention to the multiplicity of migrants residing in the Arabian Peninsula, looking at how the diversity of the population and the range of their economic, spiritual, and intellectual activity are part and parcel of the larger developments taking place in the Middle East, rather than seeing Mecca as an isolated and uniform community (2020). In this same vein, this chapter looks at the diversity of Sufi residents in Mecca's publishing scene in order to situate them within the broader developments taking place during this age of print, as well as to trace how the Naqshbandi intellectual heritage had been preserved through migrant communities. The printing metropoles of Cairo and the Levant have monopolized the story of Muslim printing, casting more shadows over other printing narratives in the region, as will be discussed in the coming section. In this chapter, I look at remote publishing houses and the men in charge of producing texts that have influenced the Naqshbandi tariqa's collectivity.

The contribution of al-Qazani is a vast one, yet it is unappreciated. There seems to be no dedicated study of his contribution to Muslim intellectual history in English or Arabic historiography. However, al-Qazani is a popular figure in Central Asian studies.[1] This scholarship is extensive, for it unveils his involvement in the realignments taking place during the early years of Soviet Central Asia vis-à-vis the Jadidi-Qadimi discourse, where al-Qazani was known as a staunch Qadimist who constantly and harshly criticized Jadidist reformers such as Musa Bigiev (d. 1949).[2] The scholarship also addresses his role as a distinguished historian of his day through his germinal work, *Talfiq al-akhbar wa-talqih al-athar fi waqa'i' Qazan wa-Bulghar wa-Muluk al-Tatar*, which led to his persecution by Soviet officials at the end of his lifetime.[3] This chapter is an attempt to trace al-Qazani's contribution to Sufism and the Naqshbandi intellectual heritage during his 36 years in Mecca (1878–1914). A study of his intellectual labor within the contours of the Meccan publishing scene, encapsulated through the pages of the *Rashahat*, is but a meager attempt to recognize a man whose legacy is vast and unappreciated. As one contemporary of his observed: "Nobody knows the value and importance of this great and humble man! He lives here [in Mecca] by the sweat of his hard work, and by the books he writes" (Ibrahim 2003, 487).

Naqshbandi Lives: A Historical and Intellectual Heritage

Strange is the Naqshbandiyya clan,
like clockwork they work– pieces encircling a chauper board,[4]
All have come to the center,
A circle of awareness, that all labour is a work-in-progress,
All toil is fledged to the *tariqa*,
And all within it understand their part.

(Fakhr al-Din ʿAli, Rashahat ʿayn al-hayat)

The inception of the *Rashahat* came as a result of a series of travels undertaken by its author, Fakhr al-Din ʿAli. The *Rashahat* was a moving text in its inception, and this was further conveyed in its circulation in manuscript and print form, as it was widely disseminated and translated in Turkish, Arabic, Urdu, and Uzbek from the original Persian. The pages of the *tariqa*'s history are filled with accounts of travel, intellectual networks and spiritual journeys, emblematic of Fakhr al-Din's life, as well as the entirety of the Naqshbandi *tariqa*. In the introduction of the text, which was written in 909/1503, Fakhr al-Din informs his reader that this humble book was intended as a *dhayl, addendum,* to ʿAbd al-Rahman Jami's (d. 898/1493) *Nafahat al-Uns*. Fakhr al-Din informs his readers of the reason behind his book's title.

[The] Beads of Dew from the Fountain of Life are everywhere in my book, for if I am ever to embark on speaking of the knowledge or wisdom of this *tariqa*, I indicate with a small circle as if it is a *rashha*, dew drop, before the name of a sheikh.

He continues by saying,

in this way, the transmitted good deeds and guidance are like a drop that refreshes the heart and gives life to the hearts, and spilling from the spring of life it brings a new joy and vitality to the hearts of sincere devoted students and dear friends.

(ʿAli 1889, 51)

The son of the well-known preacher, exegete and poet of Timurid Iran, Husayn Waʿiz Kashifi (d. 910/1505), Fakhr al-Din moved in the same intellectual networks of his father during the fifteenth century. Living in the shadow of a great father had not eclipsed Fakr al-Din's intellectual production and involvement in the scholarly community of his time. His education took place in Herat, where he studied all the Islamic sciences under the tutelage of his father (ʿAli 1889, 203,489; Storey 1933). His introduction to the Naqshbandi Sufi network was a product of his strong and close relationship with the poet Jami. Jami made sure Fakhr al-Din received both a spiritual and scholarly preparation influenced by the poet's established network of reputation

142   *Mariam Elashmawy*

all over the Persianate world of Central and South Asia, Anatolia, and the Balkans, making Fakhr al-Din conversant in mystical texts and their commentaries (Binbas 2016). His education familiarized him with the principles of the tariqa, spurring in its wake a deep yearning within Fakhr al-Din to meet the order's guide and master, *Khwajah* 'Ubayd Allah Ahrar (d. 895/149). His master's text, *Nafahat al-Uns*, a compendium of biographies of Muslim *'awliya* (friends of God), was written in 1479, and included about six hundred biographies of Sufis which cover the period between the eighth and fifteenth centuries. Fakhr al-Din's work is not as ambitious in scale, yet it does illuminate the intellectual networks in Timurid Iran, a literary work sparked by his involvement with the *Khwajah*. Encouraged by his teacher Jami, Fakhr al-Din set out on a series of travels outside the city of Herat, embroiling himself within the active networks of Naqshbandis ('Ali 1889).[5] During his travels, Fakhr al-Din had grown closer to the *Khwajah*, as well as his son and students, where after extended discussions and note-taking, encouraged by the *Khwajah*, Fakhr al-Din wrote and dedicated this book to the Naqshbandi master ('Ali 1889; Haji Khalifa 1992).

Fakhr al-Din divided the contents of the *Rashahat* into three sections. The first section is concerned with relating a brief biography of the early Naqshbandi sheikhs who had been teachers of the *Khwajah*. He cites the *silsila* through which the Khwajah had received the *dhikr* and *nisba* permission, as well as contemporaries of his time, starting with the *Muhadith* Abi Qassem al-Jurjani (d. 1036), and including the head of the Naqshbandiyya *Khwajah* Abdel Khaliq al-Fagdwani (d. 1179), Sayed Amir Kilal (d. 1370), and Bahaa' al-Din al-Naqshbandi (d. 1389), among many others. The longest entry in this biographical dictionary section is dedicated to Fakhr al-Din's master Abdel Rahman Jami, almost 22 pages narrating Jami's coming of age and the learned men he had interacted with in Timurid Iran and during his stay in the Hijaz ('Ali 1889). At first glance, the *Rashahat* would simply seem like a biographical dictionary or a short biography of the *Khwajah*. However, a closer inspection explains its popularity with Naqshbandis in different parts of the Muslim world. The second and third sections are dedicated to the person of the *Khwajah*. The entries provide a window into the *Khwajah*'s intellectual prowess at Hadith and Quranic exegesis, and the sort of transmissions and tales he had accumulated over time. One section in particular focuses on accounts of the political influence exerted by the *Khwajah* on the princes and Sultans of the Timurid period, such as Abu Sa'id Mirza (r. 1459–1469), the ruler of Timurid Iran who reunified much of the empire, which had become fractured in the aftermath of the death of his great-uncle Shah Rukh.

Fakhr al-Din's text was a reflection and a product of the time during which he was writing, where the narrative of Naqshbandi life is not circumscribed within a closed circle or a patron-subject relation but rather in a shifting circle trekking through lands, texts and languages. The motif of travel is scattered throughout the literary texts and biographies of Naqshbandis, an indication of a thriving connectivity between different actors moving like clockwork within an interconnected world (Ziad 2019). All the different iterations of the Naqshbandiyya are of a fluid nature, men and texts connecting through movement in intellectual networks. Literary networks, à la Ronit Ricci, are the medium through which we are able to trace the connections between Muslims permeating through boundaries of space, culture, and language. These literary networks of print and translation fostered a complex web of texts and interpretations that sustained Naqshbandi continuities in the Muslim discursive and collective imaginary. Hence, a study of the *Rashahat*'s circulation in the age of print does many things. We know more about its circulation in different languages and regions, as well as the role of printing in this initial episode of globalizing the history of print in Mecca. How then, can we look at this history that constitutes individuals and groups from different backgrounds grounded within a flourishing literary network?

The Importance of Being Translated

Translation is a central facet in the circulation history of the *Rashahat*, as it stimulated individuals and groups to publish different linguistic iterations of it in Istanbul, Lucknow, Tashkent, and Mecca, all cities inhabited by Naqshbandis. Al-Qazani battled with his translation projects, plagued by thoughts of insecurities as detailed in his autobiography. His thoughts littered along the paratexts of his translations illuminate the thought process behind his approach to translation, what the Arabic language means to a Muslim hailing from the Ural-Volga areas, and how he conceded to having his mastery of Arabic widely circulated among "more informed" peers for criticism. He says:

> I refrained from [translating at first] as I felt I lacked the prowess in Arabic, and a general deficiency in the literary arts. And I baffled myself even more thinking this way, and said to myself: you are lacking, because you are of no importance. Granted, there is some knowledge to be had between you and [the Arabic language], but where is the mastery of producing a certain sweetness of expressions in you? You were not given birth to by Arabs, nor do you hail from Kufa or Baghdad.
>
> (al-Sirhindi 1889, 4–5)

A particular sense of self-deprecation is apparent from al-Qazani's vocalized fears. Is this a sentiment shared by all Muslims hailing from "peripheral" centers of the Islamic world, falling under the brunt of the sword for attempting to tackle a "grandiose" language such as Arabic? Perhaps this sentiment is likely a result of him being from the "periphery" of the Islamic world. It is also possibly a result of instances, for example, when Arab intellectuals, such as Rachid Rida (d. 1935), the owner of the *Manar* periodical in Cairo, during his many travels to India, had taken issue with how "peripheral" and non-Arab Muslims spoke and wrote in the Arabic language.[6]

144 *Mariam Elashmawy*

Ta'rib, or Arabization, has yielded various translation projects across different temporal and spatial moments in history. Many works in this field have attempted to look at cultural and textual diffusion, and how texts are sites to be studied in order to trace the migration of ideas and people. As texts and their producers travel among geographically and culturally adjacent languages, Francesca Orsini illuminates the role of the "Multilingual Local" as an active actor in the demand, transmission and circulation of translated texts (2017, 345–346). In addition, Saliha Paker and Sule Demirkol-Ertürk look at the physical spaces in the Ottoman world that fostered networks that catered to minorities' translation initiatives. Ronit Ricci similarly looks at the common religious outlook that unites Muslim communities in South and Southeast Asia in their intellectual production, and demands for Arabic texts to be "retold" through translation for a wider audience and by co-existing with several languages (2011).

The eighth- and ninth*century Abbasid translation efforts fostered a flourishing scholarly movement in Baghdad, spurring textual production and the preservation of ancient Greek texts into the Arabic language. During later periods, Arab Christians communities were heavily affected by cultural and mercantile exchanges that spurred translation efforts, turning religious Orthodox books into Arabic in the eighteenth century (Radwan 1954, 12). This movement of printing and circulating translated texts inadvertently led to the circulation of the Arabic language and resulted in consolidating Arabic as the *lingua franca* of Syriac communities, to the point where Syriac languages were only understood in Mount Lebanon and small areas in Damascus (Radwan 1954, 12–13). Yet what remains center stage in the history of translation is a distinct moment in the nineteenth century within the paradigm of modernity, reform, and renaissance. The *nahda*, as reiterated by scholarship, marks an important episode in the translation history of the region, which was seen as a "political-cultural project of modernity, a renaissance, an awakening, an indigenous movement focused on the vitality of Arabic culture and the desire to expand it" (Booth 2019, 15). Translation initiatives have been previously reiterated in a nationalist fashion of historiography, particularly focused on a select group of nineteenth-century reformers and extraordinary individuals backed up by institutional channels, especially in the Arab metropoles of Cairo and the Levant.

The Levant's translation movement of the nineteenth century was focused on religious material within a printing nexus that involved missionaries and local church authorities. Maronite communities in the Levant were amongst the initial waves that embraced print in Ottoman lands. Religious texts from Europe were being disseminated amongst the communities through the American Protestant missionaries' outpost in the Levant (Auji 2016, 23). However, it was seen that their teachings were unlike that of the region's Maronite instruction. Therefore, Maronites began to establish printing presses of their own in order to print translated texts pertaining to their own religious doctrines (Radwan 1954, 85). Such ventures were heavily influenced by the strategic location of the Levant as a trading hub, a site and melting pot for exchange between different key players of the international trading and missionary network.

In tandem with these ecclesiastical translation initiatives, government-led reform in Istanbul during the *Tanzimat* reform from 1839 to 1876, and in Cairo under Muhammad Ali Pasha (r. 1805–1840), also moved to produce and circulate "official" translation projects that mirrored state needs for military, scientific and geographical texts (Booth 2019). The need for mass production of translated texts spurred the rise of institutions of schooling, such as the translation bureau *Tercemi Odasi* established in Istanbul around 1832, as well as the 1835 *Madrasat al-Alsun* in Cairo, thus creating cohorts of trained translators, equipped with the formal education and skills to edit and oversee projects of translation (Booth 2019; Heyworth-Dunne 1940).

Peter Hill and many others delved further into the translation movements during this period, highlighting actors and intellectual circles that do not necessarily fall in line with the historiography of nationalist, renaissance, or modernist tendencies found in scholarship. Hill's focus on a group of Christian intellectuals in Demietta, far from the centers of translation during the *nahda*, illuminates the often-neglected circles of intellectual production that the *nahda* discourse overshadows (Booth 2019, 95). In the same vein, an examination of Naqshbandi translation, and its overlapping nature with printing and publishing initiatives during the nineteenth century shows us how translated texts, circulating with the aid of publishing houses, were "the instrument for renewing the collective imaginary through the propaga- tion, certainly in a diffuse form, mediated by [acts of] Arabization, of new models of representing the world" (Booth 2019, 26). In his seminal article on translation and printing, Heyworth-Dunne postulated that although during the nineteenth century, "Arabic suffered through the destruction of the old madrasah-system, it gained immensely through the needs of Muhammad Ali [to modernize]" (1940, 348), a claim shared by many who have conceptualized translation initiatives as confined within the modern, Europeanized institutions, putting out renditions of Arabic translations during the state- building process. In line with scholarship that has been re-evaluating dis- missive claims of traditional institutions during the modern period, I argue that the Arabic language did not suffer at the hands of the old traditional institutions of *madrasas* and its teachers. Rather, it found a scholarly climate that acclimated to the changing scene wrought by the printing press, and in turn, fostered translation efforts that heavily responded to the publication needs of Sufi groups residing in remote parts of the Muslim world, such as Istanbul, Lucknow, Tashkent, and Mecca.

The translation of the *Rashahat* does not fall under any of the nationalist or reformist translation projects operating in the nineteenth century at the time in the Arab world. More often than not, as the previous section has shown, the intellectual and cultural weight of translation in Arab Muslim history pivots around the *nahda* (Renaissance) during the nineteenth and twentieth centuries

146   *Mariam Elashmawy*

as a result of the conceptual ramifications of western penetration and colonization. This, in turn, has spurred an abundance of scholarship on translation through a historiography of extraordinary individuals in Muslim history, as well as the institutions developed by the "modern" state to finance translation projects. I am more interested in decentralizing this approach to the history of translation. Therefore, rather than posit al-Qazani as a remarkable individual, I situate him as part of a larger cohort of Naqshbandi scholars operating in close proximity to various publishing houses patronizing the translation of seminal *tariqa* texts for different audiences.

The first printed edition of the *Rashahat* is a Turkish translation of the *Matba'a* Amirie in Istanbul (1821). It is important to note that the *Rashahat* had only been popularly printed and circulated in Anatolia and Egypt in the Turkish language ('Ali 1889; Gülşenî 2014; Balut and Balut 2007). These Turkish imprints, however, were reproductions of earlier manuscripts that had been translated and popularly circulated since the sixteenth century. The intellectual heritage of the *Rashaḥāt* in the Ottoman tradition of these translations of the sixteenth century was grounded in an established community of Naqshbandīs, who had arrived in the Ottoman capital from Transoxiana. One of the earliest had been Isḥāq Būkharī Hindī, for whom Sultan Muḥammad II (r.1451–1481) is said to have endowed the first center of the brotherhood in Istanbul, the Hindiler Tekkesi (Weismann 2007). The demand for a translation of the original Persian text came as a response to the increased demands of the established Anatolian Naqshbandis in the *tekkesi* for a more comprehensive and basic text on the *tariqa*'s founders and influential masters.

In India, Fakhr al-din's debut took place at one of the most prominent presses in Lucknow. The Nawal Kishore Press was founded by its namesake in 1858, with titles ranging from Urdu, Arabic, Persian, and Sanskirt (Stark 2007). Munshi Nawal Kishore was a member of the Indian National Congress, and his publishing interests ranged widely from producing works on Indian national culture as well as Urdu translations of some Islamic mystical texts (Ahmed 2017). By the 1870s, the press had a prominent department that specialized in translating texts for publication from Persian to Urdu (Haider 1981). The *Rashahat* had been among one of the texts undertaken by the Urdu department. It was translated by Mawlana Abul Hasan al-Laknawi (d. 1886) and was later published in 1893. This edition was followed by two more print runs in the Persian language during 1897 and 1911.

In al-Qazani's regional homeland of Central Asia, a local printing industry had been blossoming during the twilight years of imperial Russian rule. From the cracks in the Russian empire's very foundations rose Central Asian Muslim printing as an effervescent phenomenon with a flourishing publication tract in Persian, Uzbek, and Arabic (Khalid 1994). The circulation of printed texts in Central Asia predominantly relied on "imported" imprints from the movement of individuals returning from the *Haj* (pilgrimage), India, or Cairo, as well as texts from the official printing press in Tashkent. However,

Can the Qazani Speak? 147

by the end of the nineteenth century, we find the initial stirrings of private publishing houses, with the opening of Esanbay Husaynbayoghli's lithographic press in Tashkent. The first text to be printed by this private house was a commentary by the Naqshbandi *Mujadidi* Allah Yar al-Bukhair (d. 1721), an educational *tariqa* textbook titled *Sharh Sebâtü'l-âcizîn*, which had been used during the first stage of madrasa education by Turkmen, Uzbek, and other Turkic communities (Mahdum 2020).

Tashkent's presses were concerned largely with publishing recognized classics with a guaranteed audience (Khalid 1994), such as the popular *Rashahat* imprint by Arijan's Golamiya publishing house. The 1911 lithographic edition of the Newal Kishore house had travelled to Tashkent, where it formed the basis for the Uzbek edition by the steam-driven lithographic press *Golamiya*. Local editions of Persian works were supplemented by imports from India, which enjoyed great popularity in Central Asia, and served as models for local publication, whereas works in Arabic were rarely published locally, the small demand being satisfied by imports (Khalid 1992). *Golamiya* took on the project of translating the *Rashahat* into Uzbek for a wider dissemination of the book for Central Asian audiences.

Can the Qazani Speak in Mecca?

The book's survival in Turkish and Persian was problematic for Arabic speakers, once we arrive at al-Qazani's contemporary moment in the Hijaz. Al-Qazani lamented that many do not have linguistic access to the knowledge tucked between the *Rashahat*'s pages, nor has he been able to acquire an Arabic translation of the text. As a result, this led him to the conclusion that no one had undertaken the task of Arabizing the *Rashahat* yet. "Because of the Persian language of the text, many have been unable to gain access or grow close to the benefits that text contains", al-Qazani introduced the text, "and to this day I have not been able to locate another's attempt at Arabizing it" ('Ali 1889). This is an important observation on al-Qazani's behalf and for our study of the circulation and printing history of the *Rashahat*.

An earlier Arabic translation had been done by Taj al-Din Zakariya al-Hindi (d. 1640), who had been the head of the Naqshbandi order at the time. His intellectual projects also included Arabizing Jami's *Nefahat al-Uns* (al-Nabulsi 2006; al-Muhibbi 2011). However, unlike al-Qazani's and other translations, his work remains to this day in manuscript form in the Egyptian *Dar al-Kutub*. Al-Qazani's inability to locate this translation is a testament to its obscurity in Naqshbandi intellectual circles, especially because he had been known among his contemporaries for his vast library and penchant for collecting books (al-Kattani 1982). Taj al-Din al-Hindi's absent translation thus formed the impetus for al-Qazani's venture into translation.

äät-Minzälä, between Ufa and Kazan in the Ural-Volga region, began his educational tract in his uncle's *Madrasa*. There he was taught Arabic grammar,

148 *Mariam Elashmawy*

medieval logic, ethics, and theology until the age of 18 (al-Sirhindi 1889). He travelled to Kazan in 1290/1873, aiming to settle at the *Madrasa* of Shihab al-Din al-Qazani al-Murjani. Instead, al-Qazani travelled to Bukhara, and on his way, he stopped in the village of Troksy where he lived for two years in the *Madrasa* of Mulla Sharaf al-Din and Mulla Muhammad Jan. There, he studied the commentaries and glosses popular in the land of the Arabs (al-Sirhindi 1889). Once he reached Bukhara in 1293/1875, he attended the lessons of ʿAbdullah Sartawi and ʿAbd al-Shakur Turkmani. Nevertheless, he found that Bukhara, as a learning center, was not as it used to be and realized that to remain there would be a waste of time, so he left, heading to Tashkent once more before finally deciding on relocating to the Hijaz. Around 1878, he passed through Lahore, Bombay, and Karachi on his way to Mecca. Upon arrival, he sought out the Kazan community living in Mecca, which consisted of students in the madrasas, as well as influential traders. In 1880, he married Asma', the daughter of Muhammad Shah, a member of the aforementioned community. His life as a Meccan scholar was a productive one, where he taught many students coming from diverse locations around the Muslim world, specifically in the Amin Agha and Mahmudiya *Madrasas*. Al-Qazani's involvement with the Naqshbandiyya began with his becoming a disciple of the Naqshbandi Sufi Master Muhammad Mazhar, who left quite an impression on the younger al-Qazani. Mazhar had been an immigrant as well, hailing from Delhi, and settling in Mecca with his father when he was 29 years old. In the *haramayn*, he became embroiled in the Muhammadiyya, Ahmadiyya, and Naqshbandiyya tariqas, taking on a teaching position in the local *madrasa* (ʿAli 2008). Al-Qazani relates his master's involvement in the intellectual scene in the Hijaz, building a madrasa that was three stories high with a vast library, as well as a space for teaching and recitation sessions (ʿAli 2008).

The year 1884 in particular was a difficult one for al-Qazani, as two of his masters, Muhammad Mazhar and ʿAbd al-Hamid Daghistani died, leaving him bereft and in the throes of a dark episode of mourning. Fearing he would not be initiated had been a cause for anxiety, so much so that he impulsively began preparations to travel to India, yearning to be inducted in the *tariqa* from the Indian masters there (al-Sirhindi 1889). However, al-Qazani found that with the ascendency of Abdallah al-Zawawi (d. 1343/1924) in Mecca as sheikh of the tariqa, his heart eased, as al-Zawawi undertook the prospect of inducting him personally. Al-Zawawi came from an established Meccan family whose members were all part of the Naqshbandiyya *tariqa* (Abu al-Kheir 1986). His intellectual networks brought him students and disciples from India, Malay, Indonesia, China, as well as Japan (ʿAbd al-Jabār 1982, 1/140). The different ethnic communities al-Qazani was exposed to through the Naqshbandi learning circles of Muhammad Mazhar and Abdallah al-Zawawi reflect the cosmopolitan make-up of the community established in the Hijaz. Moreover, Javanese, Indian, and Meccan Sufi men were heavily embroiled in the printing scene in Mecca, working together to edit and publish texts

Can the Qazani Speak?   149

of different languages, a particular moment of publishing initiatives that has only been given its due in Arabic scholarship.

The first printing press in Mecca was established by the Ottoman Governor, Uthman Nouri in 1882 (al-Tashkandi 1999). The inhabitants of Mecca used to print their own books in Cairo (al-Dabib 2018), as well as in India, for in the first and second decades of the nineteenth century, Indian printers were prepared to publish some heritage books sought by the Arabian Peninsula's scholars (al-Dabib 2018). This familiarity with, and the cultivation of publishing, literary, and intellectual networks with the printing capitals of Cairo and Lucknow, paved the way for the initiation of the Amiriya Press in Mecca once it set off (al-Tashkandi 1999). The printing press came prepared with movable types of Arabic, Turkish, Javanese, and Malaysian (al-Tashkandi 1999). Not only that, but the catalogues listing the names of employees who had worked over the years in the printing press reveal cohorts of editors specialized in Arabic, Javanese, Malay, and Urdu. The Amiriya Press is a fascinating episode of Muslim printing that included different departments operating within it, and that produced multilingual books to cater for a cosmopolitan community in Mecca. The Amiriya press alone represented 94 percent of what was printed overall in the Arabian Peninsula by the end of the nineteenth century. Its chief productions were mainly concerned with mystical texts, followed by literary, historical, and science books.[7] The Sufi orders situated in Mecca were both the producers and consumers of these printed texts. The Naqshbandiyya in particular were heavily involved in the Amiriya Press,[8] such as Sheikh al-Dagestani, al-Qazani's teacher, who had been *Kabir al-Muhaqqiqeen* (head of the editors) there ('Ali 2008). While Abdallah al-Zawawi, Muhamad Mazhar's successor, was the editor of the Arabized *Rashahat*.

Returning to al-Qazani, al-Zawawi's new position forced him to constantly travel between Mecca and Medina, prompting Qazani's dark disposition to resurface once more. He became overcome by waves of loneliness and unease. This emotional plight in Mecca conveys the homesickness that had overcome al-Qazani, so much so that in 1908, with the publication of *Talfiq al-akhbar* in Orenberg, he speaks of this time as a moment that hindered his scholarly work, as he was burdened with homesickness and plight [*ibtila' bi al-ghurba wa al-karba*] (al-Qazani 1/26). In *Talfiq al-akhbar*, al-Qazani provides for his readers an image of the sort of scenic plains, rivers and wilderness which, we can posit, he yearned for back home:

> The best [of this land of Central Asia] is the beautiful music of nature and God's creations, that reside by the tranquil rivers such as the ducks, geese, etc. … the foreigner or he who strayed far from [this] home can keep himself from sobbing only if his heart is made of stone or steel …
>
> (al-Qazani 1/47)

Nevertheless, al-Qazani found solace in the scholarly community and religious spaces in Mecca, particularly through intellectual exploits, where his

150   *Mariam Elashmawy*

fervor for books did not abate, even during his bouts of homesickness. As part of his bookish exploits, al-Qazani came across the Persian and Turkish translations of the *Rashahat*, and from that point onwards, the book becomes his constant companion, day and night ('Ali 1886). In an effort to keep the dark thoughts at bay, he undertakes the project of translating the *Rashahat*, both to feel closer to the *tariqa* through engaging with the text, and to do something of benefit for his brothers. Although al-Qazani had undertaken this project during an emotionally and spiritually turbulent period in his life, it is clear that he had aimed to channel the education he had received, under the tutelage of Mazhar and al-Zawawi, into presenting a well-rounded text to his Arabic-speaking brethren. Al-Qazani's edition is not only a conveyance from Persian to Arabic, but it also includes interventions from the translator into Fakhr al-Din's narrations.

Within Fakhr al-Din's biographical entries of the prominent Naqshbandi sheikhs, al-Qazani interjected in order to supply a more comprehensive Naqshbandi *silsila* that he had been made aware of and taught by the learned men of his time. Hence, al-Qazani began his own biographical dictionary in between Fakhr al-Din's pages, starting with Abu Bakr (d. 634) until where Fakhr al-Din begins his biographies in the twelfth century. It is in these historical accounts, through the hadiths and narrations, that al-Qazani developed his craft as a historian, for these were the initial steppingstones that would enable him to undertake the larger project of *Talfiq al-Akhbar*. In this interjection, al-Qazani identified for his readers controversies related to the *Silsila* of the Naqshbandi. First, he pointed out that some Naqshbandis of his time had been under attack since they had traced their *Silsila* from Abu Bakr through Salman al-Farisi (d. 652). However, al-Qazani argued that this claim of a *Silsila* from Salman al-Farisi is from Sheikh Abu Talib al-Makki, and al-Qazani says "Abu Talib had lived far from the time of the founding fathers of the *tariqa*, so how would he be correct in this conjecture?" ('Ali 1886). This episode also provided an impetus for al-Qazani to correct some misconceptions about how *silsila*s are traced by the great sheikhs of the Naqshbandis. He argues that *silsila*s are not traced through hadith narrations as Abu Talib al-Makki had claimed of Salman al-Farisi's *silsila* but rather through established methods only the initiated are privy to ('Ali 1886).

Moreover, the *Rashahat* did not only serve the purpose of engaging in *tariqa* discourse but a text in which al-Qazani had sought solace. The loss of his two masters Mazhar and al-Daghestani had demoralized the young *murid* (initiate). It is thus clear why he had chosen this text in particular to translate, and more importantly, to have by his side day and night to read. The biographical entries by Fakhr al-Din heavily revolve around the emotional and spiritual connections of a *murid-sheikh*, or a student–master, relationship. It is perhaps likely that these accounts brought peace to al-Qazani during his mourning period, and as he awaits for his new master al-Zawawi to return from Medina. The book also included a long entry on a series of commandments and advice of Sheikh Abdel Khaleq al-Ghedwani (d. 1179/

Can the Qazani Speak? 151

1765) to his student that might have been al-Qazani's solace after losing his master ('Ali 1886). Perhaps reading and engaging with a text that is dedicated to anecdotes of masters and their students, such as the intimate relation between Abu'l-Qasim al-Qushayri (d.1072) and his student, Abu 'Ali al-Farmadi (d. 1043), had al-Qazani reminisce about his early years with his own Sheikh Muhammad Mazhar or provided a source of solace during the absence of his master al-Zawawi.

While al-Qazani was fighting an inner battle by translating the *Rashahat*, an *ijaza* (certification of mastery) for initiation and deputization reached him by Caravan hailing from Medina, where al-Zawawi appointed him as deputy in his stead. Feeling unworthy of this important position, al-Qazani wrote back to his sheikh imploring him to excuse him from this appointment as in his heart he does not feel part of the tariqa quite yet (al-Sirhindi 1888). Zawawi writes back refusing his request. A year later, al-Zawawi's return marked al-Qazani's official initiation into the tariqa. He then took on his role in the tariqa in a scholarly and spiritual capacity in the *Hijaz* with unmatched fervor and passion. When he was done with translating the *Rashahat* in 1889, he presented it to al-Zawawi who had been so pleased with it that he decided to finance its printing himself. It was initially printed in 1889 in the Amiriya Press, edited by al-Zawawi himself with a postface colophon in praise of the translator's prowess at unveiling the intricacies of the Persian language into Arabic. The printed text also bore a *taqriz* from the prominent Naqshbandi Sheikh, Suleiman al-Zuhdi, whose intellectual connections went as far as Southeast Asia (al-Zirikli 2007). A *Taqriz*, or an honorific, was first highlighted by Franz Rosenthal as a genre reminiscent of modern "blurbs" in the manuscript tradition (1981). When analyzed as part of the manuscript's paratexts, a *taqriz* is invaluable when constructing a social and material history of the text, providing "knowledge of the organization of past intellectual life, and the relationships among intellectuals and their role in society" (Rosenthal 1981, 189).

This presence of honorifics during the age of print is an interesting development. It stems from an already established practice from manuscript culture, where authors solicited *taqariz* for their work. It was conceived as a form of recommendation and commendation by an established scholar contemporaneous to the author. This continued practice from the manuscript age was found to be relevant by editors, such as al-Zawawi, in order to increase the scholarly value of the text when it bears the approval of one of the highest-ranking scholars of the time. Suleiman al-Zuhdi praises al-Qazani's translation, remarking upon the importance of making the *Rashahat* available for a different audience not well versed in the original language, an effort, he pointed, whose printing benefited Muslims everywhere ('Ali 1886). This Arabic translation began to circulate popularly in the publishing houses of Egypt and Anatolia, replacing the initial popularity of the Turkish translation, where it was then published in 1886 and 1887 in al-Maktaba al-Islamiya in Anatolia and Cairo's Bulaq press.

152   *Mariam Elashmawy*

Al-Zawawi also commissioned al-Qazani to follow up this scholarly endeavor by translating Imam Ahmad Sirhindi (d. 1624)'s *Maktubat* (letters) as a *tariqa* commission this time. Al-Qazani refused at first, finding it was a controversial and consuming task. However, he had already translated some of the entries of Sirhindi's letters within the *dhayl* he had attached to the *Rashahat*, particularly during his discussion of the *Mujadidi* Naqshbandis residing in Mecca, and their relation to Imam Sirhindi's teachings through his correspondences (al-Qazani 1889). It is probable that al-Zawawi had seen potential in patronizing another *tariqa* text that a translator had already found accessible and translated sections of, as a sort of follow up publication. After being finally persuaded to undertake this translation, al-Qazani writes an introduction to the three-volume *Maktubat* that is worthy of noting, as it illuminates the thought process behind how al-Qazani approaches his task of translation, both for the *Rashahat* and *Maktubat*. In the self-deprecating introduction, al-Qazani reveals his insecurities, as well as what the Arabic language means to a Muslim of the Ural-Volga region, before finally accepting for his intellect and capabilities to be widely circulated among more informed peers and masters.

Al-Qazani relates to his readers how his heart and soul calmed when he had received what he deemed as a signal from God to embark on this initiative. From here on, he begins to contemplate his approach to translating the Arabic language, and like all authors and editors, asks his readers to forgive his errors and shortcomings, concluding that "even Lord Almighty had not allowed for any book to be free of imperfections except for His book":

> I began to undertake the translation, choosing instead to focus on the second concern [of translating], I mean that of highlighting the overall meaning of the text – which to me is a finer endeavor – while also bearing in mind the first concern, i.e. the choice of wording … For the second concern allows me to bring terms into my translation that do not have an equivalent in the original language, as well as permits me to change the passive voice to an active one, and so on … through this model of translation one is able to avoid ambiguity, or induce one's anxieties – forsaking speculation and analogous methods.
>
> (al-Sirhindi 1889, 4)

The laying out of his careful method of translation echoes the previously mentioned concerns by Arab intellectuals, such as Rachid Rida, regarding how non-Arab Muslims were only able to do literal translations of Arabic texts. Here, al-Qazani, perhaps in response to these dismissive inclinations, illuminates how he does not approach the text by unveiling its literal meanings, but instead unearthing the "inner meanings" of the *Rashahat*. As a concluding word to his methodology section, al-Qazani wrote: "[I translate this] hoping it would benefit the brothers of our tariqa who have no knowledge of the original Persian language of the text, or its other translation in Turkish" (5)

Dhayl of a Dhayl

The *Rashahat*'s initial printing included a *dhayl* by al-Qazani titled *Nafa'is al-Sanihat fi Tadhyl al-Baqiyat al-Salihat* (The Jewels of Inspiration in the *Addendum* of Good Deeds). One concern in particular needs to be addressed when examining the material aspect of this *dhayl*, that is, the choice of how to present it within the primary printed text. The *dhayl* is added along the margins of the page, a material aspect that is reminiscent of how commentaries were copied in manuscripts. Islam Dayeh's work on the editing practices of the nineteenth and twentieth centuries, is among the initial studies done to complicate the material history of printing in the Muslim world, arguing that editing practices were a "burgeoning culture of textual scholarship and publishing that continued traditional Islamic scholarly methods and techniques, but also tested new techniques and forms that were made possible by print technology" (2019). This Meccan edition is a testament of the relevance of manuscript culture's influence on modern editorial practices in the Hijaz, elucidating that maintaining the basic form of a text was among the chief interests of those involved in the publishing business. This is also found in the lithographs of the *Rashahat* in Tashkent and Lucknow, as previously discussed, where the material form and decorations of the lithographs were more popular, due to their retention of manuscript form. Al-Qazani's *dhayl* is also important due to its popularity in the scholarly scene of the early twentieth century. It includes the biographies of some of the influential Naqshbandis in the nineteenth century, detailing the intellectual and social context of Indian and Central Asian migrants in the Hijaz, and elaborating on the spiritual teachings of the *tariqa*.

The work includes the biographies of al-Qazani's mentors as well as what can be constituted as a scholarly ethnographic study of Mecca in the nineteenth century. Through al-Qazani's *dhayl*, we are introduced to Mecca as al-Qazani and his fellow migrants experienced it and of the diasporic communities inhabiting the intellectual and spiritual landscape at the time. A digression is due to appreciate al-Qazani's mapping of the intellectual and social history of Mecca. It is important to note that although the nineteenth century for Hijaz had been a period where it was not under foreign rule, it still operated within the backdrop of an increased imperialist presence in the region. This is reflected in the seminal, and most utilized, ethnographic account on Meccan life in the nineteenth century by Hurgronje. Hurgronje was a Dutch scholar of Oriental cultures and languages, and Advisor on Native Affairs to the colonial government of the Dutch East Indies. His work *Mekka in the Latter Part of the 19th Century* came as a result of an increased need on the side of the Dutch government to glean information about "Pan-Islamic ideas living within Southeast-Asian community in Mecca" (Snouck Hurgronje 2007), and it has been referred to by scholars as a blueprint for daily life in Mecca (Laffan 2008). This begs the question of how nuanced Hurgronje's ethnographic account is and to what extent al-Qazani's accounts bring a different understanding to the bustling community in the Hijaz.

154   *Mariam Elashmawy*

Hurgronje's distaste for Sufi orders is quite apparent from how he describes them, referring to the popular religious orders as:

> ... absurd thaumaturgy with their noisy processions, their Central-Asiatic beggar dervishes and their Sheikhs who work only to gather numbers of adepts round them. Very rarely however does one venture to oppose one of these blind leaders of the blind when surrounded by his people.
>
> (2007, 220)

His descriptions of how different ethnic communities lived together in Mecca is a stark opposite to what al-Qazani recounts. Hurgronje writes of the unfriendly attitudes ethnic groups harbor towards one another manifested in "malicious jokes," and a lack of desire to live or study together (Snouck Hurgronje 2007). However, al-Qazani paints a different image. The intellectual climate al-Qazani paints in his experience of nineteenth century Meccan Naqshbandiyya is one that involves a wide range of Muslims. The teaching circles of Muhammad Mazhar and Abdallah al-Zawawi, as experienced and lived by him, are a multiethnic experience that included students from India, Central Asia, Southeast Asia, and various parts of the Arab world (Al-Qazani 1889). It is these multiethnic men whom al-Qazani praises for their prominent role in creating a tight-knit community, not only in Mecca, but also in the far reaches of what constitutes the Muslim world. Al-Qazani dedicated a large section of his observations to his diasporic community of the Ural-Volga region, and the scholarly and spiritual stations they have achieved during and after their stay in the Hijaz (Al-Qazani 1889). He mentions six prominent names of this diasporic community such as Sheikh Mulla Nu'man Efendi, Sheikh Muhmmad Sherif Effendi,[9] Mulla Ahmad Safa Efendi al-Tash, Sheikh Abdel al-Hanan Efendi al-Burjani, Sheikh Abdel Haq Efendi, and finally whom he calls "Our friend," Sheikh Khayr-Allah Efendi, the son of Sheikh Zein-Allah Effendi, known as al-Amir Khalifa. The curated brief biographies of these individuals reflect the established intellectual connections and networks between Central Asian and Meccan Naqshbandis during the late nineteenth century.

Moreover, al-Qazani's accounts reveal the processes through which some of these connections were forged, either through intentional planning on part of the Central Asian learned man or through God's will. Mulla Ahmad Safa Efendi, for example, had only stumbled upon the teaching circle of Muhammad Mazhar when he had been on pilgrimage. He was so influenced by Mazhar that he had arranged to return home to get his affairs in order and relocate to the *Hijaz* to embark on his spiritual journey alongside him. Sheikh Abdel Hanan Efendi, hailing from Bukhara, had completed his education there and moved to Mecca in order to be initiated into the *tariqa* by Mazhar. He remained in Mecca and Medina for several years, teaching and initiating students, until he decided to return home in Bukhara. Further examination of the life and contributions of these men is needed in order to appreciate

Can the Qazani Speak? 155

the multiplicity of actors involved in the Naqshbandiyya *tariqa* within vast spatial areas.

Furthermore, the *dhayl* includes a section on the theory and practice of Sufism for the "*murid* requiring guidance," almost as if he was writing it for himself as well as his fellow brethren. This section consists of 24 chapters on different topics relevant to any new initiate to the *tariqa*, the sum of all al-Qazani's years of studying under three different masters, such as (i) the road to repentance; (ii) how to accompany your sheikh through *muraqaba* (observance); (iii) solitary confinement; (iv) inner introspection; and (v) the circle of affection with your brethren, among other topics. Al-Qazani's explication of the Naqshbandi tariqa uses a variety of texts. He heavily relies on the *Maktubat*, citing correspondence after correspondence of Imam Sirhindi as the basis through which he relates to the young *murid* the essentials of the *tariqa*. In the end of this section he puts a disclaimer, asking those seeking answers to the mysteries of the Sufi way to peruse the important books first, such as *al-Risala al-Qushayriya* by al-Qushayri (d. 376), *'Awaref al-Ma'arif* by al-Suhrawardi (d. 1234), and *Ihya Ulum al-Din* by Ghazali (d. 1111), as his "humble text is bound to be full of errors and mistakes," hence it is best to seek out the texts of the more knowledgeable.

After 36 years in Mecca, al-Qazani decided to return to Russia with his family, where he worked in the libraries and archives of St. Petersburg and traveled around the country, collecting material for his historical work, *Talfik al-Akhbar*, which Russian Orientalists considered to be his *magnum opus*. This very same book put him in a political predicament. In 1915, his book had him arrested and sent to Siberia. Only at the cost of incredible efforts did he manage to avoid exile and return to his family, who had been residing in Orenburg. Following the years of the 1917 revolution, al-Qazani lay hidden in Soviet Russia, haunted by Soviet officials and frowned upon by the growing class of Muslim reformers. He dreamed of leaving the country, and when he managed to do this in 1919, he flew with his family to Chuguchak in Western China, where he remained until his death. Whether he was remembered for being a Naqshbandi deputy, translator, or Qadimi, it is clear that al-Qazani's repertoire left a mark upon the Muslim intellectual heritage. His translation, while undertaken to aid him in his dark moments, was both a comfort and blessing for those congregated in Muslim metropoles, or for his own emotional release.

Conclusion

Rashahat ayn al-hayat attracted the interest of Muhammad Murad al-Qazani, as well as several editors and translators of both the medieval and modern period. This chapter reveals much of its translation and printing history, and how the wide circulation of the *Rashahat* in different languages speaks of the popularity of the text and the influence of the Naqshbandi *tariqa* within the printing scene of the nineteenth century. Naqshbandis sought out and

156 *Mariam Elashmawy*

published the *Rashahat* in Urdu, Ottoman Turkish, Uzbek, and Arabic, a testament to its popularity. Additionally, the printed *addendum* by al-Qazani plays a prominent role of its own, despite its marginal location in the material text, by mapping out (i) the psychological and intellectual process of translation undertaken by al-Qazani; (ii) the journey and life of a migrant Sufi in nineteenth century Mecca; (iii) the inner workings of patronage for printing; and (iv) the intellectual scene in Mecca and the migrants seeking the Sufi path.

Al-Qazani's migration and life in Mecca involved an episode of emotional turmoil. The religious spaces in Mecca that he operated in, as illustrated in his autobiography and *addendum*, including both the learning circles and the publishing scene, provided a solace for the young Qazani. In addition, his psychological and spiritual proximity to the *Rashahat* illustrates the ways in which religion and the Naqshbandi tariqa unburdened the emotional plights of our translator.

The editorial practices and choices of printing Naqshbandi texts show us that Mecca's printing scene was an effervescent one that engaged different constituencies of migrants and scholars living in the Hijaz during the print age, and they also highlight the role of Sufi tariqa's patronage of texts to be printed. Consequently, the *Rashahat* reveals that those working in the publishing scene, printing medieval texts for nineteenth-century audiences, come from various backgrounds. The story of the *Rashahat*'s printing is a story of movement: the movement of the text across time and space, its movement through languages, as well as the movement of those working on publishing the text through migration and travel, seeking out manuscripts, migrating for knowledge and teaching, and moving through spiritual and emotional states when handling texts.

Notes

1 Much of the scholarship on al-Qazani highlights his career following his return to Central Asia in 1914, within a tumultuous time period following the Bolshevik revolution, and in a changing Muslim community. See: Abdulsait 2016; Akhunov 2004; Зямилович 2013; Akhmadullin 1917. I owe these references to Abdulsait, and the help of translations of colleagues and online resources.
2 Jadidism marked a particular moment in the history of reformism in Central Asia in the early twentieth century, and its earliest leaders was Musa Bigiev, a Tatar Hanafi Maturidi scholar. For more on reformism and Muslims in Central Asia see Khalid 1998; Tuna 2017; DeWeese 2016; Kanlidere 2010.
3 This text caused al-Qazani a lot of difficulty, which resulted in his flight to Orenberg to escape the authorities and his exile to Siberia, as it put him in direct confrontation with Soviet intellectuals who opposed his "proto-nationalist" attempts at constructing a national history of Muslim Kazan.
4 Chaupar is considered to be one of the early table-top games. It is a variation of a game of dice that first makes its debut in epic poem *Mahabharata*. The game is played by the players' attempts to move their four pieces around the board's columns in anti-clockwise motion.

5 For more on Jami's intellectual connections in Timurid Iran, see Khan 2020.
6 In Rida's *fatawa* section of the Manar, he responded to inquiries from non-Arab Muslims about the validity/prowess of non-Arab Muslims' translations, finding that they were only focused on translating meanings from the Arabic language verbatium without identifying the nuances of the language. See for example: "'Ahamm ma yajib 'ala muslimi al-a'ajim min al-lugha al-'Arabiyya [The Most Important Part of the Arabic Language Necessary for the Non-Arab Muslims]" al-Manar, vol. 29, 1929, 661–664.
7 Catalogues of the *Salnamah*. The *Salnamah* was an annual publication of the Amiriya Press, disclosing the titles of books printed during the years, first published in 1883. In its first year, the press was able to print six books, a number that expanded exponentially over the years once books of different languages were demanded.
8 A particular episode of a printing war between two Naqshbandis was mentioned by Snouck on pages 191–193, revealing a struggle of legitimacy between Suleiman Effendi and Khalil Pasha who both claimed to be Sheikhs of the Naqshbandi order. According to Snouck, both of them sought to increase the number of their adherents, especially among Turks and Malays, so a war of pamphlets and refutations erupted between the two of them until Sheikh Ahmad Dahlan intervened on behalf of Khalil Pasha, defaming the treatises and pamphlets of Suleiman Effendi (Laffan 2008).
9 He remained in Mecca until Mazhar had initiated him and given him the *ijaza*. Following that, he returned to a teaching post at a madrasa in Trosky where he began initiating others in the Naqshbandi tariqa there.

References

Ахмадуллин, Салават Зямилович. (2013) "Мурад Рамзи и его касыда о Зайнулле Расулеве." *проълемы востоковедения*, 60 (2), 73–75.
Akhmadullin, Salavat Zyamilovich. (2017) "'Talfik Al-Ahbar' by Murad Ramzi & The Censorial Report by N. F. Katanov: Circumstances & Reasons of the Ban of the Book." *Современная наука: актуальные проблемы теории и практики*. Серия: ГУМАНИТАРНЫЕ НАУКИ, 8, 4–9.
Akhunov, Azat. (2004) "'Deputy' Teacher (life path of Murad Ramzi)" 1913, Accessed on 23 February 2020, http://idmedina.ru/books/history_culture/minaret/3/ahunov.htm.
Abdel Gabar, Omar. (1982) *Siyar wa tarajim ba'd 'ulama'una fi al-Qarn al-rab'i 'As*har. Jeddah: Tuhama.
Abdulsait, Aykut. (2016) МУХАММАД МУРАД РАМЗИ (1855–1935) И ЕГО РАБОТЫ [Muhammad Murad Ramzi (1855–1935) and his Works]. *КРЫМСКИЙ ИСТОРИЧЕСКИЙ ОБЗОР* 2 (13), 8–26.
Abu al-Kheir, Abdallah. (1986) *Nashr al-Nur wa al-Zahr fi Tarajim 'Afdal Makkah*. Jeddah: 'Allam al-Ma'rifa.
Ahmed, Sumaiya. (2017) Munshi Newal Kishore Press and a New Heritage for Islamic Literature during the Colonial Period. *Islam and Muslim Societies: A Social Science Journal*, 10 (2), 66–77.
Auji, Hala. (2016) *Printing Arab Modernity: Book Culture and The American Press in Nineteenth-Century Beirut*. Leiden: Brill.
al-Babani, Ismail. (1951) *Hedayet al-'arifin*. Beirut: Dar Ihya al-Ilm.

158 *Mariam Elashmawy*

al-Bakkani, Shu'aib. (2018) *Tabaqat al-khawajakan al-naqshbandiya*. Cairo: Dar al-Risala.

al-Dabib, Ahmed. (2007) *Bawakir al-tiba'a wa al-matbu'at fi bilad al-mamlaka al-'arabiya al-seoudia*. Jeddah: Markaz Hamad al-Gasser.

al-Kattani, Abd al- Hayy ibn 'Abd al-Kabir. (1982) *Fihris al-faharis wa al-athbat wa mu'jam*. Beirut: Dar al-Gharb al-Islami.

Allāh Ṣafā, Zabīḥ (1956) *Tārīkh-i adabīyāt dar Īrān*. Tihrān: Kitābfurūshī-i Ibn Sīnā

al-Mar'ashli, Yussif. (2006) *Nathr al-jawahir wa al-durrar fi 'ulama al-Qarn al-rab'i 'Ashar*. Beirut: Dar al-Ma'rifa.

Al-Nabulsi, Abdel Ghani. (2008) *Muftah al-Ma'iyyah fi Dustour al-tariqa al-Naqshabandiyya*. Cairo: al-Dar al-Juwdiya.

al-Sirhindi, Ahmad. (1889) *Maktubat al-Imam Sirhindi*. Mecca: Matba'a al-Amirirya.

al-Tashkandi, Abbas. (1999) *al-Tiba'a fi al-Mamlaka al-'arabiya al Seoudiya*. Riyadh: Maktabit al-Malik Fahd al-Wataniya.

Balut, Ali., and Balut, Ahmed. (2007) *Mu'jam tarikh al-turath al islami fi maktabat al 'alam*. Dar al-'Aqaba: Kayseri.

Binbaş, İ.E. (2016) *Intellectual Networks in Timurid Iran: Sharaf al-Din 'Ali Yazdi and the Islamicate Republic of Letters*. Cambridge: Cambridge University Press.

Booth, Marilyn. (2019) *Migrating Texts: Circulating Translations Around the Ottoman Mediterranean*, Edinburgh, Edinburgh University Press.

Charles Häberl. (2015) *Balaybalan*, in Encyclopædia Iranica, online edition, available at www.iranicaonline.org/articles/balaybalan-language (accessed on 14 February 2021).

Dayeh, Islam. (2019) "From Taṣḥiḥ to Taḥqiq: Toward a History of the Arabic Critical Edition." *Philological Encounters* 4 (3–4), 245–299.

DeWeese, D. (2016) "It was a Dark and Stagnant Night ('til the Jadids Brought the Light): Clichés, Biases, and False Dichotomies in the Intellectual History of Central Asia." *Journal of the Economic and Social History of the Orient*, 59 (1–2), 37–92.

Freitag, U. (2020) *A History of Jeddah: The Gate to Mecca in the Nineteenth and Twentieth Centuries*. Cambridge: Cambridge University Press.

Gülşenî, Muhyî-yi. (2014) *Resehat-i Muhyi: Resehat-i 'Aynu'l-Hayat Tercumesi*. Istanbul: Türkiye Yazma Eserler Kurumu.

Haider, Syed Jalaluddin. (1981) "Munshi Nawal Kishore (1836–1895) Mirror of Urdu Printing in British India." *Libri* 31, 227.

Haji Khalifa, Mustafa. (1992) *Kashf az-zunun an asami' al-kutub va al-funun*. (1:903). Beirut: Dar al-kutub al-ilmiyya.

Heyworth-Dunne, J. (1940) "Printing and Translations under Muḥammad 'Ali of Egypt: The Foundation of Modern Arabic," *Journal of the Royal Asiatic Society* 72 (4), 325–349.

Hurgronje, C. (2007) *Mekka in the Latter Part of the 19th Century: Daily Life, Customs and Learning, the Moslims of the East-Indian-Archipelago*. Leiden: Brill.

Ibrahim, Abd al-Rashid. (2003). *'Alem-I Islam ve Japonya'da Intisari Islamiyet*. Istanbul: Nesil Yayinlari. 2 vols.

Kanlidere, A. (2010) "The Trends of Thought Among the Tatars and Bashkirs: Religious Reformism and Secular Jadidism vs. Qadimism (1883–1910)." *Orta Asya ve Kafkasya Araştırmaları* (09), 48–62.

Khalid, A. (1992) "Muslim Printers in Tsarist Central Asia: A Research Note." *Central Asian Survey* 11 (3), 113–118.

Can the Qazani Speak? 159

Khalid, A. (1999) *The Politics of Muslim Cultural Reform: Jadidism in Central Asia.* California: Univ of California Press.

Khalid, Adeeb. (1994) "Printing, Publishing, and Reform in Tsarist Central Asia." *International Journal of Middle East Studies* 26 (2),187–200.

Khalifa, H. (1986) *Kashf az Zunun an-asami al kutub va-l-funun: in 6 volumes.* Beirut: Dor ul-fikr, 822.

Khan, Ahmad. (2020) "Jami in Regional Contexts: The Reception of Abd Al-Rahman Jami's Works in the Islamicate World, Ca. 9th/15th14th/20th Century." *The Muslim World Book Review* 41 (1), 41–6.

Kurah Balut, Ali Reza. (2007) *Mu'jam tarikh al-turath al islami fi maktabat al 'alam.* Turkey: Dar al-'Aqba.

Laffan, Michael. (2008) "The New Turn to Mecca: Snapshots of Arabic Printing and Sufi Networks in Late 19th Century Java." *Revue des mondes musulmans et de la Mediterranee* 124, 113–131.

Le Gall, Dina. (2005) *A Culture of Sufism: Naqshbandis in the Ottoman World, 1450–1700.* New York: SUNY Press.

Mahdum, Abid. (2011) "On the Sources of SEBÂTÜ'L-ÂCİZÎN BY SÛFÎ ALLAHYÂR," *Türkiyat Mecmuası,* 212, 239–253.

Muhammad al-Muhibbi. (1868) *Khulasat al-'Athar fi 'Ayan al-Qarn al-Hadi 'Ashar.* Cairo: Matba'a Al-Wahabiya.

Muhammad Murad al-Qazani, (1889) *Dibaja of Maktubat al-Imam Sirhindi.* Mecca: Matba'a al-Amirirya, p. 1–5.

Mu'temedî, Mehînduht. (1989) *Mevlânâ Hâlid Nakşbendî ve Peyrevân-ı Tarîkat-ı Û.* Tehran: Matbaa-ı Amire.

Al-Qazani, Murad. (1908) *Talfiq al-akhbar wa-talqih al-athar fi waqa'i' Qazan wa-Bulghar wa-mulūk al-Tatar* (Vol. 1 and 2). Orenburg: al-Maṭba'ah al-Karimiyah wa-al-Ḥusayniyah.

Raḍwān, Abū al-Futūḥ. (1954). *Tārīkh Matba'at Būlāq Wa-lamhah Fī tārīkh Al-ṭibā'ah Fībuldān Al-Sharq Al-Awsat.* al-Qāhirah: al-Matba'ah al-Amīrīyah.

Ricci, Ronit. (2011). *Islam Translated: Literature, Conversion, and the Arabic Cosmopolis of South and Southeast Asia.* Chicago: University of Chicago Press.

Rosenthal, Franz. (1981) "Blurbs' (taqriz) from Fourteenth-Century Egypt." *Oriens* 27–28, 178.

Schulze, R. (1997) "The Birth of Tradition and Modernity in 18th and 19th Century Islamic Culture: The Case of Printing." *Culture & History* (16), 29–71.

Shahrani, M. (1991) "Local Knowledge of Islam and Social Discourse in Afghanistan and Turkistan in the Modem Period," in *Turko-Persia in Historical Perspective,* ed. Robert L. Canfield, Cambridge: Cambridge University Press, pp. 161–188.

Stark, U. (2007) *An Empire of Books.* New Delhi: Permanent Black.

Storey, C.A. (1933) "The Beginnings of Persian Printing in India." *Oriental Studies in Honour of Cursetji Erachji Pavry,* edited by Jal Dastur Cursetji Pavry, Oxford: Oxford University Press, pp. 457–461.

Tuna, M. (2017) "Pillars of the Nation": The Making of a Russian Muslim Intelligentsia and the Origins of Jadidism. *Kritika: Explorations in Russian and Eurasian History,* 18 (2), 257–281.

Weismann, Itzchak. (2007). *The Naqshbandiyya: Orthodoxy and Activism in a Worldwide Sufi Tradition.* London: Routledge.

Yazici, Tahsin. (2002). "GOLŠANI, MOḤYI MOḤAMMAD." *Encyclopaedia Iranica, Vol. XI, Fasc. 2.* 113, 125–168.

160 *Mariam Elashmawy*

Ziad, Waleed (2019). "From Yarkand to Sindh via Kabul: The Rise of Naqshbandi-Mujaddidi Sufi Networks in the 18th–19th Century Durrani Empire" in *The Persianate World: Towards a Conceptual Framework*. Leiden: Brill.

Zirikli, Khayr al-Din. (2007) *al-A'lām, qāmūs tarājim li-ashhar al-rijāl wa-al-nisā' min al-'Arab wa-al-musta'ribīn wa-al-mustashriqīn*. Beirut: Dar al-'Ilm lil-Malayin.

'Ali, Fakhr al-Din. (1886) *Rashahat Ayn al-Hayat*. Mecca: Matba'a al-Amirirya.

'Ali, Fakhr al-Din. (2008) *Rashahat Ayn al-Hayat*. Beirut: Dar al-Kutub al-'Ilmiya.

Part IV
Negotiating National Imaginaries of Belonging and Exclusion

8 Spectral Migrant Workers and the Paradox of Modern Nation-Building in Deepak Unnikrishnan's *Temporary People*

Lava Asaad

Za'atari camp, the largest refugee camp for Syrians in Jordan, is one of many places in the Middle East that accommodate the influx of Syrians fleeing their country. These camps have been drawing increasing levels of international attention. In the last two decades, migrants from Iraq, Afghanistan, and recently Syria, have dominated the migration discourse in the Middle East as the epicenter of crisis, the producer of the displaced, and the exporter of human lives. On a closer look and by resituating the observing eye towards the Arabian Peninsula, the story of migration changes its scene, actors, and producers. The United Arab Emirates, a hub of modernity and globalization where dream cities attract migrants with promises of prosperity, hosts its own labor camps, predominately for South Asian workers who are scouted by hawk agencies dispersed across South Asia. These labor camps are plentiful, exceeding thousands. The workforce is allured by agencies to the UAE, enticed by the promise of well-paying jobs, accommodation, medical attention, and other benefits that are difficult if not impossible to find in their home countries. The reality check on the other side of the shore explodes the migrant's expectations, stranding him (migrant workers are usually male) deep in the sense of obligation to make ends meet for the family back home, at any cost. Unlike refugee camps in the Middle East, labor camps are inaccessible to outsiders, let alone to the press. By and large, these migrants living and working in the Gulf are categorized as temporary economic workers with varying visa durations.

There is a dearth of literature available on these migrants. *Goat Days* by Benyamin, a 2008 Malayalam novel later translated into English in 2012, follows the life of an abused migrant in Saudi Arabia. In 2013, Mahmoud Kaabour released the documentary, *Champ of the Camp*, which enabled him access under the guise of filming a singing contest. The documentary cleverly shows the dire situation of the camp while also capturing the fleeting dreams and years of laborers scrambling to send meager wages back home. Kaabour juxtaposes the precarious conditions of migrant workers with the obscenely affluent Emiratis to differentiate the two different worlds they occupy. The importance of this documentary lies in how Kaabour managed to shed light on these ignored issues without being censored. Through singing, migrants

DOI: 10.4324/9781003301776-13

164   *Lava Asaad*

had the chance to show their plight in labor camps, their extreme poverty, and their homesickness. More recently, and the main focus of this chapter, Deepak Unnikrishnan published in 2017 his collection of short stories, *Temporary People*, for which he was deservedly crowned as the winner of Restless Books Prize for New Immigrant Writing. Born to Indian immigrants in the United Arab Emirates, moving between the United States and Abu Dhabi, Unnikrishnan continues to exist in-between. The collection of stories is loosely jointed, held together by the shared, albeit slightly different, experiences of South Asian migrants living in the Gulf. The story of migration in the UAE is by no means one-dimensional, and the variety of stories in the collection attests to that. Notwithstanding, there is an underlying ghostly, spectral, and ephemeral quality to migrant lives in the book that excludes them from the fabric of the Emirati nation while also exploiting their existence to build, serve, guard, clean, engineer, and teach, amongst other jobs, only for them to later leave, be deported, or stay illegally. Unnikrishnan is cognizant of the duplexities of the migrants' existence and role in building the oil-rich nation.

This chapter examines how the exclusion of these migrants—exasperated by their low economic class—further detaches them from belonging to their home country and from the Gulf States where governments have constructed a rigid definition of citizenship. The stories explored in this chapter trace these experiences of migrants who are forever distanced from planting roots in the Gulf States. These workers wear their scarlet letter for being *ghurabaa* (foreigners) and are compelled to endure the state of ghurba (alienation). The chapter draws on the work of Giorgio Agamben and Zygmunt Bauman to understand the surrealist narratives of workers in labor camps and to explore the lived realities of those migrants who are completely ostracized from Gulf societies and from the discourse of nation-building. To quote Agamben, these migrants are labeled as "bare lives" whose existence necessitates their exclusion and vice versa (1995). These bare lives exist in direct contrast to the true and authentic Gulf State citizens whose rights expunge the rights of others. In effort to catch up with modernity, even to surpass it, the Gulf States import what Bauman refers to as "redundant" people to swell wealth to the point of bursting (2003, 5). In legitimizing the migrants' "redundancy," the idea of a unified nation-state becomes more defendable. The second half of the chapter will further elucidate how middle-class migrants in the Gulf are allowed to lay fragile roots in the city, yet they continuously develop contested identities that romanticize their "Indianness," while always reminded by Emirati culture of their otherness. Consequently, the rhetoric of nation-building for the Gulf States has allowed violence to be at the heart of this racial clash which pits South Asian migrants against Emiratis and other Arabs.

It is vital to underline how migration theories tend to compartmentalize immigrants brutally and strictly by approaching refugees as different from economic migrants and internally displaced people. These labels are politically constructed, and they "continue to be developed in an effort to align the migrant subjects with national and international policies" (Asaad 2020, 19). Allowing bureaucratic definitions to define patterns of mobility validates the circulation of "convenient images" of who migrants are and/or how they should be treated in the host country (Zetter 2007, 173). The migrant story in the Gulf States is not completely unlike those who are labelled as economic migrants moving to Euro-American territories. However, one dissimilarity between the two stories makes all the difference. In the West, the migrant experience is entrenched within a long trope of colonial and diasporic mobilities where most migrants set roots elsewhere, or at least have the option to be naturalized, even if it takes years to accomplish. In the Gulf States, nationalizing migrants is rare, even non-existent, for strategic, national, and cultural reasonings. *Temporary People*, therefore, brings to light migrant lives, be they middle-class South Asians who have illusory connections to the city, or laborers residing at camps forever ostracized and kept far away from the cities they build. Paradoxically, the existence of necessary yet redundant people is vital to the nation that clings to an imagined and exclusive sense of community with its traditions and an assured Arab lineage.

The exclusion of these workers from the nation's discourse operates on three trajectories. First, it legitimizes the dehumanization of these workers because of their foreignness, Second, it warrants the exploitation of their cheap labor. Third, it ossifies the imaginative notions of being an authentic Gulf State citizen. While these series of exploitations have been kept under wraps, literary works like *Temporary People* expose the fraudulent underpinnings of the Gulf States' nationalistic and economic discourses that nullify the migrants for the sake of building an exclusionary circle of privilege and belonging. Highlighting literary works, therefore, is an essential first step to poke through the Gulf States' bubble of authenticity, Arabness, and imagined nationhood.

Nation Building in the Gulf States

The desire to solidify a unified image of an Emirati nation has its roots deep in colonial history. Several of the Gulf States experienced a long share of British colonial dominance beginning around 1840. Initially, the proximity to India peaked Britain's interest in keeping the Gulf region under its control. The Trucial States was the name given by the British government to a tribal confederation in Arabia under a protective treaty. However, in 1913 with the eruption of oil, Britain renewed its interest in the Gulf for geostrategic purposes, giving British companies full ownership of oil-producing concessions (Hanieh 2011, 62). Arab nationalism was at stake and became the driving force behind reclaiming control over the oil industry and, with it, territorial agency. In retaliation against colonial policies that tend to erase local identities, and because of the need to construct a unified nation with political and economic independence and a distinct national identity, the United Arab Emirates and other Gulf States inevitably recreated a romanticized image of the nation, becoming "an imagined political community—and imagined as

166   *Lava Asaad*

both inherently limited and sovereign" (Anderson 1983, 6). The political sovereignty of the state rests on politics of exclusion from other Arabs, South Asian workers, and the more privileged Western nationalities residing in the Gulf. In *Walls Built on Sand: Migration, Exclusion, and Society in Kuwait*, Anh Nga Longva understands the Gulf States through Benedict Anderson's definition of an imagined community by arguing that,

> in order for a politics of exclusion to evolve successfully, three conditions are required: first, there must be an acute sense of external threat, which presupposes that there is a sense of internal identification; second, there must be a central apparatus with the capacity to provide both the ideological and the administrative means to implement and reproduce exclusion, the best candidate for this role being the state; and third, there must be a cultural tradition favorable to the ideas of exclusion.
>
> (1997, 44)

Longva argues that these three conditions reflect the ways in which the Gulf States reshaped their policies of inclusion and exclusion by rewarding their nationals with wealth, free health care, free education, free housing, etc. The state, in return, asks its nationals for complete loyalty and obedience to strict policies. For instance, there are laws set to curb any chance to marry someone from outside the Gulf States "with the aim of preserving national identity" (Dresch 2006, 203). The idea of having a clear and clean *nasab* (relatedness) is essential in attributing nationality (Dresch 2006, 203). Nevertheless, cheap labor from South Asia became and has remained the optimal option for building the Gulf States. South Asian nations with their abundance of unemployed young men desperate to earn have proven to be the ideal labor pool for the aspirational petrostates. With such a large influx of foreigners, the external threat to local culture had to be heavily regulated and monitored.

The Gulf States' reliance on South Asian workers, too, has roots in British colonial rule. In *Capitalism and Class in the Gulf Arab States*, Adam Hanieh explores the role of the British in contributing to the overall image of a pure Emirati nation: "Britain encouraged the concentration of power within the hands of individual rulers who were connected to a wider ruling family, and could trace their origins back to one of the Arabian Peninsula tribes" (2001, 5). In this way, Gulf politics would come to resemble the British tradition of rule by a landed nobility. Furthermore, the importance of belonging to certain Arab families, a trend that dominates national policies in the Gulf, has its inception with the presence of South Asian workforce brought to the region by British companies (Hanieh 2011, 62). Initially, the flow of workers from South Asia was halted by importing laborers from other Arab countries. However, these Arab migrants soon grew to be an undesirable workforce, as Hanieh argues, "because many of [them] came to sympathize with Arab and Palestinian nationalism and began to challenge the Gulf regimes and their

Spectral Migrant Workers 167

perceived ties with the Western powers" (2001, 63). Arab migrants also posed a threat to the ruling monarchy in the Gulf by enticing anti-revolutionary sentiments against the monarchs (Chalcraft 2010, 3). As a result, particularly after the Gulf War of 1990–1991, more laborers came from the Indian sub-continent. For example, Bangladesh sent 60% to 70% of its migrant workers to the Gulf by the mid-1990s (Hanieh 2011, 64). The increasing number of foreign workers in the Gulf intensified the need to create a clear divide between Emirati citizens and migrants, be they Arab, Muslim, or non-Muslim. This created what is known as *Khaleeji* Capital, Khaleeji meaning from/of the Gulf, which "represents the development of an emerging space that reflects a shift in the social relations underpinning accumulation in the Gulf—a process of class formation located within, and occurring through, the international-ization of capital" (Hanieh 2011, 2–3). Centralizing power and wealth in one class created the *kafala* or sponsorship system where the *Kafeel* is a citizen who sponsors the importation of laborers. The Gulf States argue that these migrants are not immigrants since their contracts are temporary, but these contracts, as Noora Lori has shown in her study on the *kafala* system, are "repeatedly" renewed, which has led most workers to remain there for decades (2019, 137). Lori further argues that importing foreign guest workers in the Gulf purposefully prohibits the formation of any pathway to citizenship, which is different from other patterns of employment migration to the United States or Europe (2019, 136). Thus, guest workers remain at the mercy of their sponsors.

The *kafala* system is built on an imbalance of power that primarily feeds on migrant laborers. The loopholes in the system allow for individual employers to further exploit the law to keep an iron grip on migrants. Several case studies have even pointed out the similarity of *kafala* to human trafficking given the large number of cases in which the employer confiscates the laborer's passport, pays wages irregularly, decreases the salary, or even sends off the migrant to another employer without prior consultation (Qadri 2020). Others have equated the *kafala* system to modern-day slavery (Barkawi 2020). The agencies in South Asia recruit laborers who usually pay between 2000 and 3000 USD to secure a contract with a sponsor, which puts the migrant in debt even before arriving to the UAE (Barkawi 2020). While some Gulf States, like Bahrain, have ended the *kafala* system in 2016, the reformed policies are not vastly different from what they were before (Lori 2019, 158). Currently and because of the international outcry against the *kafala* system, some Gulf States have introduced long-term visas for highly competitive occupations (Lori 2019, 158). Nevertheless, these reforms do not apply to non-white collar laborers.

As evident by this brief historical overview of the consolidation of the Gulf States and the creation of an "authentic" Gulf State citizen, the imagined threat of the other (be it another Arab or South Asian) was already in the making. The current dehumanizing and exclusionary policies in the Gulf States regarding migrant workers have roots extending back to the original

168 *Lava Asaad*

formation of an envisioned Gulf identity that must be fortified at any cost. The following section focuses on the role of literature in collapsing and problematizing the entrenched idea of "true natives" in opposition to the dangerous and infiltrating *ghurabaa*. In this way, voicing the voiceless disrupts the illusory idea of homogeneity in the Gulf States.

Surrealist Belongings: Redundant Existence Outside the Nation-State

The storylines in *Temporary People* reflect the exploitative system that peels off the worker's worth and humanity as a precondition to enter the UAE. The characters also mirror the complexities of belonging to a nation in which migrants are inevitably caught between the (im)possibility of hybridity and the contested need for assimilation. Unnikrishnan weaves narratives together, relying on mingling English, Malayalam, and Arabic where each of these languages demonstrates the historical, political, and cultural variances of the Emirati nation. "The trilingual patois" is a remnant of the conflicting identities and does not necessarily grant its speakers access to multiple sites of belonging (Mathew 2017). Unnikrishnan's style has been compared to Kafka's, as some characters shape-shift and ignominious metamorphoses and grotesqueness abound. Others have compared him to Salman Rushdie, specifically *Midnight's Children*, as characters exist on the margins in a surreal world. The language as well as the stories themselves unpack varying degrees of struggle for non-citizens in the UAE. These multiple takes on belonging and identity are extensively analyzed in Neha Vora's *Impossible Citizens: Dubai's Indian Diaspora*, an essential ethnographic study for understanding the complexities of narratives in *Temporary People* and the anxious belonging(s) that characterize the existence of migrants in the Gulf. In a way, the characters have been expelled from their countries of origin before being ostracized by Emiratis. The anxiety of belonging begins with the home country that continues to dehumanize its citizens through extreme poverty and intensifying consolidation of power and privilege in the hands of the few. Migrants-to-be already embody a precarious existence, as Judith Butler would argue, where "certain populations suffer from failing social and economic networks of support and become differentially exposed to injury, violence, and death. Such populations are at heightened risk of disease, poverty, starvation, displacement, and of exposure to violence without protection" (Butler 2009, 25–26). The deprivation of rights in the home country pushes citizens to export their dreams elsewhere, which leads them to become a Gulf kid, a Gulf husband, or a Gulf widow, all to accumulate Gulf nickels. Their dehumanization as well as their simultaneous expulsion from the society continues in a Gulf city, be it Dubai, Abu Dhabi, or Sharjah, that further devalues migrants, even if they assimilate with the host country and forsake their roots back home. In the two stories below, the characters' attempts at planting roots in the Gulf region are continuously thwarted as they themselves are seen as disposable humans, unworthy of any legitimate and tangible sense of belonging.

Fittingly, the lives explored in Book One fall under Agamben's "bare life" and Bauman's "human waste." Relying on concepts from ancient Greek, Agamben distinguishes in *Homo Sacer* between zoe (the simple act of living and existing as a living being) and bios (political states), where he argues that modern states tend to produce zoes without political, economic, and social protections (1995). These bare lives, in the sense of their biological quality as lives, lead a vulnerable existence without being protected or feeling connected to a specific sovereignty (Agamben 1995). The laborers in the camps are already expunged from the fabric of their own nation, and are thus tossed onto global cities that continue to dehumanize them. Similarly and aptly, Bauman studies the aftermath of modernization and globalization, which have been responsible for creating "human waste" that was necessary in the process of "order-building" that outcasts some populations, and of "economic progress" that cheapens human worth for the sake of escalating modernity (2003, 4). As a result, we have an abundance of redundant people, defined by Bauman as follows:

> To be "redundant" means to be supernumerary, unneeded, of no use— whatever needs and uses are that set the standard of usefulness and indis- pensability ... To be declared redundant means to have been disposed of because of being disposable ... "Redundancy" shares its semantic space with "rejects," "wastrels," "garbage," "refuse"—with *waste*.
>
> (2003, 4)

Deemed as the scum of the earth, laborers in the Gulf States go through double exclusion, from home and from ruthless modernizing states. They are stripped of their human rights, and their livelihood only exists until their visas expire. They are disjoined beings, which means that Unnikrishnan can only write about their lives in a surreal and Kafkaesque narrative style.

The surreal image of redundancy is highlighted in Chapter Two, "Birds" where the narrative takes place at construction sites. Anna Varghese is an employee in Abu Dhabi whose sole duty is to tape people, those who fell from unfinished buildings. Her job is to stitch workers up without having the need to call for medical attention: "when workers fell, severing limbs, the pain was acute, but borne. Yet what truly stung was the loneliness and anxiety of falling that weighed on their minds" (10–11). The precarity of the workers' situation is increased with the city's incessant need to have higher buildings and lower wages. In one of her inspection tours, looking for falling bodies, Anna tries to repair Iqbal who has recently fallen. Iqbal's connection/affiliation with his home country is rapidly severing: "Home's shit," he says. His village suffocated its young, "so small you could squeeze all of its people and farmland inside a plump cow" (12). Like the rest of men in his village, Iqbal yearns to be a Gulf boy enticed by the pipedreams woven by recruiters in his village.

170 *Lava Asaad*

The story also demonstrates rapid change in the cityscape where citizens have left the old center and relocated into villas in more modernized areas:

> Hamdan, Anna's haunt, her hood, was growing, from a tiny city center to a mutating worm that refused to tire. The streets grew streets, parked next to slabs of steel and glass towering over trees planted to grown in exactly the same way. Roads were widened and swept regularly to keep them spotless and black. Imported planners erected tall, stringy American-style street lights. If you paid attention, you could hear mercenary architects barking instructions to create perfect city: *Move. This. There. That.* They never slept, shouting orders into the night, into the wee hours of the morning, never resting. The city way a board game and labor its pieces, there to make buildings bigger, streets longer, the economy richer. Then to leave. After.
>
> (19)

The city and its inhabitants expand on the shoulders of its laborers who are always seen as intruders, as outcasts. Hamdan is uncontrollably expanding, but with expansion comes exclusion. Politics of zoning are strictly structured in the Gulf States. For example, Vora clarifies the distinction between downtown Dubai, inhabited by middle-class immigrants, and New Dubai where natives and Western workers reside. Those two zones are further separated (socially, culturally, politically, and economically) from labor camps. Those who build the city are excluded from it, but this marginalization is not unique to migrant workers in the UAE, as evident in Saskia Sassen's study of belonging in Global cities in *Globalization and Its Discontents*. Sassen argues that the city deepens the cliff between corporate capital and the disadvantaged workers "whose political sense of self and whose identities are not necessarily embedded in the 'nation' or the 'national community'" (1998, XXI). Laborers move in and out of spaces without having the right to place and where the specter of departure is ever reminding them of their anxious belonging. In constructing an imagined rhetoric of the nation, these laborers are always and forever outside the circle of belonging in the Gulf State. The narrative in this story highlights how these migrants are not only deprived from claiming roots in the city, but they are also brushed off as sub-humans with no basic human rights. The literal manifestation of these laborers as "objects" to be repaired draws from the ways in which the Gulf governments refuse to see these migrants as human beings.

Similarly, the idea of disposability is sustained in Chapter 7, particularly in, "In Mussafah Grew People," where the narrative deconstructs the fantasies of "authentic" citizens by toying with the idea of what it means to be human. A Malayalee scientist, Moosa, implants seeds that grow MALLUS (Malayalees Assembled Locally and Lovingly Under Supervision). The need to increase the labor force for a cheap cost was necessary to accommodate the rising demand for laborers to build the city, since "employing more white men

Spectral Migrant Workers 171

was not an option [because] they wilted in the sun" (50). Those laborers spoke Arabic and Malayalam to not raise suspicion once the canned MALLUS are sent to employers. Unnikrishnan cleverly captures the dehumanization of the workforce who are being squeezed, exploited, and then deported. In the case of MALLUS, the lifespan, resembling most visa-staying duration, is around 10 to 12 years, after which, the MALLUS groups are rounded up and taken to the desert to be disintegrated. This allegorical representation of laborers in the UAE captures their ephemeral and unearthly existence where their final destination is always detrimental. The MALLUS are "cerebrally customized" to be dutiful workers/objects (51). However, the storyline escalates when Moosa, out of boredom, wires a new breed with critical thinking capacity. As a result, "In 2006, canned Malayalees took to the streets ... and went on strike in a country where dissent is not tolerated" (51). Unnikrishnan here alludes to migrant worker protests between 2005 and 2008 where thousands of laborers protested low wages and inhumane working conditions (Kanna 2011). The cultural and political infrastructures in the Gulf States depend on over-satisfied and loyal citizens and silent migrants where fear of being deported for any slight misdemeanor looms large and loud. These stories highlight the plight of migrants in labor camps where precarity puts them at the lowest stratum of Emirati society. Because of their disposability, and thus inhumanity or sub-humanity, they are not to be considered as a potential component of the Emirati society, which continues to gloss over this issue with total impunity.

Contested and Violent Belongings

The precarity and redundancy of migrants in the Gulf continue in Book Two, which examines migrants who are a notch above those residing in camps. These are the working class and middle class who have been in the Gulf for years and have set down flimsy, intangible, albeit temporary roots in the city. While camp laborers are denied access to social and cultural life in the city, those who occupy middle-class status are given a sneak peek at assimilation. While the predominant image of workers in the Gulf is that of single men, middle-class migrants have the option to bring their families to the UAE, but the majority of migrants cannot. As a result, low-waged migrant men (married or single) remain alone in the Gulf. Michelle Buckley writes about "Bachelor Subjectivity" where the status of being a bachelor in Dubai "refers not to one's familial status generally but to their familial status in Dubai, which acts in many cases to delineate a subordinate class position for many lower-waged foreign workers" (2015, 139), but they are still differentiated from those who reside only in labor camps. Moreover, because of the UAE's strict policies against granting citizenship to migrants, Vora studies the multifarious ways in which one can claim "citizenship" without relying strictly on legalities and where, despite the pushback against integrating migrants in the nation, these migrants leave a huge impact on the nation culturally,

172   *Lava Asaad*

socially, and economically. Interestingly and important to this chapter are the distinctions that Vora draws between the South Asian diaspora in the West versus the UAE. Many of her interviewees

> revealed several disconnect from the South Asian diaspora literature, namely their sense that Western South Asian experiences were very different than theirs, their lack of nostalgia for homeland or sense of cultural "loss," and their ambivalent positions vis-à-vis the Indian state.
>
> (Vora 2013, 23)

In 1999, India issued a new policy to incorporate its diasporic subjects in their motherland by giving them Person of Indian Origin (PIO) cards, entitling them to partake in and benefit from the economic sector as any Indian citizen would. Nevertheless, those who reside in the Middle East (except for Israel), Africa, or the Caribbean do not have PIO cards, a point Vora pauses at and writes that "it is the Indian state *in the first place,* and not the kafala system, that removes political rights from Indians in the Gulf" (2013, 27). This double exclusion, from their motherland and from the "host" country amplifies migrant workers' situation in the Gulf where "nostalgia and hybridity—are largely missing from the narratives of Dubai Indians" (Vora 2013, 65). In diasporic literature and theories, these two terms, "nostalgia and hybridity," are central to the narratives and experiences of migrants. Unnikrishnan's middle-class characters show that, while they retain an idea of India and being Indian, they are cognizant that their Indianness is fraught with otherness both at home and in the host country.

Book Two relates instances of anxious belonging. It is a book about the violence of (dis)assimilation, the intensification of racial differences, and inevitable frustrations and clashes between Emiratis and non-Emiratis. Here we find a malformation of the sense of being Indian. At the center of these stories is an inherent and inescapable racial clash between Emiratis, Arabs, and Indian migrants that can only be materialized and expressed through violence. For example, Chapter One, "Mushtibushi," takes the readers back to Hamdan Street, the city center, where the children continue to be sexually assaulted and where, we are told, media coverage would have been different if "an Emirati kid fell victim" (91). The narrator, Debashish Panicker, who has taken the responsibility upon himself to investigate the assaults, realizes his bare life status in the Gulf: "Helpless parents, myself included, had no choice but to accept these attacks as a child's rite of passage" (91). The children believe that the elevator Mushtibushi is the one assaulting children, where the kids in the apartment complex struck a deal to rotate volunteers to feed the hungry elevator. After questioning a child, Maya, about the incident, Panicker writes his formal and final report:

> The culprit, the girl believes, wore a kandoura, but it is possible she could have misidentified the garb, or even misidentified the man's nationality …

Spectral Migrant Workers 173

Given the sensitivity of the accusations, I would argue it is irresponsible to blindly believe the allusions of a distressed child ... I myself have seen Malayalee chauffeurs in kandouras driving Toyota 4×4 or dusty Land Rovers. These men speak good Arabic—accented, but good Arabic. Upon scrutiny—the shape of beards, bone structure, gait, gravitas—it is clear these men cannot and do not possess all attributes of authentic Emiratis ... What we can ascertain, if M's right, is that the man who committed this act knows Arabic and dresses like a national. We, however, do not know if he's a temporary worker or a local. We do not even know if this man is new to the country or a long-time resident, or perhaps even an illegal.

(112)

A kandoura is a traditional Emirati dress, but Panicker's hesitancy to believe the allegations is rooted in the political and economic context that has rendered people like him voiceless and without agency.

Because of the overwhelming number of non-Emiratis in the UAE, exceeding 80%, it becomes pertinent to the state to draw lines of difference between nationals and non-Emiratis. In *Fear of Small Numbers: An Essay on the Geography of Anger*, Arjun Appadurai writes about the "anxiety of incompleteness" of a nation that is always apprehended and where realizing an "unsullied national whole, a pure and untainted national ethnos" is of paramount importance (2006, 8). More alarmingly, the nationals of the UAE are *not* the majority, hence the need for state apparatuses to instill in the mind of citizens and non-citizens alike that there are quintessential Emirati traits that resemble no others. Panicker looks at "the shape of beards, bone structure, gait, gravitas" to distinguish an "authentic" Emirati from an Arab or South Asian. Ironically, Panicker blindingly convinces himself that a pure Emirati would never assault a child, despite numerous allegations brought forth. Mastering Arabic is yet another deficient qualification to distinguish a citizen from a non-citizen, or so the state and Panicker believe. Panicker's unwillingness to believe Maya only reflects the state of perpetual fear of the so-called "authentic Emirati" as a breed who is morally infallible. It is also a testimony to how the myth of building a unified national discourse based on an imagined historical purity, a specific way of dressing, and a certain linguistic variant not only proves to be replicable but also hollow. Indeed, other Arab and even non-Arab migrants can easily pass as Emiratis despite dominant nationalist discourses that racialize migrants and justify their exclusion and othering on the basis of characteristics that supposedly distinguish them from Emiratis. Xenophobia in the UAE is indoctrinated by the State when it presents migrants to its nationals as "necessary evils" (Vora 2013, 13) and a "strategic threat" (Hanieh 2011, 65). Immigrants like Panicker have internalized that any possible threat in the city must be committed by a foreigner.

Violence and unavoidable clashes between Emiratis and migrants continue in Chapter Five, "Moonseepalty." This story is a raw example of rampant

174   *Lava Asaad*

dis(assimilation) and the unattainability of hybridity. The vignette is about school Indian boys living in what they call Moonseepalty, which are "weak coffee-colored buildings housing the city's municipal offices" (143). The boys play soccer, transforming the parking lots into

> makeshift playgrounds, swaths of asphalt claimed by gangs of boys speaking multiple tongues. For a few hours we were all temporary inhabitants of Moonseepalty, an ephemeral, football-mad province of many complex cultural parts powered by nationality or race, where all of us pretended to be footballing warlords, ruling with our feet, manically protecting our tarred kingdoms.
>
> (144)

Each nationality is necessarily metamorphosed by others, yet it continues to imaginatively hold on to its own sense of identity. Hanieh writes about the strategic diversification of workers where the potentiality of solidarity becomes slim (2011, 65). The enforcement of segregation where each ethnic group gathers together, creates a disunity between the workers, perceiving the other with hostility. As a result, the workers cultivate "a spatial identity that is solely constituted through their relationship with capital means" (Hanieh 2011, 65). The Indian boys at the Moonseepalty have nurtured their own sense of Indianness, as opposed to being Emirati or any Arab national. Excluded from belonging to the city, the Indian boys hold on to their own imagined idea of what "back home" is. If they do claim any sense of being part of Abu Dhabi, this belonging is always limited and challenged by the state as evident by the roaming police, the state apparatus, around these neighborhoods. Vora also pertinently describes the paradox of belonging and exclusion for Indian workers in Dubai, opining that "it was the overwhelming Indianness of Dubai that framed Dubai's Indians' experiences of liminality—as Indians, as emigrants, and as foreign residents in the city. Old Dubai was therefore a place of both intense belonging and intense exclusion" (2013, 67). The state of exclusion dominates the ways in which these boys (the narrator, Anand who is nicknamed Tits, and others) navigate the spaces/rights that are inaccessible to them. The boys construct their identity in terms of what they lack, vis-à-vis what other Arabs are or have. The presence of the shurtha (Arabic for cops) reminds the boys of their fragility and exclusion. The shurtha objects when the Indian boys play cricket, and so they would occasionally raid the parking lots. The narrator says:

> As soon as we saw them [shurtha], we dug into our shorts, picked up our balls and threw them away. Other fuckers didn't. Arabees certainly didn't. Arabees had tungsten gonads. I wanted tungsten gonads ... Bug-eyed, we cursed him, his fucking language, and all his fucking ancestors. This was privilege the little fucker had negotiated.
>
> (146)

Spectral Migrant Workers 175

The shirtless Arab players, undisturbed by the presence of the cops, signal a sense of inclusion, of access to rights, and of maintaining self-esteem and worth. On the other hand, the Indian boys are painfully aware of their status of lack, of inferiority. "The vision of 'Moonseepalty' is a chimera, or more properly, the community to which the Indian boys belong offers only a bastardized version of municipal belonging," says Jacob Rama Berman in his review of the book (2017). The narrator's attitude, as a result, can only be shaped by feelings of hatred accompanied by the acute absence of masculinity which the Arab boys clearly manifest. Immigration, low socioeconomic status, and racial and ethnic demarcations repeat for the boys the story of *difference*. The storyline worsens as one of the gang boys (identified by the Indians as being Somali based on the shape of the skull and level of blackness) steals Tit's bicycle. Seeking help from the shurtha, the boys end up being questioned for their ID cards that prove their lawful presence. The cop says to Tits:

> "Babers" he said, switching to English.
> "Papers?"
> "You no understand? Bathaka!"
> "Student! Indian School, Indian School!"
> "Bathaka? Where batha—"
> "Please, I give Father's number. He works here. I live here. ADNOC Company! You know ADNOC Company?"
> ...
> "Zoory, habibi? For what zorry? Sbeek Arabic?"
> "No." Tits's head was hung.
> "Only English. No Arabic? In my country—"
>
> (148–149)

Tits is only released from the interrogation after the shurtha confirms that the boy has a lawful presence. The bike, nevertheless, is never mentioned again. With his immigration status, Tits cannot claim protection under the state, and his rights are forfeited since the state does not extend legal protection to foreigners like Tits. Animosity results, as Tits feels disempowered:

> "Kus Umak!" he yelled. "Kelb!" he screamed, spittle running down his lips. He then brough his palms to his crotch, cupped his balls, fingering every vein. "Motherfucker!" he yelled. "Madarchod!" He cussed them in every language he knew ...
> "Come to MY country. Choothiya! I fuck you up, COME TO MY COUNTRY!"
>
> (151–152)

Tits romanticizes his idea of his country, of the imagined powers and rights he could possess for being an Indian in India. The acute awareness of theirs versus ours dictates how he exists in the UAE where he experiences an

176   *Lava Asaad*

anxious sense of belonging to the host country and to the home country that he imagines being part of. The narrator says: "We didn't like Arabees but we rarely told them that. We wanted to talk back, we wanted to fight, we wanted tungsten gonads. We wanted all that but we didn't want to get into trouble" (152). In retaliation, Tits randomly throws a rock at an Arab boy, a weak attempt at regaining a lost masculinity and his Indianness. This coping mechanism helps second-generation migrants to construct an imagined sense of identity in a place that denies them the right to enjoy a sense of a multicultural one. Clashes continue when the Arab boy, aggravated, yells back " 'You crazy?' He spoke English now. He then held his index finger up to his temple and drew circles in the air. With Arabic, he tightened our dicks, with English he lopped them off" (152). Now that Tits is completely emasculated, he attacks the boy, only to be beaten down by the Arab's friends who severely leave Tits injured and mutilated for life. Tits' friends, unwilling to be caught breaking the law, run away. The imagined sense of belonging to an Indian community instantly shatters and Tits is left to fend for himself. The court dismisses the case by ruling it as a case of self-defense. Years later, Tits meets with the narrator at a wedding. Unable to forget the painful past as evident in the cane on which he leans, Tits ends up chewing off the narrator's ear as he whispers rapprochements of abandonment, of being betrayed by his own community. The strict immigration policies in the Gulf bring forth raw violence, committed against migrants and among migrants alike where one's purpose in the Gulf becomes concerned only with affirming one's economic and labor value without having the privilege to belong to a certain community.

"Kloon" (an Arabic pronunciation of Clown) is another story where migrants are stripped of their sense of identity and rights. More than any story, "Kloon" highlights racial discrimination in the Gulf where migrants are treated as dirty workers. The main character, Chainsmoke, takes up a part-time job to pay for his tuition. The job requires the worker to dress up as a clown to sell detergents in Abu Dhabi's supermarkets. The worker is sneered at by shoppers, harassed, and made an object of ridicule. One teenage girl warns her little sister to stay away from the clown:

> "Black clowns don't exist, Saarah. Look at his neck, fingers" she told her sister in Arabic … "Most blackies are bastards," she said. "My uncle also told me that you people don't wash. And that your farts smell like curry."
>
> (174, 180)

Chainsmoke is not only economically exploited, but he becomes a sexual fetish for a "local" woman, dressed in abaya, who asks him to ejaculate in front of her. No touching is her policy, as she reminds him of his dirty body and race. Seeing him unable to perform sexually, the local woman "cussed. Transitioning smoothly from English to Arabic, insulting his family, his future sons, his comatose prick, his cheap briefs" (172). After cussing in Arabic, "Chainsmoke's prick rose like vapor" (172). Like Tits, he feels an irreversible cultural and physical emasculation, which leads him to lash out on to a teenage girl and an old British woman who thought of him as being rude for walking in front of her in the store. Chainsmoke claims small victories at the end, but the cultural clash continues to manifest itself among migrants and citizens. Racial privileges resurface here where a Western woman is placed on a higher scale vis-à-vis brown or black migrants. These stories thus highlight the innate racial prejudices that further abase South Asian migrants who are always haunted by their sense of otherness.

Conclusion

The stories in Unnikrishnan's *Temporary People* highlight lives that exist on the margins, and lamentably, on the peripheries of a highly blinkered vision in academic discourse on migration and diaspora. Despite the shadowiness of these lives, they glue the pieces of the nation together without having the right to *claim it*. Migrant workers, economically expelled from their own countries to seek better opportunities elsewhere, hover between two irreconcilable belongings. Unnikrishnan's text spotlights this issue wherein deracinated migrants are doubly excluded from their home countries, referred to as "Veed," and from the countries they adopt. *Temporary People* ushers in a nuanced area of focus on a diasporic community in the UAE that is obliquely marginalized yet heavily exploited in the discourse of imagined nation-building in the Gulf States. Despite the attention projected onto migrants in the West, the stories of South Asian workers in the Gulf continue to be underscored as yet another unfortunate experience of economic migrants. Their plight, as this chapter elaborated, is more than suffering from an economic disadvantage. Unnikrishnan poignantly provides a narrative to an unheard or a muffled story of dismemberment and transience. If anything, the surrealist characters at least unravel the fragility of the fantastical idea of an "authentic" Gulf identity while also shedding light on the state of alienation and estrangement that these migrant workers endure. These workers are in a liminal space as they are expunged from their home and host countries, lost between their incomplete "Indianness" and the prohibition of constructing a new identity in the Gulf States.

References

Agamben, Giorgio. 1995. *Homo Sacer: Sovereign Power and Bare Life.* Stanford: Stanford University Press.

Anderson, Benedict. 1983. *Imagined Communities: Reflections on the Origin and Spread of Nationalism.* New York: Verso.

Appadurai, Arjun. 2006. *Fear of Small Numbers: An Essay on the Geography of Anger.* Duke: Duke University Press.

Asaad, Lava. 2020. *Literature with A White Helmet: The Textual-Corporeality of Being, Becoming, and Representing Refugees.* New York: Routledge.

178 *Lava Asaad*

Barkawi, Ban. 2020. "Race Protests Spark Calls for Arab States to End 'Exploitative' Migrant Worker System." *Reuters.* www.reuters.com/article/us-mideast-workers-rights-trfn/race-protests-spark-calls-for-arab-states-to-end-exploitative-migrant-worker-system-idUSKBN23F2IY

Bauman, Zygmunt. 2003. *Wasted Lives: Modernity and its Outcasts.* New York: Polity.

Berman, Jacob Rama. "Migrant Vernaculars: Deepak Unnikrishnan's *Temporary People.*" *Los Angles Review of Books*, April 12, 2017. https://lareviewofbooks.org/article/migrant-vernaculars-deepak-unnikrishnans-temporary-people/

Buckley, Michelle. 2015 "Construction Work, 'Bachelor' Builders and the Intersectional Politics of Urbanisation in Dubai." In Abdulhadi Khalaf, Omar AlShehabi and Adam Hanieh (eds.) *Transit States: Labour, Migration and Citizenship in the Gulf.* London: Pluto Press. 132–149.

Butler, Judith. 2009. *Frames of War: When Is Life Grievable?* New York: Verso.

Chalcraft, John. 2010. "Monarchy, Migration and Hegemony in the Arabian Peninsula." *Kuwait Programme on Development, Governance and Globalization in the Gulf States*, no. 12. 1–43. http://eprints.lse.ac.uk/32556/1/Monarchy,_migration_and_hegemony_%28working_paper%29.pdf.

Dresch, Paul. 2006. "Foreign Matter: The Place of Strangers in Gulf Society." In ohn W Fox, Nada Mourtada-Sabbah, and Mohamed Al-Mutawa (eds.) *Globalization and the Gulf*, J New York: Routledge. 200–222.

Hanieh, Adam. 2011. *Capitalism and Class in the Gulf Arab States.* New York: Palgrave.

Kaabour, Mahmoud, dir. 2013. *Champ of the Camp.* UAE: Veritas Films.

Kanna, Ahmed. "The Arab World's Forgotten Rebellions: Foreign Workers and Biopolitics in the Gulf." *SAMAR: South Asian Magazine for Action and Reflection*, May 30 2011.http://samarmagazine.org/archive/articles/357/

Longva, Anh Nga. 1997. *Walls Built on Sand: Migration, Exclusion, and Society in Kuwait.* New York: Routledge.

Lori, Noora. 2019. *Offshore Citizens: Permanent Temporary Status in the Gulf.* Cambridge, Cambridge University Press.

Mathew, Shaj. 2017. "Stories of Fragmented Lives in the Emirates" *The New York Times.* www.nytimes.com/2017/03/24/books/review/temporary-people-deepak-unnikrishnan.html

Qadri, Mustafa. 2020. "The UAE's Kafala System: Harmless or Human Trafficking?" *Carnegie Endowment for International Peace.* https://carnegieendowment.org/2020/07/07/uae-s-kafala-system-harmless-or-human-trafficking-pub-82188

Sassen, Saskia. 1998. *Globalization and Its Discontents.* New York: New Press.

Unnikrishnan, Deepak. 2017. *Temporary People.* Perth: UWA Publishing.

Vora, Neha. 2013. *Impossible Citizens: Dubai's Indian Diaspora.* Durham: Duke University Press.

Zetter, Roger. 2007. "More Labels, Fewer Refugees: Remaking the Refugee Label in an Era of Globalization." *Journal of Refugee Studies*, volume 20, issue 2, 172–192, https://doi-org.spot.lib.auburn.edu/10.1093/jrs/fem011

9 The Arab-African Cultural Identity in Idris Ali's *Dongola*

Rania Salem

Who Are the Nubians?

Nubians are "an ethnic group descended from one of Africa's earliest and most powerful ancient civilizations, which existed from 3700 BC to 350 CE" (Gilmore 2015, 53). Their cultural system is unique, because

> although 99% of Nubians are adherents of Islam, their culture and social structure have been described as a mosaic of Nubian and Arab-Islamic cultural patterns which borrows from and synthesizes Islamic, Arabic, Christian, and other much older beliefs into a single system of values and normative models of behavior.
>
> (Gilmore 2015, 53)

The Nubians "continue to self-identify as sharing many aspects of identity based on language, common social structures, a shared oral literature, and similar ethics, beliefs, and traditions," which led them to a share a collective notion of "We are like ourselves and others are not like us" (Gilmore 2015, 53). In other words, the Nubian community has a sense of pride in its cultural heritage as well as identity that give its members a special sense of individuation. However, this ethnic identity has suffered marginalization in Egypt. The Nubian community has been marginalized "socially by mainstream Egyptian culture as well as politically by the state system and exclusive nationalist discourses" (Youssef 2015, 77). In addition, Nubians "constitute a culturally distinctive group whose perceived racial characteristics operate as a 'boundary marker' in the social context of Egypt where they may be popularly perceived as Africans or 'Others'" (Gilmore 2015, 53). The exclusive Egyptian nationalist discourse along with the Nubian sense of collective identity have created an Arab-African identity dilemma despite the fact that Nubians have long been integrated in one cultural mosaic along with other minor communities in Egypt.

DOI: 10.4324/9781003301776-14

180   *Rania Salem*

Arab Nationalism and Nubian Literature

As a result of pan-Arabism, modern Arabic literature in general, and the Arabic novel in particular, have a strong relationship with Arab nationalism. The

> discourse of nationalism is an ideological formation whose success depends on its internalization at the level of the individual, and it is at that same level that the novel, more so than other traditional cultural forms, operates on the reader [regardless of the powerfulness of such operation].
>
> (Shalan 2002, 214–215)

The Egyptian nationalist discourse during Gamal Abdel Nasser's era (June 23, 1956 –September 28, 1970) as well as the "unitary fiction"[1] were purposefully "cultivated by the ideology of Arab nationalism in the postcolonial period"; as a result, other Egyptian identities were automatically marginalized and neglected as the state was aiming to secure "its dominance" (Gilmore 2015, 54; Youssef 2015, 83). Thus, such a unitary fiction asserted an essentialist hierarchical ideology that was on the rise during the Nasser era, which led to the marginalization of minorities in Egypt. In other words, as wa Thiongo puts it, any seemingly different writing or sub-cultural body that "gestures to the contradictions underwriting the nationalist program, particularly the fact of social and cultural difference, which was strategically deemphasized by the slogans of a unified platform of national liberation," is toned down if not eliminated by the authority (qtd. in Naaman 2011, 107). Moreover, according to Shalan, "the modern Arabic novel developed in conjunction with a specifically nationalist mode of thought ... [and] was instrumental not only in the dissemination of that thought, but in its very formation as well" (2002, 213). This is of relevance to Ali's novel as "the timeframe in which *Dongola* is set posits 'Nasserism' and Arab nationalism among the novel's central themes" (Abbas 2014, 152). Ali proposes Nasserism as a main theme in his novel to accentuate some of the "paradoxes and contradictions that underpinned" Nasserism in particular relation to the Nubians (Abbas 2014, 153). Therefore, *Dongola* reflects how Arab nationalism excluded a whole sect that is ethnically different but geographically located inside the boundaries of the imagined nation.

Unlike any non-Arabic speaking community in Egypt, the Nubians sacrificed their homeland for Nasser's national project, Aswan High Dam, with rosy promises of a proper compensation and a brighter future.[2] Unfortunately, these promises were not fulfilled. Although there is an excellent archiving of the process of saving Nubia's ancient monuments and temples led by the UNESCO, Saad states that there is scarcely an official record that documents the "deep psychological and social trauma that this project left in its wake" and such experience and trauma "were only documented in literature, never in the history books" (qtd. in Gilmore 2015, 56). Such a fact draws more emphasis on the importance of Nubian literature where the trauma of displacement is recognized and documented.

Aswan High Dam

> not only constituted an act of economic oppression—leading to mass displacement and the consequent migration to the north of a large number of Nubians who could no longer self-subsist by farming—it also constituted an act of cultural oppression: priceless monuments and artifacts of ancient Nubian civilization were drowned in Lake Nasser, the body of water that formed as a consequence of the building of the dam.
>
> (Abbas 2014, 150–151)

Gilmore states that the "perspectives and priorities of the displaced themselves were never recorded in official narratives, which tended to emphasize the dam's national benefits at the expense of its local costs" (2015, 56). As a result, Nubian literature, especially that of the third wave that started in the 1970s, attempted to voice out the "long-standing Nubian demands for equitable compensation [and] cultural recognition" in which the history of the Aswan High Dam and Nubian displacement are retold in the authentic voices of the Nubians themselves after the total submission of Old Nubia (Naaman 2011, 113). Hence, some Nubian writers and thinkers have a "sense of betrayal" because of the erasure of the Nubian displacement from "Egyptian collective memory and the lack of proper compensations or reparations made to the Nubians" (Naaman 2011, 113). Thus, the third wave explains the frustration and the struggle of the Nubians to integrate in and belong to the mainstream Egyptian community.

The term "Nubian Literature" emerged by the end of the twentieth century and was seen to consist of three main waves. According to Naaman, following Hagag Hasan Uddul's schema (a well-recognized Nubian writer and activist), the first wave started in the late 1940s and the second wave in the late 1960s where writers followed the social realist approach that was dominant in this period (2011, 114). In second-wave writings, Nubia was not yet completely submerged by the floods, "so the idea of their homeland as a lost paradise had yet to emerge," and these writers were more interested in tracing the beauty of the Nubian life and culture (Naaman 2011, 115). Third-wave writers, like Idris Ali, were more radical than second wave writers, as their writings reflected "their condemnation of the state, the reassurance of their way of life and culture, and the acute poverty plaguing many of the resettled Nubian communities" (Naaman 2011, 115). In their novels, Ali and his peers "have drawn heavily on their rich [Nubian] mythological inheritance and the centrality of the Nile to their way of life and customs" (Naaman 2011, 115). Thus, Nubian literature, particularly the third wave, voices the untold stories of a lost land that was sacrificed and documents the suffering and loss of an ethnic minority.

182   *Rania Salem*

Idris Ali

Third-wave Nubian writers wrote about Nubian displacement and the nostalgia to the lost paradise of Old Nubia. Their radicalism hit the Egyptian nationalist discourse nerve; consequently, some of these Nubian writers and novelists faced accusations of separatist tendencies that threaten the unity of the Egyptian state, as "viewing Egypt as a site of difference across ethnic, geographic, religious, class, and gender lines necessarily means calling into question the entire rhetorical architecture of the nationalist movement, which is predicated on unity and the eliding of difference" (Gilmore 2015, 57; Naaman 2011, 110). Ali refused this radicalism, as he "has shown that it overlooks the historical fact that Nubians have always been an integral part of the Egyptian people" (qtd. in Gilmore 2015, 57). Nonetheless, his protagonist Awad Shalali in *Dongola* is a radical figure. My analysis demonstrates that it is through his depiction of Awad's radicalism that Ali reflects on the misery of the non-integrated Nubians and criticizes how marginalization and exclusion have led to their agony and estrangement within Egypt, their homeland.

The way in which Idris Ali positions himself is of crucial importance in reading *Dongola*. According to Youssef, Ali

> describes himself as a "katib sha'bi" (public/popular writer) who opposed the ideal of "naqa" al- "irq al-nubi" (purity of the Nubian vein), which his people believe in, and espoused a realist literary style to write about Nubia and the daily experiences of its marginalized individuals who struggle to secure their basic needs.
>
> (2015, 79)

He did not even accept *Dongola*'s characterization as belonging to Nubian literature, as this excludes him and other Nubian writers from mainstream Egyptian literature to which he claims to belong (Youssef 2015, 79). By this declaration, Ali

> positions himself among those who seek a homogenous narrative of Egypt excluding other racial populations and at the same time departs from the essentialist position of racial pride that marginal groups embrace to resist hegemonic and exclusive discourses and enactments.
>
> (Youssef 2015, 80)

Presenting himself as an Egyptian writer reflects Ali's awareness of the Arab-African intercultural crisis. It is crucial to investigate what constitutes an Arab identity and an African identity in order to contextualize this intercultural dilemma.

What Makes an Arab Identity?

Arab nationalism is an integral notion to constituting an Arab identity. Peter Wien defines Arab nationalism as a "reference system for the shaping of collective identities, and as such it is an intrinsic part of twentieth-century culture" and a "framework of cultural references [that] circumscribes an imaginary space between the Atlantic Ocean, the southern and eastern rim of the Mediterranean, and the Tigris River" (2017, 12). According to Manduchi, Arabism ("*urūbah*, the fact of being Arabs") emerged as a "sentiment and political project in the second half of the 19th century" to "emancipate the Arab masses" (2017, 9; 11). Arab nationalism became more profound in the first half of the twentieth century and after the First World War, but "it lived its most important moment between the middle of the 1940s and the end of the 1960s," at a time when many North African countries like Egypt were working towards their independence and the pan-Arab ideology was at its epitome (Manduchi 2017, 18).

In the case of Arab identity, Manduchi admits that "nationalism" is no longer a solid concept. She acknowledges that

> all nationalistic ideas are based on the acknowledgement of the identity of a population that aims to create political unity and—if there is the possibility—a national power in line with a project of cultural and spiritual hegemony implemented by means of expansionistic or imperialistic policies.
>
> (5)

Moreover, she adds that the base of the nationalistic ideology "is identified with a group which, on the basis of a deliberate choice, shares a land, a language, and ethnic ties" (Manduchi 2017, 6–7). In addition to these, Manduchi defines the nation as "a de facto community" that is based on "a culture of belonging" (2017, 7). As we see in Ali's *Dongola*, post-colonial nations "make use of all means of communication to create and spread this unifying identity [of nationalism] to strengthen the power of the hegemonic state through the creation of a single and unifying idea." During president Gamal Abdel Nasser's rule (1956–1970), which is the time of the novel, Arab nationalism was integral to the discourse of Egyptian nationalism. Although Egyptian identity is culturally rich and encompasses various geographical, racial, ethnic, and cultural backgrounds, the rise of Arabism that Nasser relied on as a resistance tool against colonialism led to excluding and marginalizing whoever does not conform to the notion of the Arab Muslim individual. The de facto community that emerges through this process of exclusion is administered by the post-colonial state's concept of nationalism that utilizes all forms of communication to build and promote a collective national

184   *Rania Salem*

identity. The state thus reinforces its domineering authority by establishing a single unified ideology that is based on a shared land, language, and race. This ideology, in turn, enforces essentialist notions in society and legitimizes the exclusion of ethnic minorities. Therefore, Arab nationalism created a hierarchical system that, unfortunately, worked against some of the Arab communities who have different ethnic origins.

Afropolitanism: What Makes an African Identity?

In their article *"Beyond Sovereign Reason: Issues and Contestations in Contemporary African Identity,"* Michael Eze and Katja Wal believe that "African sociopolitical and cultural differences make it an uphill task to write of African identity as homogenous enterprise," since the "entrenched diversity in terms of religion, language or history symbolizes the intensity of these cultural variations and ruptures any claim that a collective African identity exhibits homogenous universal coherence" (2020, 189). In other words, Africa's immensely rich history, whether it is pre- or post-colonial, makes it almost impossible to pinpoint one collective African identity. Moreover, according to Western perceptions, the concept of the tribe is often at the heart of defining African identities and civilizations, which is an epistemological invention of colonialism (Eze and Wal 2020, 193). Eze and Wal state that the African collective identity has always been transient in accordance with cultural and religious traditions, and since culture is in a continuous state of evolvement, the African identity that is drawn from them changes as well to accommodate these alterations (2020, 194). These cultural alterations, in terms of customs, helped preserve a sense of identity and, at the same time, permitted for an identity assimilation that was natural and unnoticed (Eze and Wal 2020, 194). Furthermore, African societies were, and still are, very rich with traditions and extremely diverse, where people might belong to a variety of ethnic groups with various extents of affinity that imbricate numerous social, religious, and political affiliations (Eze and Wal 2020, 194). Therefore, African identity has a unique quality of flexibility through the ability to contain, embrace, and integrate multiple ethnicities, religions, and customs.

One of the main factors that have affirmed African identity is the colonial experience. The "project of colonialism thrived by politicizing differences using divide and rule policies. Different cultures, traditions and histories were forcefully divided or integrated, in 'radically different degrees,'" which resulted in a collective self-determination that "was measured through the medium of shared experiences of colonialism and revolting against it" (Eze and Wal 2020, 196). Unfortunately, however, post-colonial African citizenship developed a fragmented identity as a result of inheriting this sort of segmented collective: "the citizen was both an ethnic citizen among her group and a stranger in another native authority," which is the case of the protagonist in *Dongola* (Eze and Wal 2020, 196). In order to demolish the colonial conception of African identity and clarify the concept of Afropolitanism,

The Arab-African Cultural Identity   185

Eze and Wal believe that crossing the geographical border does not negate one's Africanness since the concept of the border is in and of itself a subjective transcendence of geographical inevitability. They add that a significant consequence of such restriction is the dogmatic inference that one's identity is intrinsically linked to geographical fatalism, which has enormous sociopolitical and economic ramifications (2020, 201). Thus, being an African human is essentially defined by one's geographical imaginary, even when no affective relationship or commitment to that region exists, and is foremost a product of these constraints on subjective mobility (Eze and Wal 2020, 201).

Gehrmann defines the Afropolitan as a "human being ... who has realized that her identity can no longer be explained in purist, essentialist and oppositional terms or by reference to the African continent" (qtd. in Eze and Wal 2020, 202). Consequently, Afropolitanism

> invokes the following credentials: it is cosmopolitan, yet unlike Western cosmopolitanism it is discursive and "antiessentialist, open to cultural and intellectual hybridization, but endowed with a particular consciousness for Africa's historical wounds," yet, inspiring a political moment, one that would contribute to complete the "unfinished decolonization process of Africa."
>
> (Eze and Wal 2020, 202)

In other words, beyond racial solidarity, Afropolitanism presupposes social and cultural cohesion since it abandons racial solidarity as the basis for modern African collective identity in favor of a new notion of collective African identity that is neither antagonistic to the West nor a residual narrative, but rather a "subjective space of contemporaneous identification" (Eze and Wal 2020, 203). Therefore, the Afropolitan can be perceived "as an African who refuses to be marginalised, prototyped, and cast as the antithetical Other on the cosmopolitan ground of Western modernity" (Knudsen and Rahbek 2016, 16).

Since cultural identity is complex and multilayered, looking into two of the main components that constitute the current Nubian identity, that is, Arabism and Afropolitanism, helps in understanding the complexity as well as the conflict that are embedded in such an identity. Arabism and Afropolitanism are not conflicting concepts; however, their intercultural intersection may result in an ideological struggle due to essentialist ethnic and nationalistic concepts that encourage exclusion to grow among Arab-African societies. This is why in *Dongola*, Awad decides to focus on what negates his Arab identity after it fails him due to his ethnicity, and chooses to prioritize his national belonging to the lost African Dongola.

Dongola

This chapter's reading of *Dongola* argues that Idris Ali seeks harmony and recognition rather than separatism. Ali attempts to show how an essentialist

186   *Rania Salem*

identity can be "inherently constraining" (Alcoff 2000, 319). Gilmore believes that *Dongola* is

> grounded in the social realist tradition, using the Nubian experience of displacement, poverty, and injustice as the starting point for a broader materialist critique of the failure of the nationalist movement to bring about social change and improve the conditions of the rural classes and peripheral groups in Egypt.
>
> (2015, 68)

Naaman further elaborates that Ali's novel "serves more as a symbol for the collective experience of disenfranchisement experienced by the Egyptian underclasses than as the articulation of a unique experience of ethnic or racial marginalisation" (qtd. in Gilmore 2015, 68). In *Idrīs ʿAlī: ʿabqarī Al-riwāyah Al-Nūbīyah*, El Gayar considers *Dongola* a first-class political novel that discusses a model of Nubian politicians who were accused of communism in the 1960s. Al Gayar states that Ali himself admits that "the sorrows, the tears, and songs would never restore the land that had been drowned, the identity obliterated, or the unhurried saviors—because they were here, not there" (Mawsili 2011, 18, 29). El Gayar adds that Ali cleverly presents what Awad Shalali suffered in prison, then in Nubia, and then in his work on a ship that roams the shores of the world to finally reach a long-sought realization. Through Awad, Ali shows that a dream that attempts to restore the past is no more than a nightmare because the past, which is not repeated again in history, does not return, and such a dream leads to the protagonist's slow disintegration and soul decay (Mawsili 2011, 18). The theme of return is echoed in *Dongola*, which reflects the failure of Awad's return in restoring balance. Awad dreamed of returning back to his village to restore the glory of the past; however, he fails because he does not realize that his salvation is not in a nostalgic place that he belongs to, but within himself.

Indeed, *Dongola* offers a striking example of the modern production of the novel apart from the restricted and colossal view of the nation-state that is offered in modern nationalist Egyptian novels. It shifts the focus towards "the cultural experiences of individuals from the ethnically and religiously marginal communities whose histories and languages are often overlooked due to dominant cultural discourses and reductive historical narratives" (Youssef 2015, 75). In other words, Ali's novel attempts to highlight an untold reality that is toned down, if not neglected on purpose. The novel participates in testifying "to the more complex reality of the intersections of class with race, ethnicity, religion, gender, sexuality, culture, and language by bringing these intricacies to the forefront of its literary undertakings" (Youssef 2015, 76). In this way, Ali's novel advocates recognition and appreciation rather than separatism.

Dongola is written in three parts. The first part, "Separated Man," is the most intensive in its depiction of the protagonist's crisis. The title conveys the

The Arab-African Cultural Identity   187

act of marginalization against Nubians, which Ali wants his readers to recognize. The novel is set around the time of Egypt's defeat in the 1967 Arab-Israeli War (Setback), which was a traumatizing experience for all Egyptians and led to collective frustration. As a Nubian and a follower of Nasser, Awad's identity crisis is linked to this political and social atmosphere and the collective marginalization faced not only by Nubians but also by other disenfranchised classes.

Before Part One, Ali starts with a dedication to his "friends and loved ones, the people of the north" in a poem where he offers all that he has: papers and voice. His plee to keep his papers and voice without conviction complements the protagonist's dilemma in the novel by demanding recognition and endorsement. According to Abbas,

> the "culture" that Ali mentions in the poem refers to the Arab-Egyptian culture of northern Egypt and the "people" that are signaled in the final line of the epigraph, and with whom Ali identifies (for they are his "people," whose "sorrows" he shares), are the Nubians of southern Egypt.
>
> (2014, 148)

It can be argued that the distinction between an "I" and a "you" does not have to signal a notion of separatism but, as Abbas suggests, "points to Ali's complicated identity as a Nubian author writing in Arabic" (2014, 148). Most probably, the distinction signals Ali's awareness of his position in seeking an acceptable integrated identity. As Dimeo argues, the "stark choice that forces the author to alienate himself from one of the two populations between whom he seeks to mediate is dedicated by a nationalist grammar that contains no mechanism for expression of the Nubian identity" (2015, 74). Clearly, the usage of such pronouns emphasizes what Bakhtin refers to as a dialogic tension that reflects how the protagonist, or the author, feels alienated and estranged.

Before Part One in the Arabic version of the novel and the first thing in Part One in the English translation, Ali has two subtitles: "Illumination" and "Disgrace," respectively, which are both historical. In the "Illumination" part, Ali cites the famous Egyptian journalist and politician Dr. Muhammad Husayn Haykal where the latter talks about how Caliph Umar sent his troops to Nubia; he describes the battle between the two armies and then the truce they had: "the Nubians gave the Muslims slaves, and the Muslims gave the Nubians food" (1). The "Disgrace" part is a historical account of the Arab tribes who settled near Nubia in the early centuries of Islam and how the Arab captivated and "trafficked in slaves from Nubia" to the extent that "slaves were so plentiful with their owners, that when one of them had his hair cut, he gave the barber a slave" (2). Ali's Dedication, Illumination, and Disgrace reflect the sense of Nubian bitterness and lack of proper recognition. This part in *Dongola* tackles the theme of slavery and blackness and recalls how the non-black North Africans "other" black Africans, which emphasizes Awad's estrangement.

188   *Rania Salem*

In Chapter 1, "Separated Man," Ali deals with Awad's situation after his release from prison, an imprisonment that lasts ten years of torment, as well as his decision to return to the south. Ali leaves the protagonist as a tourist in Cairo for several hours to criticize the prevailing reality of the city and its people, a reality represented in a way that anticipates the defeat in the 1967 War (Mawsili 2011, 19). The first chapter ends with Awad taking the train to reach the south, then fleeing his arrest attempt to Sudan and escaping to Europe for nine more years (Mawsili 2011, 19). "Separated Man" affirms how Awad is othered by the people of Cairo, referred to as "the northerners" throughout the novel.

The first pages of "Separated Man" reflect a very subtle categorization of the Cairene or northern people that Ali constructs in his novel and Awad's perception of them after being released from prison. Awad hates the authority—the people who imprisoned and tortured him—but loves the people and streets of Cairo because, according to the postcolonial Egyptian map, "Awad reasons, he is an Egyptian and the [1952] revolution promises freedom for all Egyptians" (Dimeo 2015, 75). He gets confused and sees "all these northerners as spies," but at the same time, "he was seized by a violent nostalgia for the places he loved" in Cairo (4). During his morning expedition, he was shocked as "these were not the people of Egypt, not with these scowling faces, pursed lips, cold smiles, and bad jokes" (4). Awad keeps wondering "what had happened to this once-laughing city? ... They called it the 'Mother of the World,' now she was eating her children" (4). Ali repeats the same thought to highlight Awad's awe: "he had been part of it [Cairo] all. It was they who had turned him in and soiled his innocence" (5).

The narrator openly refers to Awad's awareness of his sense of estrangement and the love–hate relationship that he has with the north and its people: "stranger in a strange city" (6). The same place he "had an addict's love for" was his exile and "the key to his crisis" (4, 6). Dimeo suggests that since Awad is "rejected as an Egyptian nationalist, [he] falls under the sway of his cousin Bahr Jazuli, who once dreamed of serving the Egyptian government, only to be driven by police harassment to seek refuge in his Nubian identity" (2015, 81). Thus, the rejection and "abandonment" that Awad experiences "first at the hands of the northern Egyptians, then from the Communist party," and later on by the people of his own village and the Sudanese Nubians during his attempt to revive the ancient Kingdom of Dongola, fall in contrast to Awad's accepting his forced identity, which prevented him from coming to terms with his intercultural identity as an integral Nubian Egyptian citizen.

In order to achieve recognition and acceptance, Awad's first move after being released from prison was "pining for a lost fixity and [being] compulsively focused on the source of [his] victimization" instead of handling his "internal heterogeneity" to avoid being entrapped in any set of categories; Awad Shalili, whether he acknowledges it or not, is a victim to the fictitious

The Arab-African Cultural Identity   189

strategic essentialism that basically "invites elitism and courts incoherence" (Alcoff 2000, 323–325). Indeed, he makes the same mistake that the people of the north did: basing the truth of who he really is and his identity on "overgeneralizations of the human experience and social praxis," as "in every encounter with the northern authorities, he sees Mamluks, slave traders, pharaonic or Arab invaders as he continually refashions himself to fight wars of past decades, centuries, or millennia" (Alcoff 2000, 325; Dimeo 2015, 83). The Nubia-Cairo relationship within Awad's scope represents a highly charged emotional baggage; while heading to the south, to his home after a 10-year imprisonment, "he would break his ties to the north ... with all its good and bad" (13–14).

Part One emphasizes Awad's oppression and attempt to regain the ancient victory of his ancestors to heal the wounded part of his identity as a Nubian. Ali uses this Part to demonstrate the traumatic "Cairene" experience of not only Awad but also his father, his uncle, and his cousin Bahr Jazuli. Awad was nostalgic about the submerged lost Nubia. Again, "Return" as salvation is strongly present in *Dongola*. However, return is misleading since Awad realizes his own fragility and inability when he returns to his Nubian village and attempts to recreate the Old Nubian Kingdom which is rejected by his own Nubian fellows. Awad was bitter about the Nubian sufferings as, for him, Nubia "was a forgotten land, which the world had erased from its map, to serve a reservoir for its water ... He grew angry and hateful, and a never-ending sorrow entered his heart" (24). For him, "the north had glory and leisure; the south, death and floods" (38). It can be suggested that he belongs to "those who, possibly by virtue of membership in multiple politically salient groups, often find themselves and their interests distorted by restricted definitions and understandings; their interests, rather than transparent, are 'opaque'" (Hames-García 2000, 104). Consequently, Awad's "opaque" interests clash with dominant "national" interests, as his "political interests thus often appear opaque insofar as they differ from those of the hegemonic members of the politically salient social groups to which they belong," which is demonstrated in the following pages (Hames-García 2000, 104).

As previously mentioned, Awad has a love–hate relationship with the Cairenes. At the beginning of the novel, he was threatened by the people of the north whom he saw as "spies" (4). As a kid, his mother, Hushia, used to warn him of Cairo and the women of the north. He recalls her voice telling him, "my boy, don't go to the land of that snake [his Cairene stepmother, Ruhia]," but he, as a "boy in school," considered Cairo to be "his holy place" (9). He loved Cairo as a kid, but as a grown-up man, he became bitter and saw "the people of the north without heads" and "the whole north as corrupt, where only cowards and informers got any glory— death to decent men" (9).

In time, Ali makes it clear that Awad can see that he is not the only oppressed individual among even those bullying him. When the "Bulaqi" (i.e.,

190   *Rania Salem*

Cairene) informer brags about his grandparent owning black slaves, Awad realizes that it is "slaves owning slaves!" (19). This reflects the multileveled class and racial oppression that Awad faces. The Bulaqi informer does not belong to a high social class and is himself subject to class oppression, but he bullies Awad because of the latter's skin color. After this encounter, Awad heads to the Nubian café in Abdien to look for "some old friends," just to find a Nubian band singing in the praise of the Aswan Dam and the revolution, "they were not the descendants of the bowmen of the glance. They had lost Nubia, their past, and their present" (19). He is disconnected from Nubians as well as Cairenes and experiences a bitter sense of betrayal and abandonment because none of these people accepted him with all his dreams and aspirations. However, within his heated emotions and thoughts, Ali intentionally surrounds him with a crowd of Cairenes excited about a football match. Awad here, after "dunk[ing] his head in the water [of the river Nile] and [feeling] totally recovered," has a moment of realization that allows him to understand his marginalization from a more nuanced perspective:

> He saw things with a clarity that lifted fog around simple truths: those marching figures were not invading soldiers, but weary northerners going home after a hard day, and they were not hostile or hateful. They were not all the murderers of Bahr Jazuli. The murderers were a terrible minority who made no distinction between northerners and southerners, infidels and believers, Muslims and Copts. Nor had they any hand in the destruction of the south or the enslavement of its valiant people … Yes, Cairo was beautiful, and its people were full of goodness and tolerance. Those who had invaded the south and laid it waste had done that with older cultures and more powerful nations.
>
> (21)

Ali fluctuates between his bitterness and reality, and this is reflected in how he depicts the thought process of his protagonist. A few pages after Awad's moment of realization, he wonders why he "had never been able to understand the mentality of the northerners"; for him, "some of them were so brilliant as to be virtual prophets, while others were the lowest of the low" (50–51). Awad here falls into the same pitfall that feeds the racism of northerners: he attempts to stereotype them as they stereotype him and other Nubians. In other words, Awad categorizes the northerners into two categories: virtuous and evil, and he is bewildered when he meets a northerner who does not fit into any of these two categories. He thus thinks in an ethnic binary opposition and fails to humanize the "different" Other. Interestingly, this alienation keeps invading Awad until he feels completely alienated from his own people. Cairo for him is a geographically alienating space that heightens his inability to belong and perform his identity as a citizen and that also questions his essentialist notions of identity.

Awad Shalali and Authority

Awad's rejection of authority is linked to ethnic and class discrimination, on the one hand, and to his defeated dream (i.e., Nasser's era) and lost Nubia on the other hand. His encounters with the authorities reflect nothing but oppression and discrimination. The first encounter with the police is a flashback where he recalls the dialogue between himself and the police officer:

'Where are you from?'
'Halfway between north and south, in the area where Cambyses' army perished, where the army of the Muslims retreated in defeat, its' soldiers' eyes gouged out. Now it's all become a water reservoir for the north.'

(8–9)

Awad's nostalgia to a glorious past he did not witness but in which he remains engrossed is reflected in this interrogation where the tone is edgy and bitter. Although his answers sound vague to the investigator, the reader can clearly observe the sense of pride and loss in his words. Moreover, Awad's words reflect how his identity is geographically and religiously pined. He is defeated and alienated by the Cairenes because of his blackness; consequently, he grounds himself in the ancient glorious Nubian kingdom and rejects his present.

A couple of pages after this flashback, Awad recalls another investigation where "the security men pounced on [him and his comrades on the train]. He invited them to a southern wedding. They led him to a northern massacre" (15). Awad recalls the investigation:

'I insist on reading the transcript of the interrogation. I'm not illiterate.'
'We're the ones who taught you how to read, you son of a slave.'
'I object. My mother is a free Nubian lady.'
'I want to read it first.'
'The government was wrong to give you people schools. If we had left you savages, you'd still be our waiters and doormen. Take this man away and teach him some manners.'

(15–16)

Again, the condescending and racist tone of the officer highlights Awad's pride, as a literate and a free human being, as well as a rebel against the northern biased accusations. This interrogation echoes Bakhtin's dialogism since it demonstrates a "constant interaction between meanings, all of which have the potential of conditioning others" (1984, 426). The power struggle between Awad and the interrogator demonstrates how each one of them tries to assert his authority. Moreover, this dialogue indicates that color is another factor in Awad's identity that leads him to be perceived as inferior to the light-skinned

192 *Rania Salem*

Cairenes. As a result, he is always in "pursuit of 'roots' as a symbolic counterweight to the processes of [his] exclusion and marginalization" (Hall 2019, 56). His roots are symbolized in the dream of "Return" to Dongola.

Awad's blackness arises in each encounter with authority, for he is not only marginalized but also humiliated because of his blackness. In another incident where he reports his cousin Bahr Jazuli missing after the latter's imprisonment, Awad is insulted by almost everyone in the police station where the emphasis on his skin color is clear (17).

Bahr Jazouli—Awad's cousin—is always somewhere in the latter's stream of thoughts, especially during his encounters with the authority: "the day they arrested [Bahr] he was Egyptian, but he died a Nubian" (25). Bahr was arrested as an Egyptian who believed in the post 1952 ideals and dreams; however, when he was in jail because of his Egyptian-ness, he resorted to his ethnic Nubian origins to face the racism that he was subjected to. In prison, an "arrogant young officer" insulted Bahr: "your heart is as black as your face," to which Bahr replied "my blackness is a fact—I know where it comes from! Not you—I think you'd better ask your grandmother where those blue eyes of yours came from," and this is how Bahr "[grew] even blacker—even more authentic" as the soldiers joked torturing him (25–26). Ali here mixes between the personas of Awad and the narrator. Clearly, Awad's alienation and marginalization because of his blackness is confirmed by the death of his cousin Bahr.

Awad's frustration and disappointment in his Nubian fellows starts to grow even more when he arrives in Qirshah, the Nubian village he comes from. He wonders "how had they submitted to this reality and grown accustomed to it" and how "not one of them knew any of their forgotten history or had any enthusiasm for it" (2, 39). The scene where Awad's mother, Hushia al-Nur, receives him demonstrates the intensive mixed feelings of "a belated celebration of nationalist mourning to grieve over drowned Nubia" (28). However, in the midst of Awad's disappointment, Demerdash appears. According to the people of Qirshah, Demerdash is a drunkard smuggler and is never taken seriously due to his extremist tendencies (41). Supporting Awad's cause, Demerdash argues against all of the village and recognizes the legitimacy of Awad's demands saying "the man is only asking that we get some agricultural land and reasonable compensation" (42). This scene is a glare example of Awad's alienation from his own Nubian people. His essentialist understanding of identity created a barrier between him and his own people to the extent that they cannot relate to his own dream, and he cannot relate to their everyday reality.

Part One, which covers more than half of the novel, ends with Awad fleeing to Sudan after things get heated in Qirshah, a reminder to the reader of the significance of the title of this part "Separated Man." Awad's own people do not accept his ideas except for Demerdash who flees with him. On his way to Sudan, the desert guide asks him about his identity: "if Awad knew who he himself was, he would tell him. After breaking off from his past, would he be

The Arab-African Cultural Identity   193

able to learn who he was?" (58). Not knowing who he is, "Awad Shalali was leaving thirty-nine villages behind him. He was defeated. This was an exodus of the vanquished" (59). Ali here prepares his readers for the fading away of Awad Shalali in the coming and last part in the novel. Awad no longer appears except in some dry brief lines sent to his wife Halima. By abandoning all his beliefs and people, he abandons himself.

The Fading of Awad Shalali

The second part, entitled "The Trial of Awad Shalali," is about Awad ten years after fleeing Nubia. It shows how Awad "manages to transform himself thoroughly after each experience of rejection" (Dimeo 2015, 83). The situation in Nubia did not change for the entire ten years of his absence, as evident in Ali's description of the status quo:

> The life of these people, which consisted of perpetually waiting for absent people scattered all through the world seeking the livelihoods lacking [in Nubia]. They had been quickly dispersed and discarded at the base of Silsilah Mountain, middle-aged people and widows. They were granted small allowances, and the able-bodied were left idle and loitering, and so they left on an essential migration, leaving their mothers and wives to guard the stone houses in what was called their new homeland.
>
> (60)

Although change did not color Nubia in those ten years, Awad has gone through changes that unravel hidden aspects of his identity. Dimeo summarizes the main three stages of the process in which Awad's identity is de-/re-constructed. First, he "becomes intoxicated with 'the north' [and] determined to embrace the Egyptian identity assigned him by virtue of the modern political map"; this stage reflects Awad's willingness and desire to integrate the different elements of his identity as an Egyptian (Dimeo 2015, 73). However, the second stage takes place when Awad's blackness "marks him as an 'other' in the imagined community's neat census categories, despite his embrace of Egyptianism. ... Awad revives Nubian nationalism, only to find his resurrected nationalist vision beyond the imagination of Nubians in both Egypt and Sudan" (Dimeo 2015, 73). The final stage follows Awad's failure to pursue his roots when he "abandons with contempt Egypt, Nubia, and Africa altogether, finding acceptance only in a post-nationalist Western Europe. Yet even this multicultural grammar of tolerance proves incomprehensible to the imaginations of the family he leaves behind, voiceless, in Nubia" (Dimeo 2015, 73). Therefore, the last stage exemplifies Awad's inability to perform his identity as an integrated individual and citizen in Egypt. He continues—to "search or reinvent" himself in order to find a fitting place that he can wholeheartedly belong to (Dimeo 2015, 83). However, the result is the same because each identity that he attempts to recreate is too rigid and essentialist to help

194   *Rania Salem*

him negotiate and come to terms with the ideological formations in which it is implicated. In other words, it is as if Awad keeps reinventing the same identity in different forms.

Awad Becomes His Worst Nightmare

The third and last part of the novel focuses on the abandoned Nubian women in Awad's life: his mother, Hushia, and his wife, Halima. According to Abbas, "while Dongola presents a Nubian challenge to Arab-Egyptian nationalism through Awad's perspective, its engagement with and representation of gender issues ultimately frames this challenge ironically" (2014, 160). Awad, most probably subconsciously, repeats the scenario of his rejection by the northerners in role reversal; he is the one who abandons and leaves Hushia and Halima behind, which makes them his subaltern in the same way in which he is the northerners' subaltern. Abbas further elaborates as follows:

> On the one hand, therefore, Awad's diasporic outlook is set in opposition to, and represents a critique of, Arab-Egyptian nationalism. On the other hand, Awad's own counter-discourse—in so far as it marginalizes women—seems to mirror the exclusionary practices of a nationalist perspective. This, in turn, alludes to the paradoxical relationship between diasporas and nationalism.
>
> (2014, 161)

His tragedy is reflected in the family he leaves behind: two women desperately waiting for their man to come back to "his" home, but "this absentee had a heart of stone … a man without a home port" (92–93). Ali starts the third part, entitled "The Sorrows of Hushia and Halima," by Halima who "waited and her waiting grew long because she was like the other forsaken women in Nubia" (92). Despite being the shortest part in the novel, it importantly shows how Awad's own tragic fall affects the two women and unleashes the worst in them, leading Halima to kill Hushia.

Conclusion

This chapter has attempted to demonstrate how an extremist and an essentialist pursuit of the individual's ethnic and/or cultural roots, as a metaphoric opposition to processes of exclusion and marginalization, leads to the loss of the individual's inner cohesion and balance. Hence, investigating the uniqueness of each individual identity in relation to the cultural environment gives further insight into the forces that keep shaping and re-shaping this identity. In *Dongola*, Awad holds essentialist views on identity and fails to solve his own intercultural dilemma. After being socially and politically rejected by the system that advocated Arab nationalism, he becomes attached to his African identity, which connects him to the strong and triumphant cultural heritage of the ancient Nubian Kings. Awad faces racism, injustice, and rejection; however, he never questions his situation. Instead, he keeps acting according to his agony and anger until he flees away to the West leaving behind everything that he really belongs to; that is, his family and what he claimed to be his beliefs. Awad fails to be an African, and, definitely, he fails to be an Afropolitan since he is incapable of understanding himself through previous and present experiences, interactions, and geopolitical locations: he holds to his nostalgic roots and disregards his present experiences. This chapter has attempted to give voice to these silenced aspects in relation to Arab-African cultural disintegration in *Dongola*. Further research on the Arab-African cultural identity in the region would make it possible to untangle false and essentialist ethnic notions that prevent the integration of individuals like Awad who could be assets to their own communities.

Notes

1 Unitary fiction here refers to the nationalist discourse that aims to unite people under one major umbrella; that is, the welfare of the nation.
2 According to Gilmore,

> in the case of the estimated 50,000–70,000 Egyptian Nubians displaced from forty-four villages along the Nile to the designated resettlement site known as "New Nubia"—seventy-five kilometers north of Aswan (Dafalla xvii)—resettlement was meant to offer a new beginning. Nasser promised the crowds assembled at Abu Simbel in 1960 that "If the Nubian people are leaving their smaller home of Nubia for the prosperity of the republic ... they will find stability, prosperity and a decent life" in Kom Ombo (Fahim, Egyptian Nubians 36), where they would have access to utilities such as piped water and electricity for the first time as well as better access to health care and education.
>
> (2015, 55)

References

Abbas, F. (2014) "Egypt, Arab Nationalism, and Nubian Diasporic Identity in Idris Ali's Dongola: A Novel of Nubia," *Research in African Literatures*, 45(3), 147–166. doi:10.2979/reseafrilite.45.3.147.

Alcoff, L.M. (2000) "Who Is Afraid of Identity Politics?" in Moya, M.L. and Hames-Garcia, M.R. (eds.) *Reclaiming identity: realist theory and the predicament of postmodernism*. Berkeley, CA: University of California Press. pp. 312–344.

Ali, I. (2006) *Dongola: a novel of Nubia*. Translated by P. Theroux. Cairo: The American University in Cairo Press.

Bakhtin, M.M. and Emerson, C. (1984) *Problems of Dostoevsky's poetics*. Minneapolis: University of Minnesota Press (Theory and history of literature, v. 8).

DiMeo, D. (2015) "Unimaginable Community: The Failure of Nubian Nationalism in Idris Ali's Dongola," *Research in African Literatures*, 46(1), 72–89. doi:10.2979/reseafrilite.46.1.72

196 Rania Salem

Eze, M.O. and Wal, K. (2020) "Beyond Sovereign Reason: Issues and Contestations in Contemporary African Identity," *JCMS: Journal of Common Market Studies*, 58(1), 189–205. doi:10.1111/jcms.12979

Gilmore, C. (2015) "A Minor Literature in a Major Voice: Narrating Nubian Identity in Contemporary Egypt," *Alif (Cairo, Egypt)*, 35(35), 52. Available at: https://go.exlibris.link/t8XXCZ35.

Hall, S. (2019) *Essential essays. Volume 2: Identity and diaspora*. Edited by D. Morley. Durham London: Duke University Press.

Hames-Garcia, M.R. (2000) "Who Are Our Own People?" in Moya, M.L. and Hames-Garcia, M.R. (eds.) *Reclaiming identity: realist theory and the predicament of postmodernism*. Berkeley, CA: University of California Press. pp. 102–129.

Knudsen, E.R. and Rahbek, U. (2016) *In search of the Afropolitan: encounters, conversations and contemporary diasporic African literature*. London; New York: Rowman & Littlefield International.

Manduchi, P. (2017) "Arab Nationalism(s): Rise and Decline of an Ideology" *Oriente moderno*, 97(1), 4–35. doi:10.1163/22138617-12340137

Mawṣilī, F. (2011) *Idrīs ʿAlī: ʿabqarī al-riwāyah al-Nūbīyah*. al-Ṭabʿah 1. al-Qāhirah: al-Majlis al-Aʿlá lil-Thaqāfah.

Naaman, M. (2011) *Urban space in contemporary Egyptian literature: portraits of Cairo*. 1st ed. New York: Palgrave Macmillan.

Saugestad, F. (2009) *Individuation and the shaping of personal identity: a comparative study of the modern novel*. Wiesbaden, Germany: Reichert Verlag.

Shalan, J. (2002) "Writing the Nation: The Emergence of Egypt in the Modern Arabic Novel," *Journal of Arabic Literature*, 33(3), 211–247. doi:10.1163/15700640260496695

Wien, P. (2017) *Arab nationalism: the politics of history and culture in the modern Middle East*. London; New York: Routledge, Taylor & Francis Grou

Youssef, M. (2015) "The aesthetics of difference: history and representations of otherness in al-Nubi and Wahat al-ghurub," *Alif (Cairo, Egypt)* (35), 75. Available at: https://go.exlibris.link/9h8wnbdz.

Index

Note: Endnotes in this index are indicated by the page number followed by "n" and the note number e.g., 63n2 refers to endnote 2 on page 63.

äät-Minzälä 147–148
Abdülhamid II 25, 31–32, 38
abolition, of slave trade/slavery 26, 28, 29–30, 31–32, 40, 41, 53–54, 56, 63n2
Abu Dhabi 19, 70, 74, 76, 164, 168, 169, 174, 176
Abulhawa, Susan 16–17, 63n3, 84–98
Abu-Lughod, Lila 77, 85, 90, 97, 98
adab al-luju' 17, 102, 103, 104
adab al-mahjar 8–9
adab al-manfa 101, 104
adab al-tahjir 12, 15, 17, 26, 32, 102, 112, 114, 115
affect 5–6, 19, 26, 28, 42n6
African descent 15, 49, 52, 53, 54, 60, 62
African identity 182, 184–190
Afropolitanism 184–190
After the Last Sky 91
Against the Loveless World 16–17, 84–98
Agamben, Giorgio 103, 110–111, 164, 169
age of print 138–157
Ahmed, Sara 70, 73–74, 79–80
al-Din ʿAli, Fakhr 18, 138, 141–142, 146, 147, 150
al-Fadila tantasir 18, 123, 126, 127, 128, 129, 130, 131, 133, 134–135
al-Huda, Bint *see* al-Sadr, Amina
Ali, Idris 19, 179–195
Ali, Muhammad 30, 36, 38, 145
Ali, Rozina 89, 97, 98
alienation: of Awad 190, 192; in exile 1, 3, 4, 5, 6, 11–12, 12–13, 15, 16, 17, 19; gendered pious consciousness 125, 127, 132, 134, 135; *Ghurba* and exile 101, 107–108, 112, 113, 114–115; at

home 1–2, 5; and memory 78; and religion 18, 138–157
al-Ightirab fil Thaqafa al-Arabiyya 5
Al-Nakba see Nakba
al-Qazani, Muhammad Murad 18, 138–157
al-Qazwini, Khawla 18, 123, 125, 131–134, 135
al-Sadr, Amina 18, 123, 124, 125, 126–131, 134–135
al-Sirhindi, Imam 138, 143, 148, 151, 152, 155
al-Tanturiya 16, 67–81
Amiriya Press 149, 151, 157n7
Amiry, Suad 15–16, 47–63
Amoudah is Burning 106
An Adventure 15, 25–43
Anatolia 116n12, 142, 146, 151
ancestors 27, 86, 97, 174, 189
anti-black racism/anti-blackness 16, 49–50, 53, 58, 62, 63n3; *see also* Arab racism
anti-slavery literature 15, 25, 26, 28–29, 30, 34, 36–39
anxiety 58, 85, 135, 148, 168, 169, 173
anxious belonging 19, 168, 170, 172
Appadurai, Arjun 114, 173
Ar. riqq, ʿubüdiyya 52, 53; *see also My Damascus*
Arab culture 4, 52, 124
Arab Enlightenment 12
Arab identity 12, 54, 182, 183–184, 185
Arab migration writings, contemporary shifts in 103–105
Arab nationalism 11–12, 106, 165, 183, 184, 194–195; and Nubian literature 180–181

198 *Index*

Arab racism 15, 16; *see also*
 anti-blackness
Arab women, popular religious novels
 by 123–136
Arab-African cultural identity 19,
 179–195
Arab-Egyptian nationalism 194
Arabian Peninsula 18, 61, 140, 149, 163,
 166
Arabic literary studies 10, 11, 13, 14
Arab-Israeli War 9, 187; *see also Naksa*
Arabization 144, 145
Arabness 165
Aram 106
art of storytelling, and Susan Abulhawa
 85–86
Ashour, Radwa 16, 68, 69, 72, 81
assimilation 5, 17, 43n17, 54, 95, 112,
 168, 171, 172, 174, 184
Aswan High Dam 180–181
asylum 13, 16, 17, 72; *Ghurba* and exile
 102, 103, 104, 105, 107, 108–114, 115,
 115n6, 116n15; literature of 17, 102,
 103, 104
authoritarianism 2, 101
authority 26, 29, 33, 42n12
autobiography 14, 26, 42n11, 108, 139,
 143, 156
Awad 182, 185, 186, 187, 188–190,
 194–195; and authority 191–193;
 fading of 193–194; tragedy of 194
Aydınlanma 12, 26, 29, 30, 32, 38, 41,
 42n13

Barakat, Halim 5, 12
"bare lives" 164, 169
Baroudi family 47, 48, 49, 50–51, 52, 53,
 55, 56, 57, 58, 59, 60–61, 62
Ba'th Party 123–124, 125, 126, 127, 128,
 130, 134–135
Bauman, Zygmunt 111, 164, 169
belonging 2, 6, 12, 17, 18, 19, 79, 80, 102,
 183, 185; in *Against the Loveless World*
 86, 90, 93, 97; anxious 19, 168, 170,
 172; within asylum regime 108–114;
 contested 171–177; in *My Damascus*
 51, 53, 54; not 123, 134; surrealist
 168–171; in *Temporary People* 164,
 165, 166; violent 171–177
Beyond Sovereign Reason 184
Bilad al-Sham 47
biography 15, 25, 28, 29, 30, 42n5;
 Naqshbandi 138, 142–143, 150, 153, 154

blackness 15–16, 50, 58, 175, 187, 191,
 192, 193; anti- *see* anti-black racism/
 anti-blackness
bondage 49, 52–53, 55, 56–62
Bulaq press 30, 36, 151

Cairo 36, 38, 39, 107, 132; *Dongola*
 188, 189, 190, 191, 192; Naqshbandi
 migrants and translators 139, 140,
 143, 144, 145, 146, 149
camps: labor 163, 164, 170, 171; refugee
 67, 71, 72–73, 74, 75, 76, 77, 78–79,
 80, 85, 107, 163
capitalism 10, 14, 133
*Capitalism and Class in the Gulf Arab
 States* 166
Celal 31, 33, 34, 35, 36, 37, 39, 40,
 43n19, 43n20
Cevher 27, 33, 39–40, 43n20
Champ of the Camp 163
characters 15, 16, 18, 52, 60, 62, 102; in
 Against the Loveless World 85, 86–87,
 91; and gendered pious consciousness
 125, 129, 130, 132, 133, 134, 135, 136;
 in *Sergüzeşt* 25, 27, 29, 31, 34, 39,
 42n16; in *Temporary People* 168–169,
 172, 176, 177
cheap labor 94, 165, 170–171
checkpoints 48, 89, 96, 97
Christianity 28, 71, 74, 144, 145, 179;
 see also Maronites
citizenship 2, 19, 43n17, 94, 112, 114,
 133, 184; in *Temporary People* 164,
 167, 171–172; in *The Woman from
 Tantoura* 68, 71–72, 73, 80
civil war, Lebanese 16, 68, 69, 70, 71,
 74–76
class 19, 32, 67, 87, 135, 155, 164, 167; in
 Dongola 182, 186, 190, 191; economic
 92, 96, 164; middle- 19, 164, 165, 170,
 171, 172; in *My Damascus* 47, 48,
 59–60
Classics Debate, of *Tanzimat* writers
 42n13
collective identity 17, 86, 179, 184, 185
collective memory 69, 70, 77, 81, 84, 138,
 181
colonialism 7–8, 9, 10, 11, 12, 15, 32,
 42n11, 84, 87, 183, 184; settler 16, 79,
 81; trans-imperial 41
Committee on Union and Progress 38
concubines 25, 33, 58
containment 73, 75, 77, 81, 130

Index 199

contested belongings 171–177
control 7, 8, 28, 31, 47, 72–73, 76, 88, 92, 98, 165
corruption 18, 36–37, 38, 106, 126, 127, 130, 131, 189
cosmopolitanism 7–8, 14, 15, 18–19, 107, 148, 149, 185
creativity 11, 12, 13, 68, 77, 88, 108–109, 134
criticism 6, 7, 10, 11, 13, 29, 103, 134, 143
crossing borders 48
cultural identity, Arab-African 19, 179–195
Cultural Politics of Emotions, The 73–74
Curse of the Russian Doll 115

Dakkak, Nadeen 93, 95, 101
Damascus *see My Damascus*
da'wa 128
dehumanization 57–58, 60–61, 165, 168, 169, 171
desire 25, 33, 37, 39, 40
detachment 3, 4, 5, 19, 56
dhayl 141, 152, 153–155
diaspora 1, 3, 5, 8, 9, 13, 14, 86, 97, 123, 131, 172, 177; *Ghurba* and exile 101, 103, 104, 105, 106, 107, 109, 113–114
Dilber 27, 33, 35, 36, 37–38, 39, 40, 43n20
discrimination 6, 7, 60, 68, 73, 106, 110, 135–136, 176, 191
disintegration 9, 186, 195
dislocation 1, 2, 3, 4, 5, 6, 11, 12–13, 14–15, 19, 20, 70, 97, 103
displaced people 2, 84, 85, 101, 104, 114–115, 164
displacement: forced 12, 15, 17, 26, 32, 102, 112, 114, 115; mass 13, 112, 181; Palestinian 12, 17
disposability 169, 170–171
dispossession, Palestinian 9, 11, 16, 17, 48, 77–78, 81, 86, 95–96; *see also Nakba*
division of labor 88
domestic slavery 52, 53; *see also My Damascus*
Dongola 19, 179–195
double estrangement 11–12
double exclusion 19, 169, 172
double marginalization, of Kurdish people 17
Dubai 168, 170, 171, 172, 174

economic class 92, 96, 164
economic migrants 164–165, 177
Effects of the First Travel, The 34–35
Egyptian Turks 15, 27, 32, 34–36, 41
elites 88, 91, 124, 135; in *My Damascus* 52, 55, 56, 58, 59; in *Sergüzeşt* 26, 28, 38, 40, 42n9
emancipation 12, 32, 183
embroidery 93, 96
Emirati nation 164, 165, 166, 168
emotions 1, 3, 4, 5, 14, 17, 33, 86, 112, 134, 189, 190; Naqshbandi 138, 139, 149, 150, 155, 156; in *The Woman from Tantoura* 67, 68, 69, 73–74, 76, 79, 81
Enlightenment 12, 26, 29, 30, 32, 38, 41, 42n13
enslaved mother: 34, 41; double time of 26–27, 30–32
enslavement 28, 29, 30, 31, 32, 39, 52–53, 57, 190; *see also* slave trade; slavery
epistemology 11, 184
equality 30, 32, 59, 114
estrangement 1–2, 3, 4, 5, 6, 7, 8, 11–12, 19, 79, 177; in *Dongola* 182, 187, 188; *see also ghurba*
ethics 97, 113, 148, 179
ethnic minorities 106, 181, 184
ethnicity 59–60, 87, 88, 110–111, 185, 186
eunuchs 33, 34, 36, 38, 39, 41, 42n10
Eurocentrism 7, 10
European modernity 8, 9, 11
exclusion 6, 16, 17, 19, 49; in *Dongola* 182, 183, 184, 185, 192, 194; *Ghurba* and exile 101, 106, 110–111; in *Temporary People* 164, 165, 166, 169, 170, 172, 173, 174; in *The Woman from Tantoura* 69, 70–72, 73, 76, 77, 80
exile 1, 5, 11, 101, 104, 110, 114; external 12; internal 12–13; trauma of 68, 69, 70, 73, 75, 78, 80, 85, 90, 95, 97, 102, 104, 109
exilic literature and writers 8, 9, 11, 13
exilic slaver 34–36
exogamy 53–54
external exile 12
Eze, Michael 184–185

Fatima 47, 55, 132
Fear of Small Numbers 173
female mobility 47, 48, 49, 56, 61
female slaves 15–16, 30, 55, 57, 59–60, 61

200 Index

fiction: intimate bio- 26–27, 29, 41; religious 18, 123, 124–125, 134–135, 135–136
first religious novel 126–131
forced displacement 12, 15, 17, 26, 32, 102, 112, 114, 115
forced migration 3–4, 13, 16, 103, 106, 113
foreign slave mother 27–28, 41
foreign workers 92, 94, 167, 171
foreigners 2, 15, 71, 94, 164, 166, 175
foreignness 4, 6, 134, 165
freedom 54, 88, 101, 103, 128, 188; political 131–134; in *Sergüzeşt* 30, 32, 38, 39–40
French Enlightenment 32, 41

gender 17, 20, 42n11, 48, 51, 182, 186, 194; in *Against the Loveless World* 86, 87, 88, 91–92
gendered pious consciousness 123–136
General Intelligence Services 106–107
generational trauma 95, 96
Ghabra, Shafeeq 86, 88, 89, 92–93, 95, 96–97
Ghalia 47, 49, 51, 52, 55, 56, 57, 59, 60–62
gharb 3, 132, 134
ghurba: psychological 17, 19; rewriting of 14–20; of slaves 27, 32–33; spiritual 18; theorizing of 3–8; in *When a Man Thinks* 131–134; *see also* estrangement; exile
global capitalism 10, 14
global migration crisis 101–116
global South 6, 7, 8, 10, 103, 115; *see also* Third World
globalization 113, 143, 163, 169
Globalization and Its Discontents 170
Greater Syria 47
Gulf States 7, 18–19, 72, 93, 164, 169, 170, 171, 177; nation building in 165–168
Güven, Güler 30, 31, 36, 38, 42n3, 42n5

Halabi, Zeina 11, 12
Halima 193, 194
Hanieh, Adam 7, 165, 166–167, 173, 174
harem eunuchs 34, 38, 39
harem slavery 52
Hassan 69, 74–75, 80
Hassan, Waïl 10–11, 18
hegemony 9, 10, 77, 81, 123, 182, 183, 189

hijab 124, 130, 133
Hijaz 18, 56, 61, 138, 139, 140, 142, 147, 148, 151, 153, 154, 156
hijra see migration
Home and Away 79–80
home re-making 67–81
homecomings 48
homelessness, trauma of 88
homogenization, of people of African descent 53, 58
honorifics 151
hospitality 17, 102, 103, 110, 114
Hostages of Sin 106
hostility 17, 49, 71, 73, 74, 76, 80, 174
human rights 85, 89, 103, 169, 170
"human waste" 169
humanity 29, 37, 38, 49, 57, 168, 171
husayniya 123, 130
Hushia 189, 192, 194
Hussein, Haitham 17, 101–116
Hussein, Saddam 94, 124, 126, 131

Ibrat al-ru'b 106
identity: African 182, 184–190; Arab 12, 54, 182, 183–184, 185; Arab-African cultural 19, 179–195; collective 17, 86, 179, 184, 185; national 2, 165–166; Palestinian 17, 74, 77, 80, 81, 96
ightirab see alienation
İlk Seyahatin Tesiratı 34–35
imaginaries 19, 79
imagined nationhood 165
(im)mobility 6, 7
imperialism 7, 9, 10, 15, 26, 30, 84, 153, 183
inclusion 14, 16, 19, 51, 52, 73, 92, 166, 175
Indama yufakkir al-rajul 18, 123, 131–134, 135
Indianness 164, 172, 174, 176, 177
inhumanity 171
injustice 51, 57, 89, 90, 106, 186, 195
insanity, civil war and invasion as 75
insistent return, of traumatic events 116n7
integration 12, 19, 53–54, 58, 60, 109, 111, 112, 116n17, 127
intellectual labor 138, 140
internal exile 12–13
intersectionality 15, 51–52, 53, 80, 185, 186
intifada, Shia 131
intimate biofiction 26–27, 29, 41

intradiegetic history 31
invisibilization 103
Iran 124; Timurid 138, 141, 142, 157n5
Iranian Revolution 124, 136
Iran/Iraq war 124
Iraq 17, 18, 87, 94–95, 101, 163;
  gendered pious consciousness
  123–124, 125, 126, 127, 128, 130, 135,
  136
Islam: law of 30, 54, 59; Shia 18, 123,
  124–125, 126, 127, 128, 130, 131, 132,
  134–135, 136; Sunni 127
Islamicization 27, 130
Istanbul 15, 107, 143, 145, 146;
  pieds-noirs of 27, 34–36; in *Sergüzeşt*
  31, 32, 36–37, 38, 39, 40, 41, 43n19

Jordan 7, 16, 47, 51, 71, 87, 90, 94, 95,
  97, 98, 116n17, 163
journeys 17, 40, 42n3, 48, 56, 61, 69;
  Ghurba and exile 102, 108, 112, 114;
  Naqshbandi 138, 139, 141, 154, 156

Kaabour, Mahmoud 163–164
kafala system 167, 172
Kanafani, Ghassan 67, 68, 91
Khaleeji Capital 167
Khwajah 142
kul 52
Kurds, Syrian 16, 106–107, 116n9,
  116n10, 116n13
Kuwait 16, 17, 18, 72, 131, 133, 135; in
  Against the Loveless World 84, 85, 94,
  95, 96, 97, 98; boom years in 91–94;
  Palestinians in 86–89

labor 7, 29, 54, 55, 56, 85, 87, 92, 166;
  cheap 94, 165, 170–171; division of 88;
  intellectual 138, 140
labor camps 163, 164, 170, 171
large-scale institutional slavery 52
Lebanese civil war 16, 68, 69, 70, 71,
  74–76
Lebanon, Palestinian refugees in 67–81
legal status, of Palestinian refugees 71–72
*Letters and Correspondences of Ahmad
  al-Sirhindi, The* 138, 152, 155
Levant 8–9, 16, 139, 140, 144–145; in
  My Damascus 47, 48, 49, 50, 51, 52,
  55, 61, 62
liberation 90, 91, 94, 180; *see also*
  Palestine Liberation Organization
  (PLO)

liminality 11, 15, 60, 93, 174, 177
literary criticism 13, 134–135
literature: abolitionist 26, 28, 30, 41;
  anti-slavery 15, 25, 26, 28–29, 30,
  34, 36–39; of asylum 17, 102, 103,
  104; of exile 13, 101, 104; of forced
  displacement 17, 102; by immigrants
  8–9; Naqshbandi 138; Nubian *see*
  Nubian literature; Ottoman anti-
  slavery 26, 36–39; Palestinian 11, 67,
  68–69, 86; resistance 67
livelihoods 88, 169, 193
living conditions, of Palestinian refugees
  71–72
Longva, Anh Nga 166
loss, trauma of 67
love objects 25, 26, 27, 41
love story, *Against the Loveless World*
  as 98
Lucknow 143, 145, 146, 149, 153

madrasas 145, 147–148, 157n9
Maghreb 49
Mahmud 126, 128, 129
*Maktubat Imam al-Rabbani Ahmad al-
  Sirhindi* 138, 152, 155
Malayalam 163, 168, 171
manfa see exile
manumission 28, 30, 41, 54
marginality 11, 18, 77, 81
marginalization 3, 6, 15–16, 17, 18, 19,
  49, 123, 135, 170; in *Dongola* 179,
  180, 182, 187, 190, 192, 194; *Ghurba*
  and exile 101, 110, 116n17; of
  Palestinian refugees in Lebanon
  70–72; structural 67–81
marriage 28, 31, 33, 48, 54, 88, 93,
  130, 132
Mashreq 49, 62
mass displacement 13, 112, 181
masters 25, 39, 42n2, 50, 59, 62, 138,
  146, 148, 150, 151, 152, 155
maternal slavery 15, 25–43
matricide 25, 28, 41
Mauritania 49–50
Mecca, Naqshbandi migrants and
  translators in 18, 138–157
Medina 149, 150, 151, 154
memory: in *Against the Loveless World*
  84–98; collective 69, 70, 77, 81, 84,
  138, 181; Palestinian 67, 68, 77–78,
  97, 98; among Palestinian refugees in
  Lebanon 77–80; site of 77, 80, 81

202   *Index*

Men in the Sun 91
metaphor of water 32–33, 40
metropoles 8, 13–14, 140, 144, 155
middle-class 19, 164, 165, 170, 171, 172
Midhat, Ahmet 26, 42n3
migrant workers 7; spectral 19, 163–177
migrants: economic 164–165, 177;
    Naqshbandi 138–157; redundancy of
    164, 169, 171; South Asian 7, 19, 164,
    177
migrants-to-be 168
migration 5; crisis of 101–116; forced
    3–4, 16, 103, 106, 113; precarious 3–4,
    13, 16, 103, 106, 113; South–North 7;
    South–South 7; theories of 164–165
military-administrative slavery 52
minor groups, monetization of 51
missionaries 28, 144, 145
mixed-race people 16, 54, 60
mobility 2–3, 5, 6, 7, 13, 15, 51, 103, 165,
    185; female 47, 48, 49, 56, 61; social
    27, 28, 32, 33, 39; *see also* diaspora;
    displacement; exile; migration
modern nation-building, paradox of
    163–177
modernity 2, 12, 14, 27, 29, 139–140,
    144, 185; entanglements with slavery
    and racism 49, 62; European 8, 9, 11;
    in *Temporary People* 163, 164, 169;
    Western 12, 185
monetization, of minor groups 51
mosques 123, 128, 129, 130, 135, 136
motherhood 27, 30, 48
mothers 25–26, 27, 28, 29, 30, 34, 41, 50,
    58, 88, 193
mughtarib 4, 5, 134
Muhammad 131, 132, 133–134, 135
mukàtaba 28, 30, 41, 54
Mukhabarat 106–107
multiculturalism 48, 54, 176, 193
multilingualism 138, 139, 144, 149
murid 150, 155
Muslim world 18, 71; in *My Damascus*
    47, 50, 51, 53, 54, 58, 60; Naqshbandi
    138, 139–140, 142, 143, 144, 145–146,
    148, 153, 154, 155, 156n1, 156n2,
    156n3; *see also* non-Arab Muslims;
    popular religious novels by Arab
    women
My Damascus 15–16, 47–63

nafy see exile
nahda 101, 144, 145–146

Nahr 86, 87, 88, 89, 90, 91–92, 93–94,
    95–96, 97, 98
Nakba 9, 16, 101; in *Against the Loveless
    World* 87–88, 88–89, 90, 92, 95, 96, 97,
    98; in *The Woman from Tantoura* 67,
    68, 69–70, 73, 75, 77, 78–79, 80, 81
*Nakba: Palestine, 1948 and the Claims of
    Memory* 85, 98
Naqa 126, 127, 128, 129, 133
Naqshbandi: literature 138; migrants
    138–157; *tariqa* 141, 155, 156, 157n9;
    translation 145
Nasser, Gamal Abdel 123, 180, 183, 187,
    191, 195n2
nation and woman, conflation of
    132–133
national identity 2, 165–166
national imaginaries, of belonging and
    exclusion 163–177, 179–195
nationalism: Arab *see* Arab nationalism;
    without a nation-state 84, 89–91
nation-building, in *Temporary People*
    163–177
nation-state: nationalism without 84,
    89–91; redundant existence outside
    168–171
Nawal Kishore Press 146
Needle of Horror, The 106
New Woman 124, 126, 127
No One May Remain 17, 102, 108, 109,
    110, 114
non-Arab Muslims 18, 143, 152, 157n6
not belonging 123, 134
novels: first religious 126–131; popular
    religious 18, 123–136; as secular genre
    125
Nubians 19, 179, 180–181, 182, 187, 188,
    190, 193, 195n2
nuzuh see displacement

odalik 29, 33, 39, 41
official story, challenging the colonizer's
    89–90, 96, 97–98
oil industry 7, 91, 92, 101, 164, 165
oppression 11, 12, 18, 57, 103, 106, 131,
    133; in *Dongola* 181, 189, 190, 191; in
    The Woman from Tantoura 68, 71, 73,
    80, 81
Orientalism 8, 10, 32, 34–35, 36, 38, 41,
    104
othering 15–16, 49, 58, 68, 173; of
    Palestinian refugees in Lebanon
    70–72, 73, 76, 81

Index 203

Ottoman Empire 15, 26, 27, 31–32, 42n3, 48–49, 139; anti-slavery literature 26, 36–39; reformism 25–43; slavery 25, 26, 28, 29, 32, 52–56, 63n2

Palestine: displacement 12, 17; dispossession 9, 11, 16, 17, 48, 77–78, 81, 86, 95–96; exile in Lebanon 70–80; identity 17, 74, 77, 80, 81, 96; Liberation Organization (PLO) 71, 73, 75, 94; literature 11, 67, 68–69, 86; memory 67, 68, 77–78, 97, 98; refugee communities 72; women 16–17, 68, 69, 78, 79, 81; *see also Nakba*
Palestinians: in Kuwait 86–89; in Lebanon 67–81
Palestinians in Kuwait 86
paradox of modern nation-building 163–177
Persian language 18, 31, 138, 141, 146, 147, 150, 151, 152
Person of Indian Origin (PIO) cards 172
Phalange 73, 74, 75
physical appearance 58
pied-noirs of Istanbul 27, 34–36
piety 18, 54, 123–136
PIO (Person of Indian Origin) cards 172
pious consciousness 123–136
place-making practices 78
PLO (Palestine Liberation Organization) 71, 73, 75, 94
political freedom 131–134
political rights 71, 92, 172
politics 48, 52, 62, 73, 77, 80, 93, 105, 114, 123, 166, 170
popular religious novels by Arab women 18, 123–136
postcolonialism 7, 8, 9–10, 11, 13, 14, 68, 71, 80, 115n5, 180, 188
post-structuralism 134–135
power 11, 13, 15, 87, 98, 103, 106–107, 136; in *Dongola* 180, 183, 190, 191; in *My Damascus* 53, 54; in *Sergüzeşt* 28, 38, 42n9; in *Temporary People* 166, 167, 168, 175; in *The Woman from Tantoura* 67, 68, 71, 74, 81
precarious migration 3–4, 13, 16, 103, 106, 113, 168, 169, 171
pregnancy 30, 42n3, 59, 88, 107, 133
printing presses 125, 144–145, 146–147, 149
psychological *ghurba* 17, 19

public space 18, 124, 125, 127, 129, 135, 136

Qad la yabqa ahad, aghatha kristy 17, 102, 108, 109, 110, 114

race 20, 39, 54, 59, 62, 174, 176, 184, 186; mixed- 16, 54, 60
racial anxiety 58
racial assimilation, through sexual relationships 54
racialization 16, 49, 51, 57, 58, 62, 173
racism 6, 15, 47, 49, 73, 110, 190, 192, 195; anti-black 16, 58, 62, 63n3; Arab *see* Arab racism
radicalism 19, 182
Raha'in al-khati'ya 106
Rashahat 'ayn al-hayat 18, 138, 139, 140, 141, 142, 143, 145–146, 147, 149, 150–151, 152, 153, 155–156
redundancy, of migrants 164, 168–171
Reflections On Exile 84–85, 104–105
refugee camps 67, 71, 72–73, 74, 75, 76, 77, 78–79, 80, 85, 107, 163
refugeedom 102, 114
refugeeism 103–105, 114
refugees: Palestinian 16, 67–81; as Russian Dolls 101–116
religion 2, 18, 127, 136, 156, 184, 186; *see also* Christianity; Maronites; Shia Islam; Sufism; Sunni Islam
religiosity 130
religious awakening 18, 124, 127, 135, 136
religious consciousness 123, 125, 136
religious fiction 18, 123, 124–125, 134–135, 135–136
religious novels, popular 18, 123–136
religious spaces 17–18, 123, 126, 127, 130, 139, 149–150, 156
religious turn, of Saddam Hussein 124
re-making of home 67–81
remembrances 29, 80, 85
Renaissance 101, 144, 145–146
repression 17, 101, 106, 107
resettlement 102, 108, 195n2
resistance, in *Against the Loveless World* 16–17, 84, 90–91, 97–98, 129–130, 183
resistance literature 67
Rewriting the Story of the Palestinian Radical 89
rights 57, 68, 75, 80, 87, 94, 111, 126; citizenship 71–72; human 85, 89, 103, 169, 170; political 71, 92, 172;

204   *Index*

in *Temporary People* 164, 168, 174, 175–176
rituals of survival 86–89
roman de filiation 29
romantic exile 102
Ruqayya 69–70, 71, 72–73, 74–75, 76, 77–79, 80
Russian Doll: Curse of 115; refugee as 101–116

Sabra refugee camp 75, 78
Sa'di, Ahmad 77–78, 85, 90, 95, 97, 98
sahwa 18, 124, 127, 135, 136
Said, Edward 11, 13, 84–85, 90, 91, 97, 98, 104–105
Sajeda 47, 49, 51, 52, 53, 55, 56–58, 59–60, 61, 62
Salih, Ruba 79
Salih, Tayeb 10
Sami 54, 56, 57–58, 58–59, 59–60
sanctuary 110, 130, 132, 133, 134
Sassen, Saskia 170
Season of Migration to the North 10, 113
self-deprecation 143
Sellman, Johanna B. 9, 13, 14, 17, 102, 109, 113
Separated Man 186–187, 188, 192–193
Sergüzeşt 15, 25–43
servitude 49–50, 57, 58, 59
Setback *see Naksa*
settler colonialism 16, 79, 81
Sezai, Sami Paşazade 15, 25–43
Shalali, Awad *see* Awad
shatat see diaspora
Shatila refugee camp 75, 76, 78–79, 80
Shia Islam 18, 123, 124–125, 126, 127, 128, 130, 131, 132, 134–135, 136
silsila 142, 150
Sirhindi, Imam 138, 143, 148, 151, 152, 155
site of memory 77, 80, 81
Six Day War 85, 87, 92, 94
slave markets 33, 37, 61
slave mother 27–30, 40, 41
slave narratives 15, 26, 28, 42n6
slave trade 15, 26–27, 28, 30, 31, 32–33, 39, 40, 55, 189
slavery: domestic *see* domestic slavery; harem 52; large-scale institutional 52; in late Ottoman Empire 52–53; maternal 15, 25–43; military-administrative 52; Ottoman 25, 26, 28, 29, 32

slaves' *ghurba* 27, 32–33
slave's unmournable mother 39–41
social mobility 27, 28, 32, 33, 39
solidarity 6, 32, 69, 86, 104, 115, 123, 128, 136, 174, 185
South Asian migrants 7, 19, 164, 177
South Asian workers 163, 166–167, 177
South–North migration 7
South–South migration 7
South–South paradigm 10–11
spectral migrant workers 163–177
spiritual *ghurba* 18
statelessness 85, 89, 90–91, 92, 95, 110
staying put 2
storytelling, art of 85–86
strangers 1, 4, 5, 18, 70, 80, 96, 108, 111, 125, 184, 188
structural marginalisation 67–81
sub-humanity 171
Sudan 10, 27, 28, 32, 33, 38, 39, 41, 49, 51, 101, 188, 192–193
suffering 30, 32, 40, 97, 98, 105, 111, 115n6, 177, 181
Sufism 18, 138–139, 140, 141, 145, 148–149, 154, 155, 156
suicide 27, 32, 39–40, 132, 133
Sunni Islam 127
surrealist belonging 168–171
surveillance 71, 73, 89
survival 70, 84, 86–89, 90, 93
Syria 17, 47, 71, 72, 75, 101, 104, 107, 108, 109, 110, 128, 163
Syrian Kurds 16, 106–107, 116n9, 116n10, 116n13

Tanzimat reform period 25, 29–30, 33, 41, 41n1, 42n12, 42n13, 145
taqriz 151
Ta'rib 144, 145
tariqa 138, 139, 140, 141, 142, 146, 147, 148, 150, 151, 152, 153, 154, 155, 156, 157n9
Tashkent 143, 145, 146–147, 148, 153
tatreez 96
Temporary People 19, 163–177
Third World 6; *see also* global South
Timurid Iran 138, 141, 142, 157n5
Tits 174, 175–176
Toledano, Ehud R. 28, 30, 31, 33, 50, 52, 53, 54–55, 56, 58, 59–60, 61
trading 33, 48, 53, 145; *see also* slave trade
trans-imperial colonialism 41

Index   205

translation 25, 29, 138, 143–147, 155
trauma 16, 25–26, 28, 42n6, 84, 91,
116n7; and Arab-Israeli War 187;
and Aswan High Dam project
180–181; dealing with effects of
113; of exile 68, 69, 70, 73, 75, 78,
80, 85, 90, 95, 97, 102, 104, 109;
generational 95, 96; of homelessness
88; of loss 67
traumatized mother 25, 27, 33, 41
Turkey 17, 107, 116n12

UAE *see* United Arab Emirates
(UAE)
underclasses 92, 93, 186
United Arab Emirates (UAE) 17, 19,
107; in *Temporary People* 163, 164,
165–166, 167, 168, 170, 171, 172,
173–174, 175–176, 177
United Nations Relief and Works
Agency (UNRWA) 71
Unnikrishnan, Deepak 19, 163–177
UNRWA (United Nations Relief and
Works Agency) 71
Urdu 138, 141, 146, 149, 156
'Ushba darra fi-l-fardus 108
Uzbek 138, 141, 146, 147, 156

victimization 16, 188–189
violence 6, 37, 89, 97, 106, 110, 124; in
Temporary People 164, 168, 172,

173–174, 176; in *The Woman from
Tantoura* 67, 68, 69, 74, 75, 76, 77, 81
violent belongings 171–177
Virtue Prevails 18, 123, 126, 127, 128,
129, 130, 131, 133, 134–135

Wal, Katja 184–185
Walls Built on Sand 166
waqi'iiya 129
war: Arab-Israeli *see* Arab-Israeli War;
Lebanese civil 16, 68, 69, 70, 71,
74–76; Six Day 85, 87, 92, 94
water metaphor 32–33, 40
water tanker, in *Men in the Sun* 91
Weed in Paradise, A 108
Western modernity 12, 185
Westernization 15, 130, 132–133; in
Sergüzeşt 27, 32, 34, 35–36, 37, 38,
39, 41
When a Man Thinks 18, 123, 131–134,
135
woman and nation, conflation of
132–133
Woman from Tantoura, The 16, 67–81
women's mobility 47, 48, 49, 56, 61

Za'atari refugee camp 163
Zilfi, Madeline 28, 32, 42n2, 53, 55, 57,
61
Zionism 67, 68, 69, 71, 72, 77, 88, 95,
96, 97

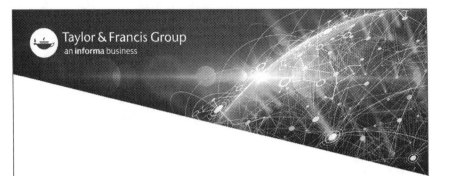